A BOOK TO FILL YOUR CUP OF KNOWLEDGE TO THE BRIM

Who were the first peoples to drink coffee and tea, and how did consumption of these bliss-filled brews spread over the entire world? What can you expect when you buy coffee from Brazil, or Kenya, or any of the host of other places where it is produced? What is the most celebrated and costly tea in the world? How can you avoid rip-offs when paying high prices for supposedly rare coffees? How long will tea remain full-flavored when stored? What kind of grind brings out the best in coffee, and should you percolate it, filter it, or even boil it? What teas are best with milk, with sugar, and just by themselves? What do such exotically enticing names as Mocha, Lapsang souchong, Arabian, Keemun and other elegant appellations really mean?

Here is a book that offers a pleasure in reading second only to the pleasure that will be yours when its knowledge is put to delightfully practical use in your kitchen and in your cup.

PETER QUIMME is the author of the highly praised THE SIGNET BOOK OF AMERICAN WINE and THE SIGNET BOOK OF CHEESE. He writes frequently on gourmet topics for leading magazines, including *New York* and *House Beautiful*. An inveterate epicure, Mr. Quimme lives in New York and travels as much as possible.

THE SIGNET BOOK OF COFFEE AND TEA

by

Peter Quimme

A SIGNET BOOK
NEW AMERICAN LIBRARY
TIMES MIRROR

SIGNET TRADEMARK REG. U.S. PAT. OFF. AND FOREIGN COUNTRIES
REGISTERED TRADEMARK—MARCA REGISTRADA
HECHO EN CHICAGO, U.S.A.

SIGNET, SIGNET CLASSICS, MENTOR, PLUME AND MERIDIAN BOOKS
are published by The New American Library, Inc.,
1301 Avenue of the Americas, New York, New York 10019

First Signet Printing, September, 1976

1 2 3 4 5 6 7 8 9

PRINTED IN THE UNITED STATES OF AMERICA

for Bill and Sharon

Acknowledgments

Whatever merit this book has is due in large part to the generosity of a great many people involved with coffee and tea who freely gave me their time, expertise, and encouragement over the past two years. In particular I would like to thank the following individuals: Frank Cho, President of Formost Tea Corporation and current member of the United States Board of Tea Experts, and William H. MacMelville, President of George Friedman Co., Inc., and former Chairman of the United States Board of Tea Experts, for sharing their considerable expertise with me at the tasting table and for taking the time to read the chapters on tea-tasting and the world's teas; P. V. Ramaswamy, Director of Tea Promotion of the Consulate General of India, for supplying me with information on Indian tea and giving the chapter on tea cultivation and processing a critical reading; Robert H. Dick, United States Supervisory Tea Examiner for the Food and Drug Administration, for taking the time to answer my inquiries and supplying me with information on the Tea Act; John M. Anderson, Executive Director of the Tea Council of the U.S.A., Inc., and the Tea Council's helpful staff, for letting me use their library and supplying me with much useful data; and Sharon McCoy of Tokyo, Japan, for researching a number of aspects of Japanese tea and collecting samples for me.

I owe a particular debt to Saul Zabar of Zabar's Gourmet Foods in New York for his willingness to take the time to share his coffee expertise and enthusiasm with me, covering everything from green beans to grinders; to him I owe many pleasant hours at the sampling table. I would also like to thank Sterling A. Gordon, coffee broker, for giving me the benefit of his expert palate and knowledge of the world's coffees, and Dr. William C. Struning, Director of Marketing and Economic Research of the Pan-American Coffee Bureau, for providing me with much useful statistical data and arranging for me to use the bureau's library. These three

gentlemen were kind enough to give most of the coffee chapters a critical reading. In addition, I would like to thank John Adinolfi, former Director of the Coffee Brewing Center of the Pan-American Coffee Bureau, for reading the chapter on coffee preparation and lending me much useful material; Erna K. Guerrieri of B. C. Ireland, Inc., and Dennis Acer of Acer and Korbin, Inc., for answering my inquiries; and the staff of Harry H. Wolfe & Sons, Inc., trade roasters, for letting me study their operation in detail. I would also like to thank F. A. Briscoe, Manager of the Coffee Industry Board of Jamaica and a most knowledgeable guide and thoughtful host, for letting me have the opportunity to see coffee cultivation and processing firsthand in the Blue Mountain district of Jamaica.

Many of these people made invaluable suggestions for improving this book, but none, of course, is responsible for any statements contained herein. The enthusiasms and opinions expressed are mine alone, as are any errors of fact, which may, unfortunately, have escaped my attention. In preparing this work, I have leaned heavily on the technical literature that exists in the field, and the authorities cited from time to time in the text (Wellman, Harler, Sivetz and Foote, Haarer, Ukers, etc.) will be found in the annotated list in the appendix under Further Reading. In particular I would like to acknowledge my debt to William Ukers' great encyclopedic works *All About Coffee* and *All About Tea*. Written some forty years ago, they are a testament to the fascination of the subject and an inspiration even where they are, alas, no longer reliable guides.

Finally, I would like to thank Nancy Newhouse for stimulating my interest in writing about two of my favorite beverages by suggesting I write articles on coffee and tea for *New York* magazine; the New York Public Library for its admirable research facilities; Susan Sachnoff for invaluable last-minute assistance in preparing the manuscript; and William Peter Burns for his continuing encouragement.

PETER QUIMME

March, 1976

How to Use This Book

Part I of this book discusses coffee; Part II concerns tea.

Part I begins with a brief history of coffee, discusses its cultivation and processing, and describes how to taste and evaluate it. A comprehensive tasting guide to the world's coffees is followed by detailed information on shopping, storing, grinding, preparing, and serving coffee.

Similarly, Part II covers the history of tea, how it is grown and made, discusses tea-tasting and evaluation, and gives a comprehensive tasting guide to the world's teas. How to shop for, store, prepare, and serve tea are discussed in depth.

The appendix suggests books for further reading and tells how to order fine coffees and teas by mail.

Although this handbook has been written to be read straight through, the subject matter has been arranged to allow the reader to dip into the text at almost any point by using the contents and index as a guide to coffee and tea types, terms, and topics of interest.

Contents

PART II: TEA

MAPS / ILLUSTRATIONS

CHAPTER ONE

Introduction: The World of Coffee and Tea

Tea and coffee are produced from the leaf and the bean, respectively, of two remarkable tropical plants. Both beverages are of ancient origin, the stimulant properties of the leaves of the tea bush and the seeds of the coffee tree having first attracted attention centuries—perhaps millennia—ago. Today we know the stimulant property tea and coffee share is due to the caffeine both contain—a biochemical substance that activates the higher levels of the brain and banishes drowsiness. The early histories of both plants revolve around legends of the discovery of their use as antidotes to sleep and the subsequent widespread belief in their supposed medicinal properties. At first, the respective parts of the plants were simply chewed for effect; later the discovery of the illimitable fragrance and flavor of the infused beverages that could be made from them made their use commonplace in the East. Once introduced to the West, they were accepted universally so rapidly that it is difficult now to realize they were once regarded as Eastern exotica whose consumption was medically questionable.

Coffee and tea have long been the world's most popular beverages. Only water is consumed in greater quantities by the world's population. The size of the world market for coffee and tea gives them an enormous impact in international trade in addition to pervasive influence on the social life of many nations. In the United States alone, some 450 million cups of coffee disappear down American throats each day, about 2.2 cups per capita. This enormous craving for coffee requires that the country import almost three *billion* pounds annually, a good third of the world's exportable production. Tea consumption in the United States is slightly less awesome, about one-half cup per capita daily—but that's still forty billion servings a year and that makes the United States the second-largest tea-importing country.

PRINCIPAL COFFEE- AND TEA-PRODUCING COUNTRIES OF THE WORLD

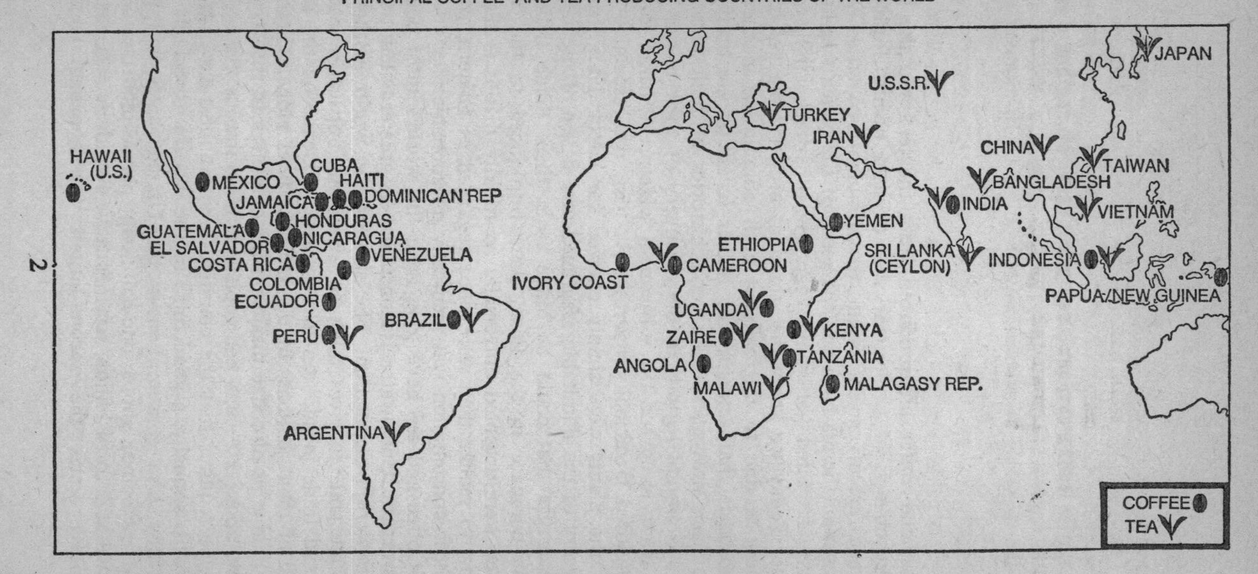

Yet Americans are by no means as passionate about coffee as the Swedes, who average almost three and a half cups daily per person, or as keen on tea as the British, who drink five cups daily per capita.

One or another (or both) of these beverages is a fixture on the tables of probably the majority of the world's peoples. It is hard to believe that they would have reached their present popularity solely as exotic stimulants. It is their taste that makes one or the other of them a seemingly necessary staple in the diets of so many people; warm, satisfying, aromatic, a cup of coffee or tea soothes, awakens, uplifts. Unlike stronger drinks, both offer mild elation without depression or side effects, and although few coffee or tea lovers would want to do without their favorite beverage, neither causes physical dependence.

Coffee and tea are the two greatest nonalcoholic drinks known. Fine coffee and tea offer the variety, subtleties, and complexities of fine wine, but at a far, far lower price. Considering the gastronomic pleasures that can be had in a cup of, say, high-grown Kenya coffee or vintage Darjeeling tea, it is surprising that so few people are really discriminating about the coffee and tea they drink.

In past centuries coffee and tea were expensive luxuries only the rich could enjoy, but modern cultivation, processing, and shipping put them within financial reach of virtually everyone. What few people realize is that the rare and exquisite growths, two and three times more expensive than the cheapest, most ordinary coffees and teas, are still among the least-expensive beverages obtainable. Fine wines—as many of us don't need reminding—can cost dollars a glassful. Even a stingy three-ounce glass from a two-dollar bottle of Mountain Red represents twenty-five cents. But truly fine, connoisseur-quality coffee and tea—as different from supermarket brands as fine wine is from *vin ordinaire*—is absurdly cheap, rarely more than a nickel a cup! Fine coffee and tea, as many people are discovering (and quite a few have known all along), are probably the only gourmet bargains left.

These inexpensive luxuries—kept under lock and key two centuries ago—are difficult neither to find nor to obtain, though the best are not found sitting on every grocery shelf, any more than the finest wines are found in every corner liquor store. These days more and more fine coffees and teas are showing up in specialty stores, gourmet departments, and, yes, even supermarkets. But those who want to explore the world of aromatic coffees and delicate teas need

to know their way around the burlap bags of exotically named beans and colorful tins (sometimes even chests) of loose tea taking up the corners of retail outlets. Fine coffees and teas are a world apart in taste from their simple supermarket cousins—and need to be bought, prepared, and appreciated with care and attention if they are to reveal all the fabled qualities for which they are famous.

Yet, considering how much coffee and tea is consumed, it is surprising that there are no reliable guides to the *connoisseurship* of these beverages. The technical literature on tea and coffee, although of great interest to the planter, processor, and those in the trades, contains little that would interest the enthusiastic amateur, who, after all, is interested primarily in the end product—the brew in the cup. Of books addressed to the layman, most have dealt with the colorful histories of these commodities, giving scant regard to their taste characteristics, the details of proper preparation, and to topics such as how to shop for the best values, how to store coffee and tea properly, or—most important—how to tell a good cup from a bad one.

But then, coffee and tea drinkers are not all the same. Many would simply like to know how to spot values, others are confused about preparation and want to know how they can prepare a better-tasting pot. Many are curious to explore intriguingly named growths like Sumatra Mandheling or Lapsang Souchong, but wouldn't mind knowing before buying what these might taste like. Others, having discovered the delights of wine, cheese, and other foodstuffs that range from quite ordinary to quite sublime, are delighted to find another gourmet area in which to expand their taste buds. What all these people need is a Baedeker to the world of coffee and tea.

Thus, this book. The following pages are a novice's introduction to coffee and tea and a gourmet's guide to the best of each. Written as a handbook, it is intended for anyone who wants to know how they can find, prepare, and enjoy a more satisfying cup of coffee or tea than they are now drinking. For convenience as a reference, the book is divided into two parts: Part I deals with coffee, Part II with tea. Each is completely self-contained, and each begins with a brief capsule history of the drink and an outline of the cultivation and processing of the plant, so that the reader can have some acquaintance with the fascinating and romantic background of these beverages and an enhanced appreciation of the difficulties involved in producing fine coffee and tea.

The midsection of each part concerns the tasting of these beverages, and it is here, if anywhere, that this book pretends to any originality.

The tasting and appreciation of fine coffee or tea, like the tasting and appreciation of wine, require that the novice have some idea of how to begin sorting out the delightful impressions fine brews give to the nose and mouth, and some idea of what to look for in the drink. Coffee-tasting and tea-tasting are not esoteric skills and, like wine-tasting, are a great deal of fun, rewarding the enthusiast with considerably enhanced enjoyment of his or her favorite cup. The sections on tasting are followed by comprehensive guides to the taste characteristics of the principal coffees and teas of the world. Although reading these sections will not make you an expert taster, any more than reading a book about wine-tasting will make you a wine expert, it will certainly tell you how to tell good coffee or tea from bad, and there is enough detail to give the most passionate enthusiast all he or she needs to develop a highly critical coffee or tea palate. The last chapters of Parts I and II tell how to purchase, store, prepare, and serve coffees and teas to bring out their best.

A word on preferences. Some people like coffee, others prefer tea. There are coffee drinkers and tea drinkers who wouldn't touch a cup of the other beverage. I enjoy both equally, and I find it puzzling that someone who esteems one wouldn't enjoy the other. To me this seems as odd as someone claiming to appreciate only red or white wine, but not both. It is true there are differences in taste in coffee and tea, but both offer considerable taste rewards to the open-minded gastronome; the palate attuned to one is rarely completely unreceptive to the other. I find that coffee drinkers who claim to find tea an insipid, weak brew usually have never tasted a properly prepared cup of fine, flavory tea. Tea drinkers who find coffee a muddy, bitter cup usually have never had a carefully prepared serving of fine, aromatic, high-grown coffee. (Not to mention the poor souls who have never had a decent cup of either!) It's my hope that those who are fans of one of these unique beverages will dip into the section in this book on the other, and perhaps be persuaded to sample some of the sublime taste experiences *each* offers.

PART I

Coffee

CHAPTER TWO

A Brief History of Coffee

Legendary Beginnings

The coffee tree from which finer coffees come, *Coffea arabica,* is known to be indigenous to Ethiopia. When and how coffee's property of preventing sleep was discovered, however, is a matter of conjecture and legend, whose authenticity is enhanced only by constant repetition. The most popular legend attributes the discovery to Kaldi, a young Ethiopian goatherd, and his goats.

According to this tale, one day Kaldi noticed his goats bounding about the hillsides in a strange manner after they had eaten some red berries from a hillside shrub. Even the oldest and weakest were frolicking wildly and frantically with heretofore unknown energy, so Kaldi, feeling rather tired and troubled, tried eating some of the berries himself. Immediately he began to prance and cavort with his goats, his troubles and tiredness banished. From then on, Kaldi and his goats cheered themselves each day by eating more of the berries. When the head of a nearby monastery happened to see Kaldi and his goats dancing about one day, he asked for an explanation of the strange behavior; after sampling some of the fruits himself, the monk immediately felt exhilaration flow through his weary frame. In one version of the legend he himself hit on the idea of boiling some of the berries to make a liquid for the monks to drink so they could more easily stay awake during religious services; in another version, Muhammad appeared to the monk later that night as he drowsed during prayer, and instructed him to boil the red berries in water and drink the resulting liquid in order to stay awake and pray.

Within a short time the news of this magical drink reached all the monasteries in the kingdom, and devout monks drank it in order to spend more time praying. The drink became known as *Qahwah,* which means "invigorating

and stimulating." (Since it is also the word for wine, prohibited by Muhammad, the drink eventually was called the Arab's wine.) In another legend even more closely linked with Islam, the Angel Gabriel comes to Muhammad in a dream and reveals to him the nature of the berry and its possibilities as a drink to stimulate the prayers of his disciples.

An ancient Arabian chronicle (preserved in the *Abd-al-Kadir* manuscript), the first to mention the origin of coffee, gives yet another legend relating the discovery of coffee to a follower of Islam, this one including the tradition of roasting the berries and the use of coffee as a medicine. According to one version of the tale, the dervish Omar, known for his ability to cure the sick through prayer, was exiled from Mocha to a desert cave near Ousab. Starving, he chewed the berries from nearby shrubs; but they were bitter, so he tried roasting them to improve their flavor. When they became hard, he boiled them in water in an attempt to soften them. Only a fragrant brown liquid resulted, but Omar was so hungry that he drank it; the beverage immediately revitalized him and sustained him for many days. Eventually patients from Mocha came to the cave in Ousab for medical advice from the exiled healer, tried this drink as a medicine, and were cured. When stories of this "miracle drug" reached Mocha, Omar was asked to return and was made a saint.

Besides the variety of legends accounting for coffee's discovery, there is a good deal of confusion in tracing coffee's uses and beginnings because of the number of different words thought to refer to it in early times. The earliest possible reference to coffee, under the names *bunn* and *bunchum*, are Arabian, and it is in Arabia that the first planting and actual cultivation of the coffee tree apparently took place. Since the coffee tree grows wild in Ethiopia, where much coffee is still gathered from wild trees, not in Arabia, some authorities believe the Ethiopians might have brought seeds to Arabia when they occupied Yemen in the early sixth century, but this remains conjecture.

Some hints as to how coffee was probably first used can be found in observations made by the nineteenth-century botanists who codified other, less flavorful species of the coffee tree in parts of central Africa. Tribes in these areas had early along discovered the stimulant properties of coffee berries; crushed berries mixed with animal fat and shaped

into balls were called "iron rations" and were taken by warriors and travelers on long journeys.

It thus seems likely that coffee was first eaten as food in Ethiopia and Arabia too, and only later was boiled with water to make a beverage. It is also possible that in early times a wine was made from the fermented pulp of the ripe berries. Some authorities think this may be the reason why *Qahwah* (which means both coffee and wine) is the word for coffee; coffee as a beverage may have started as a wine. Sun-dried beans probably inspired the idea of roasting, but exactly how and when coffee developed from a food to a nonalcoholic beverage made from boiling water and roasted, ground coffee beans is simply a matter of historical conjecture.

Coffee in Arabia and the Middle East

The first references to coffee in Arabia suggest its first use was as a medicine. Rhazes, a ninth-century physician, astronomer, and philosopher who compiled a comprehensive encyclopedia of cures for diseases, mentions *bunchum* (a word thought to refer to coffee) as having healing properties. Avicenna, an Islamic physician and philosopher of the eleventh century, has this to say of *bunchum:* "It fortifies the members, it cleans the skin, and dries up the humidities that are under it, and gives an excellent smell to all the body" (quoted in Ukers).

In spite of the auspicious beginnings of coffee as a cure-all, it was principally religion that spread coffee-drinking throughout the Middle Eastern world. A learned *imam,* or holy man, Sheik Gemaleddin of Aden, tried coffee in Ethiopia about 1450, and later, in poor health, sent for some coffee to help him recover. Revitalized, he quickly endorsed its use by dervishes during religious exercises. An endorsement from such a famous man encouraged others to try the beverage; throughout Yemen those who worked or journeyed at night also began drinking coffee, and one renowned physician began to prescribe it for a variety of ills. Dervishes, as well as other travelers, spread the word about the new drink that would help one stay awake. The drink they introduced to the holy cities of Mecca and Medina was probably no longer a decoction made by boiling leaves and cherries of the coffee tree in water; it seems likely that by

this time roasted beans were ground fine with a mortar and pestle, boiled in water, and the result consumed—the grounds along with the liquid.

From Mecca, the center of the Islamic world, dervishes took coffee to Egypt, Persia, and Syria; soon, drinking coffee had become a part of Muslim religious ritual; while chanting prayers during religious services, each dervish received a sip of coffee from a consecrated bowl before the bowl was passed to those in the congregation. For many thus introduced to coffee, it quickly became a secular beverage as well; the first coffee houses, later called *kahveh kanes* by the Turks, opened in Mecca, and students, travelers, musicians, and storytellers gathered there to play games, sing, dance, talk, and drink coffee. Although strict, pious Muslims condemned such use of a religious drink and were scandalized by the exuberant nature of coffee-house activities and arguments, coffee houses opened in all the major Arabian, Egyptian, and Persian cities. Experiments in brewing coffee eventually resulted in a more appealing drink. Roasted beans were still pounded in a mortar and pestle and boiled with water, but now were decanted into pots and served, reheated, with cinnamon or cloves.

During the two main periods of Muslim expansion between the eleventh and the sixteenth centuries, coffee followed the establishment of Islamic law. Turkey, southern India, the Balkan states, Spain, and later, northern Africa came under the sway of the Koran, and coffee became known as "the drink of Islam." But although coffee appeared in the cities in these countries and areas, it was always in roasted form. The Arabs zealously guarded their monopoly on coffee by prohibiting the exportation of green coffee beans—seeds—so that coffee trees were cultivated only in Arabia. Eventually, however, Muslim pilgrims took coffee seeds to the coast of India, where the first coffee trees were planted early in the seventeenth century.

Everywhere coffee was introduced, coffee houses sprang up, often to the dismay of the more pious Muslims. In almost every country where coffee houses flourished throughout the Middle East (and later Europe), there is a history of attempts to suppress them as places full of dangerous radical behavior and ideas. By 1511, the critics of the coffee house in Mecca had won out. The governor of the city, representative for the sultan of Egypt, became convinced that coffee was an exhilarating drink that inspired men and women to break Islamic laws. Leading citizens concurred,

and physicians, fearing the loss of patients now that the health drink was readily available, felt indiscriminate coffee-drinking should be condemned altogether; it was decided that the safest course was to close the coffee houses, forbid the sale of coffee, and burn the coffee already in the warehouses. But the coffee-drinking habit was far too widespread for this edict to be effective, and many continued to drink the forbidden potation in private, rejoicing when the sultan, a lover of the brew, promptly ordered the edict revoked.

Two decades later, the feeling against coffee broke out in Cairo, where a leading expounder of Islam preached that those who drank it were not true followers of the Prophet, despite the legends. His followers ransacked and burned coffee houses, until the chief justice summoned those for and against coffee and served coffee to the entire group, "reuniting the contending parties."

In the opulent and luxurious coffee houses of sixteenth-century Constantinople, patrons reclined on soft pillows as they were entertained with tales from *The Arabian Nights* and watched sophisticated professional singers and dancers. The democratic nature of the coffee house fostered much free and open discussion of all issues, by all classes of society; and as the price of admission was the price of a cup of coffee—about one cent—the coffee houses were constantly jammed despite the large numbers of new ones that kept opening. Among all classes of Turks, coffee was considered one of the necessary items of life. At the marriage ceremony, men promised to provide coffee for their wives throughout their lives, and their failure to do so allowed women to sue for divorce.

Eventually even sophisticated Constantinople had to contend with religious zealots, particularly imams and dervishes, who wanted the popular coffee houses closed so that people would return to the now nearly empty mosques. All sorts of justifications for banning coffee-drinking were suggested, including the assertion that ground, roasted coffee was a kind of charcoal that the Koran specifically mentioned as unsanitary food. Finally, coffee was prohibited as being in the same class as wine because of the word used for it, but because the decree proved impossible to enforce, the coffee houses reopened. They were the source of much government revenue until they were closed again for political reasons by Grand Vizier Kuprili in the mid-seventeenth century. The punishments for being caught made the ban on coffee-drinking and coffee houses effective: first violators were

cudgeled; second violators were sewn in leather bags and thrown in the Bosporus. But coffee-drinking was not destined to be forbidden forever. When a Frenchman, Antoine Galland, visited Constantinople at the end of the century, he reported that, on the average, twenty cups of coffee per person per day were consumed. Of all the coffee-drinking countries in the Middle East, only in Persia were the coffee houses never suppressed, largely because the wife of the shah appointed official teachers to sit in the coffee houses and expound only on noncontroversial political topics.

Coffee in Europe

In spite of the popularity of coffee as a general beverage in the Middle East, it was still regarded as a medicine to some degree. This view of coffee's purpose was passed on to the European visitors and ambassadors to the Turkish Empire in the latter part of the sixteenth and early part of the seventeenth centuries; their descriptions of it as "a very wholesome liquor" with decided medical benefits ensured its eventual importation into all the countries of Europe. A Swedish traveler wrote of coffee after a visit to Constantinople, "This is a kind of pea that grows in Egypt, which the Turks pound and boil in water, and take it for pleasure instead of brandy, sipping it through the lips boiling hot, persuading themselves that it consumes catarrhs, and prevents the rising of vapours out of the stomach into the head." Although a German doctor and botanist, the famous Leonhard Rauwolf, was the first to write about coffee in 1582, it was the Venetians who first imported actual beans in 1615.

Italy

Before the Spanish and Portuguese built ships capable of sailing great distances, trade with the East was funneled to Europe primarily through Venice, whose navy and treaty with the Turks gave her ships control over the Mediterranean. Since silks, spices, and other products of the Levant had been brought to Europe through Venice, it is not surprising that Venetian traders, with their knowledge of the ports of the Turkish Empire, brought in the first coffee for Europeans. An extremely expensive drink, coffee was first used as a medicine and was sold at apothecary shops. By

the middle of the century, however, it was sold in the street by lemonade vendors, along with other beverages such as orangeade, chocolate, and herbal infusions. Throughout Italy it became a commonly seen drink.

But although coffee enjoyed almost immediate acceptance, as tradition has it, there were some religious fanatics (this time Christian), hostile to Islam and its prophet, who denounced it as an "invention of Satan." They petitioned the Pope, asking to have coffee forbidden to Christians. It was an evil potation, the denouncers reasoned, because Muhammad had provided it as a replacement for wine and had no doubt forbidden his followers to imbibe the fermented juice of the grape because it was a Christian beverage sanctified as the blood of Christ in Holy Communion. However, when the Pope tried a steaming cup of it, so the tale goes, he thought it was such an excellent drink that he remarked, "We shall fool Satan by baptizing it and making it a truly Christian beverage."

Whether or not this imprimatur was actually given by the Pope, coffee flourished as a drink, and with it the coffee houses that first appeared on the Piazza San Marco in Venice by the end of the seventeenth century. Although these first *caffè* were poor affairs, consisting only of small windowless rooms, they were frequented by all but the poorest classes of society. In the mornings meeting places for conversation among workers, physicians, vendors, and other employed people, the *caffè* were the center of entertainment and scandalous gossip for ladies and gentlemen of the leisured classes in afternoons and evenings. In the tradition of the coffee houses of the Turks, Persians, and Arabs, they encouraged the spread of radical ideas; one coffee house even planned to install a reading room to educate the general public.

One famous *caffè,* still surviving in the piazza, dates from the early eighteenth century, when fashionable *caffè* with gilt mirrors, tile floors, and outside sections were built to attract aristocratic patrons. The Caffè Florian, opened in 1720 by a friend of the sculptor Canova, soon became the center of information in the city for both the aristocracy and fashionable visitors. In the days before post offices or city directories, patrons entrusted itineraries, messages, and important letters with Florian to be passed on, and travelers knew Florian would be able to help them find a particular person in the city. Trusted with confidences and asked for matchmaking advice, Florian and his *caffè* were

among the most important features of eighteenth-century Venice.

By the end of that century, though, the cycle of history prepared to repeat itself. Reformers charged the *caffè* in Venice and other Italian cities with purveying vice, corruption, and immorality. Italy, however, and the Italians had adopted the *caffè* as their own, and all attempts to suppress and close them failed.

France

The first coffee brought into France was all for private consumption. M. de la Roque, after a trip to Constantinople with the French ambassador, is credited with bringing both coffee and a Turkish coffee service to Marseilles in 1644, and in 1660, Marseilles merchants returning from several years in Turkey, unable to imagine life without coffee, brought still more beans. The merchants were soon importing coffee into Marseilles for general use, inspiring the merchants of Lyons to do the same. When coffee houses opened to great success in these cities, the doctors were among the first to denounce the new and popular drink. They announced that coffee was harmful to the local inhabitants, claiming it "burned up the blood, and so induced palsies, impotence, and leanness," and was "a vile and worthless foreign novelty," whose value as a remedy was nil. But the public, drinking more and more coffee, was unimpressed with these indictments; merchants began importing green beans in enormous quantity to supply the popular taste.

Surprisingly, the center of French fashion, Paris, was slower to appreciate the Muslim beverage, in part, no doubt, because Louis XIV, who tasted it in 1664, was not impressed. Although Jean Thévenot introduced coffee and methods of preparing it in his book published in Paris in 1657, it took the coffee parties at the rented palace of Suleiman Aga, the Turkish ambassador who arrived in 1669, to convince the Parisians of coffee's possibilities as a fashionable drink. Descriptions of these parties convey the exotic atmosphere of black slaves, gorgeous Oriental costumes, fabulous gold and silver dishes, and steaming black, fragrant coffee. One can understand why he was able to establish the coffee-drinking habit firmly in the year and a half he remained in Paris.

In a scant two years, coffee was being sold in Paris in a booth at the spring fair of St. Germain, by an Armenian

named Pascal. His waiters even carried trays with cups of coffee into the crowds to encourage fairgoers to try the drink. Although the coffee shop he then opened was not a success, his waiters did a good business hawking coffee, which they kept hot in jugs, from door to door. Other coffee houses were opened; most used as a model the Oriental-style coffee house frequented by the lower classes, and thus attracted only the poorer classes of Paris, not the fashionable, on whose patronage they depended if they were to become a success. Until the first Parisian café opened in 1689, the most successful purveyors of coffee were those who sold it door to door. A cripple known as Le Candiot was a fixture of the streets at this time and sold cups of coffee for two sous, including sugar.

By 1685, doctors were refuting the notion that coffee was a dangerous beverage. In Grenoble, a famous physician lauded the effects of *café au lait* as a medicine, while a group of doctors in Paris published their assertions that coffee cured scurvy, promoted the flow of urine, and relieved smallpox and gout. They even suggested gargling with coffee to improve the voice.

The Café de Procope, opened in 1689 by François Procope, was across the street from the Comédie-Française, so this first Parisian café to cater to the intelligentsia was well located. Within a short time, it was a literary salon; its patrons included the most celebrated dramatists, poets, actors, and musicians of the times: Rousseau, Diderot, and Beaumarchais drank coffee there, and Voltaire consumed forty cups of his favorite drink, coffee mixed with chocolate, at the Procope every day. Later, during the French Revolution, Marat, Robespierre, and Danton met there, and the young Napoleon Bonaparte, while an artillery officer, once was forced to leave his hat as security while he went to find money to pay his coffee bill.

The opening of the Procope was the beginning of the vogue for coffee in Paris; portable coffee-making kits designed to fit in pockets were the rage; those who wanted coffee prepared for them had many new cafés to patronize, such as the Café de la Régence and the Royal Drummer, frequented by Louis XV and Marie Antoinette. Among the loveliest were those situated in the galleries and gardens of the Palais-Royal. Chess was one of the favored occupations of the café patrons, even though it cost extra for candles to light their chessboards. As new cafés opened, new entertainments to win customers from rival cafés were invented; the cancan,

performed first at one café with bloomers and later, at a rival one, without, originated in this fashion. In the reign of Louis XV, there were already six hundred cafés in Paris. Cafés developed reputations for attracting artists or students or politicians; some began to serve food. To supply the vast coffee requirements of the population, coffee trees were taken to the French West Indies.

By 1760, the French had developed a more European method of coffee preparation, infusion, and various ingenious coffeepots were invented. The cafés of Paris, like the coffee houses in Turkey, fostered radical political discussions, which finally resulted in the French Revolution of 1789. The speech that precipitated the fall of the Bastille took place outside the Café Foy and so inspired the patrons that they marched off immediately to do their duty, presumably after downing the coffee in their cups. Michelet, a historian writing in the nineteenth century, waxed lyrical about the role coffee as a mental stimulant played in the Revolution: "Danton, the terrible Danton, took several cups of coffee before mounting the tribune. 'The horse must have its oats,' he said." By 1843 coffee and the café had been truly assimilated into French society. There were more than three thousand cafés in Paris, and French inventors turned their hands to the development of more elaborate drip coffeepots and the first percolator.

The English Coffee House

Among the first European travelers to Arabia, Turkey, Persia, and Egypt were many noted Englishmen: Samuel Purchas, Sir George Sandys, and Sir Henry Blount ("the father of the English coffee house"); all published their impressions of coffee, coffee houses, coffee-drinking customs, and of course expounded its medicinal virtues. While some medical men, notably William Harvey, who discovered the circulation of the blood, apparently drank coffee for its benefits in the early seventeenth century, the translator of an Arabian physician's medical assessment of coffee assured the reader coffee "causeth vertiginous headheach, and maketh lean much, occasioneth waking . . . and sometimes breeds melancholy," and warned against taking milk with coffee as it might cause leprosy.

But although it seems likely that many Englishmen were drinking coffee in the early seventeenth century, the first written account of coffee-drinking in England is found in

John Evelyn's diary notes for 1637. While at Oxford, he made the acquaintance of a student from Crete, Nathaniel Conopios, who had fled from Turkey when his patron, the Patriarch of the Greek Orthodox church, was murdered. At Balliol College, Oxford, he was granted refuge. Conopios was in the habit of drinking coffee every morning and served it to his friends.

Perhaps it was this introduction to coffee that encouraged the opening of a coffee house in Oxford—the first in England—by a Lebanese called Jacob, in 1650. Patronized by enthusiastic students, the coffee house was a great success, encouraging coffee-drinking to such a degree that, by 1655, students had convinced a local apothecary to sell coffee beans and even formed the Oxford Coffee Club (later to become the Royal Society).

It was in London, however, that the coffee house was destined to become a social institution, influencing for two centuries the manners, customs, and business institutions of the English. Pasqua Rosée, an Armenian, opened the first coffee house in London in 1652, and by 1660 the many coffee houses throughout the city had become the meeting places of the day for men. As they became the popular forums of free discussion for the commoner, tavern attendance declined, and with this came a decline in tax revenues from taxes on alcoholic beverages. The government placed a fourpence tax on each gallon of coffee sold and insisted on licensing the coffee-house establishments. But the popularity of coffee was assured; the tax had no effect on sales. In fact, the drink was so popular, and small change in circulation so scarce, that by 1670 coffee houses created and purveyed their own coffee tokens, which were used instead of money. (Even the Great Plague of 1665 was not sufficient to close these social centers, although each man entering was queried closely about his family's health!)

Part of coffee's popularity as a drink both in the coffee house and in the home, in spite of the high prices originally paid for it, was as a result of the claims made for its medical benefits. As early as 1657, coffee was advertised as "a very wholsom and Physical drink, having many excellent vertues, closes the Orifice of the Stomack, fortifies the heat within, helpeth Digestion, quickneth the Spirits, maketh the Heart lightsom, is good against Eye-sores, Coughs, or Colds, Rhumes, Consumptions, Head-ach, Dropsie, Gout, Scurvy, Kings Evil, and many others" (quoted in Ukers, p. 53). Doctors for the most part were not happy that a cure-all

once purveyed exclusively by them was becoming a common beverage rather than a medicine only they could offer, and they invented complicated and bizarre cures that must have done much to discourage general coffee consumption. Walter Rumsey's "Cophy Electuary" recipe appeared in 1657, designed to be taken before and after use of the "Provang," a formidable instrument to cleanse the stomach invented by Rumsey. For the electuary, Rumsey wrote, "Take equal quantity of Butter and Sallet oyle, melt them well together, but not boyle them; Then stirre them well that they may incorporate together: Then melt therewith three times as much Honey, and stirre it well together: Then add thereunto powder of Turkish Cophie, to make it a thick Electuary." After a substantial dose of this decoction was swallowed, the "Provang," a two- to three-foot-long piece of whalebone with a button at the end, was to be inserted anally and worked vigorously to produce its salutary effects. Rumsey invented a number of other coffee medicines, but in spite of them, coffee continued to be a popular drink, both as a beverage and a medicine.

Owners of the now-less-popular taverns and alehouses were not happy about the growing use of coffee either, and sought to win back their customers with propaganda campaigns. They issued broadsides that described coffee as "a loathsome potion, not yet understood, syrrop of soot, or Essence of old Shoes," "Turkey gruel," "ninny broth," and "a crust charkt into a coal."

The coffee controversy in England also divided the sexes for the first time. Women were barred from coffee houses in England (though not from owning them), a practice different from the custom on the Continent, where women were welcome in cafés. In 1674, women issued "The Women's Petition against Coffee," a document that claimed coffee made men as "unfruitful as the deserts where that unhappy berry is said to be bought," threatening the human race with extinction, and expressed their resentment at the many hours their husbands passed in coffee houses drinking coffee and talking. Men responded to this attack by claiming coffee's "virtues as a non-alcoholic beverage for those desiring sobriety rather than drunkenness" and as a beverage to maintain health.

But the coffee controversy was not over yet. Charles II spoke against the coffee houses in 1672, believing they were "seminaries of sedition," and began to talk of suppressing them. As in other countries, the English coffee houses did

foster radical discussions of democracy and republicanism; they were known as "penny universities," because for only the penny required for entrance (and the twopence for a cup of coffee or tea) any man could educate himself through listening to discussions between some of the most-learned men of the day and reading the newspapers available. Finally, in 1675, disregarding the caution of his advisers, Charles issued a proclamation ordering the closing of the coffee houses beginning on January 10, 1676, using the women's petition as one of his excuses. Before this date, however, there was such a public outcry that the king was forced to revoke the proclamation on January 8 unless he was prepared to put down the demonstrations of discontent. (Later, English historians were to call this one of the first victories of free speech.)

Attendance at the coffee houses grew, and by the end of the seventeenth century there were nearly two thousand coffee houses in London. Political issues continued to be discussed and disputed; the Turk's Head was the first to settle discussions by placing votes in their own invention, a ballot box. Soon each coffee house was attracting its own special clientele: the Bastons and Garraway's were the meeting places of physicians, surgeons, and apothecaries, and patients came to consult them there; at the Chapter, booksellers gathered and playwrights and authors came to sell them the copyrights to their works; at the Baltic, brokers and merchants in Russian trade met and bargained; at the Will's, Dryden held court. As men with similar commercial interests began to congregate at particular coffee houses, the coffee houses became the center of business transactions in the city. According to Edward Brahmah, Lloyd's of London, the insurance firm, is one of the modern enterprises that grew out of a seventeenth-century coffee house. Edward Lloyd's coffee house in 1688 was a meeting place for seafarers and merchants; soon, for the convenience of his customers, Lloyd began to keep lists of what ships were carrying, when they were leaving, and which needed to buy insurance. Underwriters came to sell insurance to those who were leaving, while merchants came to learn of the whereabouts of particular ships. Thus began two Lloyd's institutions: the Lloyd's insurance company and Lloyd's Register of Shipping. Today, in Lloyd's insurance offices, uniformed attendants are still called "waiters" as they were in the original Lloyd's coffee house.

But just as the end of the seventeenth century saw the expansion of importance of the coffee house in English public life, so the end of the eighteenth century saw its decline. Commercial groups began to find it more useful and convenient to establish offices; political parties and social groups sought more exclusivity by forming private clubs. While a few coffee houses were still centers for intellectual life in 1775—Samuel Johnson's literary club still met at the Turk's Head—others now served alcohol and had degenerated into rowdy, disreputable places. A proposal by the coffee-house proprietors that they be the purveyors of all news and the newspapers be shut down further contributed to their decline as the general public condemned and ridiculed this idea.

Although coffee was still the well-established breakfast and dinner drink of English upper- and middle-class homes, tea was rapidly gaining in popularity; the London Tea Gardens, which admitted women, proved a powerful competitor to the coffee house. The afternoon tea parties given by women were encouraging the spread of tea-drinking, and these, plus the advertising campaigns begun by the British East India Company, whose trade was primarily tea, to encourage more tea-drinking, had some effect. Tea became the most popular beverage served at the gardens and became fashionable at Court. (For the rise of British tea-drinking habits and its nearly complete replacement of coffee as the British drink, see Chapter Eight.)

Holland, Scandinavia, and Germany

One of the few countries in Europe where no controversy over coffee's influence occurred was the Netherlands, perhaps as a result of the fact that Dutch traders captured the first world's market for it. As early traders in all kinds of goods, they were acquainted with coffee as soon as the Venetians imported it, and Dutch ships sought, as early as 1614, direct coffee-trading possibilities with the Arabs. By 1640, the Dutch were offering their first commercial shipment of coffee from Mocha, before coffee had even been introduced into France. The enterprising Dutch were the first to plant coffee in the colonies they controlled, first in Ceylon, and later Java as well. A governor of the Dutch East India Company sent the first Arabian coffee seedlings to Java in 1696, but it was the second shipment in 1699 that began the coffee trade of the Netherlands—a trade that made Java coffee a household word. A plant sent back

to Amsterdam from Java, in fact, became the progenitor for most of the coffee of the West Indies and America, since it was from this plant that a seedling was sent to the Jardin des Plantes in Paris (see "The Tree" and de Clieu).

The Dutch probably brought coffee to the Scandinavian countries, though it seems not to have been known in any Scandinavian country before 1700. During the eighteenth and early nineteenth centuries, coffee was the center of considerable controversy. In 1746 a royal edict was issued in Sweden against "the misuse and excesses of tea and coffee drinking"; beginning in 1747, coffee and tea drinkers there were required to declare themselves and pay an excise tax, or suffer the penalty of having their cups and dishes confiscated. Coffee-drinking was prohibited in 1756; eventually the ban was lifted and import taxes were imposed when the government couldn't stop the coffee-smuggling trade. Further attempts to suppress coffee occurred until 1822, when the government finally recognized the inevitable. What makes this seem ludicrous today is the fact that more coffee per capita is drunk currently in Sweden than in any other country.

Although a German author, Dr. Leonhard Rauwolf, was the first European to mention coffee in print—in a book about his travels in the Middle East, published in 1582—coffee-drinking was not introduced into Germany until about 1670. An English merchant opened the first coffee house in Hamburg in 1679, and in rapid succession coffee houses opened in Leipzig, Stuttgart, Augsberg, and Berlin. By the time of Frederick the Great, there were over a dozen coffee houses in Berlin alone.

The coffee controversy in Germany took on a curious note; it was primarily Frederick the Great who opposed its general use, on the grounds that too much money was being paid to foreign coffee merchants, thus depriving his court of possible revenues. Despite the fact that by the 1750s coffee rather than warm beer regularly appeared on breakfast tables, Frederick sought to restrict its use to the wealthy and the aristocracy. He encouraged the use of expensive accouterments that the poorer classes could not afford and prodded the doctors into a propaganda campaign against coffee-drinking on the basis that it caused sterility. The *Coffee Cantata* written by Bach in 1732 was a musical protest against such propaganda efforts.

But Frederick was adamant: coffee had to be banned. In 1777, he issued a manifesto against coffee which is ex-

tremely amusing to read today, considering the place coffee now holds in Germany. Ukers quotes the document:

> It is disgusting to notice the increase in the quantity of coffee used by my subjects and the amount of money that goes out of the country in consequence. Everybody is using coffee. If possible, this must be prevented. My people must drink beer. His Majesty was brought up on beer, and so were his ancestors, and his officers. Many battles have been fought and won by soldiers nourished on beer; and the King does not believe that coffee-drinking soldiers can be depended upon to endure hardship or to beat his enemies in case of the occurrence of another war.

In spite of royal proclamations and manifestos, people drank coffee, and finally, the king was forced to forbid its roasting except in royal roasting establishments in order to enforce his prohibition. Naturally, coffee-roasting licenses were issued to the nobility, and the possession of the license became a kind of badge of membership in the upper class. Those in the poorer classes who attempted to roast coffee in secret were spied upon; Frederick employed wounded soldiers as "coffee sniffers" whose duty was to follow the smell of roasting coffee in the city streets in order to find those who were roasting it without permits.

But the home of the *kaffee-klatsch* would not tolerate such prohibitions for long, and by the beginning of the nineteenth century coffee had become one of the Germans' favorite beverages.

Vienna

Coffee was indirectly introduced to the Viennese by the Turks. In 1683, the army of 300,000 men sent by Muhammad IV to conquer Europe reached Vienna, so the story goes, and quickly cut the city off from the rest of the country. Not far away, waiting for aid from the Polish army, were 33,000 Austrians who, when help came, planned to besiege the capital and save Vienna. To send secret information on the enemy strength and positions in Vienna, the Viennese commander employed a Pole, Franz George Kolschitzky, who had lived among the Turks, as a messenger. Disguised as a Turk, Kolschitzky passed through enemy lines four times, even swimming the Danube to get to the waiting Austrians.

Largely because he brought back information on the signals this army would give when they prepared to attack the Turks, so that the Viennese commander could be prepared to do battle at the same time, the Turks were soundly defeated. They fled, leaving behind all their supplies, including many sacks of green coffee, at that time unknown among the Viennese. No one wanted the coffee, but Kolschitzky, having lived among the Turks, knew its purpose; he claimed the beans as the reward for his services in saving Vienna.

Kolschitzky began at once to peddle coffee door to door and later petitioned the municipal council to give him a shop—in addition to the coffee beans he had already received—as payment for his valor. After much controversy this was granted, and Kolschitzky opened the first Viennese coffee house.

Now honored in Vienna as the patron saint of coffee houses, Kolschitzky began an "institution" that continued to grow; by 1839, there were over eighty coffee houses in the city; today, one of the most pleasant occupations for a Viennese afternoon is to frequent one of the coffee houses that dates from that time.

Coffee in America

Captain John Smith, whose book, *Travels and Adventure* (1603), mentions coffee briefly, was probably the first person to bring a knowledge of coffee to North America, when he founded the Colony of Virginia at Jamestown in 1607. However, there is no historical evidence that coffee was available in early America until much later in the century, although some seem to think the mortar and pestle brought over on the *Mayflower* may have been used to grind coffee beans. Actually the first of the new Eastern beverages to arrive on the mainland appears to have been tea, brought by the Dutch to New Amsterdam. Chocolate and coffee soon followed, and according to Ukers, the first solid references to coffee appeared in 1668 and 1670. William Penn wrote of buying green coffee beans in New York (New Amsterdam was renamed after the British occupied it in 1664) for the stiff price of $4.68 a pound in 1683. This is actually higher than it sounds; something like twelve cents a serving at a time when a good meal could be bought for the same sum!

As cities grew, the colonists began to adopt European and particularly English fashions, including that of the coffee house. The history of the early American coffee house soon leads one to the conclusion that similarities between the coffee houses of Europe and those of early America were brief and fleeting. Like those of the Old World, the New World coffee house became a meeting place, a center of business activity, the place where gossip was disseminated, and a hotbed of radical ideas. In many cases, however, the "Coffee House" was really only an inn or tavern with an eye on the fashions of the times, and despite what it might call itself, primarily dispensed beer and ale, applejack, rum, meals, and lodging. The first license to sell coffee (and "cuchaletto"—chocolate) was issued to Dorothy Jones of Boston, though whether she sold the beans or the beverage is not known. The most famous of these coffee-house-tavern-inns (at least in New England) was the Green Dragon, in operation from 1697 to 1832 on Union Street in Boston. Daniel Webster called it the "headquarters of the Revolution." Certainly it numbered most of the important political figures of the day among its patrons, from John Adams and Paul Revere to the conspirators of the Boston Tea Party. In fact, the early coffee houses did more to spread commerce and revolution than coffee, but the latter gave coffee a tremendous boost in an indirect manner when tea became an unpatriotic drink as a result of its association with the British and the noxious Stamp Act (see Chapter Eight). It took tea years to recover from this precipitous slide in fashion, and by that time coffee was firmly entrenched on the American table.

The American coffee house, like the English coffee house, was soon absorbed into other social institutions, the ingredients of its atmosphere developing into separate entities: business associations, clubs, stock exchanges, banks, meeting halls, political groups, and so on. Unlike the café, which found a stable niche in Mediterranean countries, the coffee house faded into taverns, coffee shops, hotels, and restaurants.

The coffee house may have been no great success, but coffee itself was. As prices fell to levels where it could become a popular beverage, it did so with alacrity. It went west on the wagon trains, it went to California during the Gold Rush, it joined the cavalry. According to Uribé, it even became popular with American Indians, and one tale has it that the present site of Laramie, Wyoming, was swapped for tools, rifles, and a few bags of Java beans. The Northern

soldier in the Civil War received ground coffee with his rations, which was mixed with sugar and boiled in a pot over a campfire.

Coffee became important commerce, and in the 1880s attracted speculators who made several dramatic attempts to corner the coffee supply, though these attempts were often brought to a crashing conclusion with the arrival of a ship from Brazil. Throughout the nineties coffee grew in importance, and by 1900 consumption had reached nearly nine hundred million pounds total, or about nine pounds per head of population annually. By 1920 imports were triple that of 1880, about 1.3 billion pounds and per-capita consumption was up to eleven pounds. The peak was reached in 1946, when over twenty pounds of coffee per person was consumed annually in the United States. Thereafter, per-capita consumption began to slide as coffee faced strong competition from other beverages, including tea, until now it stands at just over thirteen pounds per capita. Population growth has kept total imports growing, however. In 1973 some three billion pounds of coffee were brought into the United States to meet demand, about one-third the world's supply.

"The Tree" and de Clieu

Latin America, particularly Brazil, is so closely indentified with coffee cultivation that it is easy to forget that the vast coffee lands stretching from Mexico to Central America, through the West Indies and down into South America, were all started with considerable effort only several hundred years ago—a comparatively new development in the history of the beverage. What is particularly astonishing is to discover that probably most of the billions of coffee trees now grown in these regions derive from a single coffee plant presented to Louis XIV.

In the late sixteenth century a great deal of information on coffee was brought back to the West by European travelers and traders, and as early as 1614 the Dutch began looking into the prospects of coffee cultivation; in spite of the Arabs' reluctance to part with coffee seeds or trees, the Dutch managed to obtain one tree from Mocha that they brought to Holland for study in 1618. Seedlings from the Indian coast plantings begun by Arabs as well as seeds from Mocha were brought by the Dutch to Java in 1699;

by 1706 a Java coffee tree was proudly received at the Amsterdam botanical gardens, and thrived there.

The French had not been blind to the commercial potential of growing coffee in their own colonies, and in 1708 took seed from Mocha to Réunion Island off Madagascar, where it eventually flourished. The French were less successful with the plants in their homeland, however, having failed to induce a coffee tree to take root in European soil in Dijon. They were not even able to get young plants obtained from the Amsterdam gardens to survive in Paris. Finally, in 1714, a healthy five-foot-tall coffee tree was presented as a gift by the burgomaster of Amsterdam to Louis XIV, who, while no lover of coffee (it was his successor who made the drink fashionable at Court), recognized its value sufficiently to order the first greenhouse in France to be built to house it. It was received by the royal botanist and kept at the Jardin des Plantes in Paris, where it was tended with the care due a plant of its rarity. According to Frederick Wellman, Louis XIV desired that its seeds be distributed throughout his tropical empire. This was done, and the tree became known as The Tree, the progenitor of most of the coffee of South and Central America, Mexico, and the French colonies. From 1715 on, seeds or seedlings from The Tree were dispatched to Haiti, French Guiana, parts of India, Réunion Island, and even French Equatorial Africa. Many of these attempts to spread coffee propagation were not successful; either the plants died in transit, refused to grow, fell prey to disease or disaster, or simply failed to flourish.

The most successful single seedling from The Tree was the one stolen from the Jardin des Plantes and taken to Martinique by a young French naval officer, Captain Gabriel de Clieu. While de Clieu's tree was not the first coffee plant to be brought to the New World, his was one of the most successful and influential attempts to do so. His example thus acted as something of a catalyst in encouraging further attempts to propagate coffee, something that had not always been successful prior to this time, and this in turn ensured that seeds and seedlings from his plant were spread throughout the region. The story of de Clieu and his tree, as Ukers puts it, "is the most romantic chapter in the history of the propagation of the coffee plant."

Gabriel Mathieu de Clieu, captain of the infantry on Martinique, apparently conceived the idea of introducing the coffee plant to that island while on a visit to France, sometime about 1720. By some accounts he was said to have

been inspired by patriotic zeal to find some way that France might have her own source of coffee, then growing rapidly in popularity, instead of having to rely on the Dutch and their high-priced East India coffee. At that time the only coffee plants in France were several small seedlings of The Tree growing in the hothouses of the Jardin des Plantes. De Clieu is said to have been rebuffed in his attempts to obtain seeds or seedlings of this rare plant from the royal botanist, Jussieu, who by that time had undoubtedly grown protective of The Tree and its progeny. The story becomes unclear at this point; it is not known whether de Clieu was able to persuade the royal physician, M. de Chirac, of the noble purpose of his plan, or whether he was able to persuade a "lady of quality" to impose the request upon M. de Chirac. What is clear, however, is that at least one seedling was removed by stealth at night from the Jardin des Plantes and de Clieu soon set sail for Martinique with his small precious plant in a box covered with a glass top to protect it from the cold salt air but allow it to be warmed by the sun. Historians quibble over whether de Clieu set sail in 1720 or 1723, whether he made more than one attempt to transport plants, and whether he took one or several, but de Clieu's own account (quoted in Ukers) has it that he successfully managed to take one small plant, against great odds, to Martinique.

"It is useless," he wrote, "to recount in detail the infinite care that I was obliged to bestow upon this delicate plant during a long voyage, and the difficulties I had in saving it from the hands of a man who, basely jealous of the joy I was about to taste through being of service to my country, and being unable to get this coffee plant away from me, tore off a branch." Fending off the would-be sabotage of anticoffee passengers was not the only difficulty Captain de Clieu faced; narrowly escaping capture by Tunisian pirates, the ship nearly foundered in a raging storm only to become becalmed for days on end. The water supply practically exhausted, what little remained was severely rationed, and by some accounts, the commander of the ship refused to allow the fading coffee plant a share, despite de Clieu's earnest petitions. Thus the captain was called upon to make his most generous sacrifice, and for more than a month was forced to share his "scanty ration . . . with this my coffee plant upon which my happiest hopes were founded and which was the source of my delight."

De Clieu's dogged determination won out, and his droop-

ing little plant was duly planted on his Martinique estate. Having brought it through so much, he was not about to have it fall into the hands of any anticoffee islanders. "My first care," he tells us, "was to set out my plant with great attention in the part of my garden most favorable to its growth. Although keeping it in view, I feared many times that it would be taken from me; and I was at last obliged to surround it with thorn bushes and to establish a guard about it until it arrived at maturity. . . ."

In spite of his fears, the good captain was rewarded with a harvest in 1726. Now able to complete his noble mission to bring coffee to the New World, he began spreading seeds and seedlings far and wide.

> Success exceeded my hopes. I gathered about two pounds of seed which I distributed among all those whom I thought most capable of giving the plants the care necessary to their prosperity.
>
> The first harvest was very abundant; with the second it was possible to extend the cultivation prodigiously, but what favored multiplication, most singularly, was the fact that two years afterward all the cocoa trees of the country, which were the resource and occupation of the people, were uprooted and totally destroyed by horrible tempests accompanied by an inundation which submerged all the land where these trees were planted, land which was at once made into coffee plantations by the natives. These did marvelously and enabled us to send plants to Santo Domingo, Guadeloupe, and other adjacent islands, where since that time they have been cultivated with the greatest success.

By 1777 there were said to be nearly nineteen million coffee trees in Martinique alone! De Clieu's gift to the New World (and the Old) was widely recognized, and at his death in 1774, his praises were duly sung. The soaring popularity of coffee houses in Europe created an enormous demand for coffee, ensuring that seeds and seedlings from de Clieu's plant would be eagerly planted all over the Caribbean—Jamaica, Guadeloupe, Haiti, Puerto Rico, Cuba, and later throughout Latin America, including Guatemala, Costa Rica, Venezuela, Colombia, and Mexico. By the 1750s, the West Indies shipped millions of pounds a year to Europe. A century later, Latin America—and in particular, Brazil—would make these figures seem extremely modest.

Ukers comments, "So tiny a plant to produce in the end all the rich estates of the West India islands and the regions bordering on the Gulf of Mexico!—What luxuries, what future comforts and delights, resulted from this one small talent confided to the care of a man of rare vision and fine intellectual sympathy, fired by the spirit of real love for his fellows!" Fired by de Clieu's story, he adds, "There is no instance in the history of the French people of a good deed done by stealth being of greater service to humanity."

Brazil

About the same time that de Clieu was attempting to smuggle coffee plants out of France, the Dutch brought coffee seeds to Surinam (Dutch Guiana) from Java. The French, in neighboring French Guiana, quickly started rival coffee plantings—again, with seedlings from The Tree. In any event, these two colonies jealously guarded their fledgling coffee industries, forbidding exportations of beans or seeds under pain of death, despite the fact that coffee was being planted all over the West Indies. When a border dispute between the two colonies broke out, to avoid the interruption that warfare would mean to their commerce, the French and the Dutch appealed to the Brazilians to arbitrate their disagreements. Francisco de Melo Palheta, a lieutenant colonel in the Brazilian army, was sent on this delicate diplomatic mission, which proved amenable to his talents. So did the wife of the governor of French Guiana, who presented him with a gift when his mission was over: a bag of coffee seeds and several seedlings.

Melo Palheta resigned his commission on his return to Brazil and planted his beans in Pará in 1727; cultivation soon spread to Amazonas and Maranhão, and within fifty years had spread south to where most of Brazilian coffee is planted today. As the news that the soil and climate of Brazil were ideally suited to coffee began to spread and the demands of the world market continued to grow, more seeds and cuttings were imported and the government encouraged planting. The bishop of Rio de Janeiro, Joachim Bruno, declared himself a patron of the plant and gave his blessings to the spread of the plant in São Paulo, Rio de Janeiro, and Minas Gerais.

By 1800 the first exports from Brazil were ready: thirteen bags. But by 1881 Brazil produced a crop of six million bags of coffee. A century and a half later—1959, to be exact—Brazil's total output for the year was 44,330,000 bags of coffee. This extraordinary leap forward in tropical agriculture, requiring the transformation of thousands of square miles of forest into cultivated land, came about as the result of a number of factors.

Until 1888, when slavery was abolished, there was no shortage of labor for such projects, and the soil and weather in most cases were ideal. From the equator to the Tropic of Capricorn, forests were simply hacked down and burned, and the resulting mixture of volcanic soil and ash planted to coffee. Some of the largest *fazendas* (estates) had five million trees. According to Uribé, after the slaves were freed and the last emperor of Brazil, Pedro II, abdicated in 1889, the Brazilian coffee industry found itself overextended, but not for long. Workers from Italy, Portugal, Spain, Germany, and elsewhere flocked to Brazil, the land of limitless opportunity, to carve their own plots out of the forests and plant coffee.

Despite the fact that almost all the methods of cultivation were quite primitive (and remain so to a large extent today), the coffee found a market; with every price rise, more coffee was planted. By 1900, however, the first of a series of boom-and-bust cycles began. These were to occur on the most dramatic scale in Brazil, but were repeated with no less impact in smaller producing countries as well. Oversimplified, the boom-and-bust cycles were brought about by overproduction causing a fall in prices, leading ruined planters to abandon thousands of acres of coffee trees; this eventually led to shortages, soaring prices, and thousands of farmers, eager to reap profits, planting even more acreage than before to start the cycle all over again.

In Brazil the size of the coffee industry made a dip in coffee prices a crisis for the entire country. At that time, 90 percent of the country's wealth was in coffee. In 1900 a fall in world coffee prices brought about havoc in the industry as planters fell behind in paying laborers, and labor shortages ensued, followed by currency inflation. Despite the lack of labor, plantings were at an all-time high and in 1906 the harvest was expected to reach twenty million bags. Unfortunately, the world market was already flooded with coffee, and the demand was estimated at only fourteen million bags. The Brazilian government began buying the

coffee from the planters, and eventually had to buy eleven million bags before prices stabilized. However, 1907 and 1908 yielded bumper crops as well. Despite the huge and ever-growing stockpiles, planters were pleased at the high prices coffee was commanding and stepped up their plantings. Only the small crops of succeeding years and several severe, killing frosts saved the situation and enabled the stockpiles as well as new crops to be sold. In the twenties, the government had to begin buying coffee all over again to support the industry, and again, with prices maintained at attractive levels, planters began planting. By the 1930s Brazil simply started burning its coffee stockpiles, a solution that continued to 1944. Uribé states that altogether some seventy-eight million bags of coffee were destroyed. All efforts to find another use for the beans—as cattle feed, locomotive fuel, home heating—failed. Coffee was even pressed into plastic sheets—"caffelite"—but no coffee byproducts proved commercially feasible.

Despite new government checks and balances on the coffee industry, it continued to grow at a rapid rate; supplying almost two-thirds of the coffee consumed between the two world wars, Brazil benefited from postwar demand, and soon further plantings were undertaken, this time even into the frost belt in southern Paraná. By 1961 almost one million square miles were planted to coffee in Brazil, an area that included something like 4.8 billion trees! If the ups and downs of the world coffee market can be hard on the planter, nature can be equally unkind. The last frost, in July 1975, was the worst in fifty years; it destroyed 70 to 80 percent of Brazil's trees. Although today Brazil supplies less than she once did (currently about one-quarter of the world supply), news of a frost is more than enough to start prices leaping upward for fear of shortages, no doubt the source of the saying that "When Brazil catches cold, the rest of the coffee world catches pneumonia."

New Coffee Lands

By the middle of the nineteenth century vast areas of Latin America were under coffee cultivation. These soon eclipsed the coffee-producing lands inaugurated by the Dutch in the East Indies—particularly after the dreaded "coffee blight" (*Hemileia vastatrix,* or leaf-rust disease) com-

pleted its devastation of the coffee plantings in Sri Lanka (Ceylon) described in Chapter Eight, and ravaged the low-altitude plantings in India and Java. The disease, a type of fungus, attacks *arabica* coffee but not the less-flavorful species of coffee native to Uganda and Zaire (the Congo), the major variety of which is *robusta* coffee. The disease, although not crippling to stands of *arabica* coffee planted at high altitudes (due to cooler temperatures), caused the Dutch to replant the low-altitude stands of Java to the newly discovered *robusta* species in 1900, and growers in India had to do likewise. Total coffee exports from Asia and Oceania now account for a mere 5 percent of total world exports.

The new coffee lands of world importance are the nations of East and West Africa. Total African exports now supply 35 percent of total world exports, much of it *robusta* rather than the flavorful *arabica* or "mild" coffees. The industries of all these countries (with the exception of Ethiopia) are quite new. All species of coffee are native to Africa, but *arabica* grew only in the Ethiopian highlands until missionaries brought seeds to Réunion Island about 1890 and later planted it on the slopes of Mt. Kilimanjaro in Tanzania in 1900, the same year it was planted in the highlands of Kenya. Today, *arabica* has been planted successfully at higher altitudes throughout East Africa.

CHAPTER THREE

How Coffee Is Grown and Processed

The Botany and Cultivation of the Coffee Tree

Most coffee drinkers give little thought to the origin of the ground coffee used to make the beverage in their cup. Some are vaguely aware that coffee comes from trees, fewer still what part of the tree is used. Doubtless there are many who have never seen coffee in bean form. Of course, a detailed knowledge of how and where coffee is grown, the steps it undergoes in processing, and the path it takes from tropical tree to breakfast cup, is by no means a prerequisite to the enjoyment of it as a hot drink. But knowing in broad outline how coffee is produced gives one an enhanced appreciation of those unique and attractive qualities it has when brewed.

In a sentence, coffee is a beverage prepared by adding boiling water to the ground, roasted seeds of the fruit of tropical evergreen trees of the *Coffea* family. There are four species of coffee grown for commerce, but only two of worldwide importance: *Coffea arabica* (called Arabian coffee or *arabica*—pronounced ah-ra′-bee-kah or ah-rah-bee′-kah) and *Coffea canephora* (commonly called *Coffea robusta* or *robusta* coffee). While *robusta* is of growing importance as a source of cheap blending coffee and because it is valuable in the manufacture of soluble (instant) coffees, *arabica* remains the sole source of fine coffee, as it has been throughout the history of the beverage. The two other species of coffee, *Coffea liberica* and *Coffea excelsa,* are both grown in West Africa and considered to produce poor coffee.

Coffee trees vary greatly in size from dwarf trees to thick-trunked forest giants twenty feet or more in height. Intolerant of frost, they grow only in the tropics and have

handsome, shiny dark-green leaves. All bear an abundance of "cherries" (actually berries) that vary in color, some yellow, some pink, but most bright red. Each coffee cherry contains two nutlike seeds; after picking and drying the fruit, the hulls are removed and the hard kernels or the seeds—green coffee—are shipped throughout the world to be roasted, ground, brewed, and consumed.

As with any crop, the quality of coffee depends on the variety grown, the climate, the altitude, the soil, and the care taken in processing. Coffee requires moderate rainfall (seventy-five inches a year) and grows best in volcanic soil and with moderate sunshine. All other things being equal, the higher the altitude at which the tree is grown, the finer the quality of the coffee will be. The influence of elevation appears to be primarily a moderating one, slowing down the growth of the coffee in a tropical climate, which at lower elevations would stimulate abundant growth but lower quality. Processing, at its best, simply retains the quality inherent in the fruit of the tree; poor processing, on the other hand, detracts considerably from the potential quality of the coffee.

Coffee is cultivated primarily in frost-free jungly areas from sea level to over six thousand feet in some seventy countries around the world, from Mexico, Central and South America and the Caribbean to East and West Africa, the Arabian Peninsula, India, Indonesia, the Philippines, New Guinea, and Hawaii. The colorful history of the spread of *arabica* coffee throughout the tropics has been covered in Chapter Two, but it should be noted that *arabica* is native to Ethiopia and *robusta* is native to Uganda and Zaire (formerly the Congo). (*Robusta* cultivation today is still largely confined to these countries, in addition to Angola, West Africa, and parts of Java, India, the Malagasy Republic [Madagascar], and the West Indies.) It can be said that coffee originated in Africa, was made into the beverage we associate with it by the Arabs, was spread throughout the world by the West, and today finds its principal home in Latin America. Much of the world's coffee is produced on small holdings by farmers who have a tiny orchard of coffee trees attached to their farms and take their crop to co-operative factories to be processed, but a good portion is produced, as might be expected, on enormous plantations. A surprising amount of it is still picked from trees growing in the wild, particularly in Ethiopia.

Many varieties of *arabica* and *robusta* exist, some differ-

ing only slightly in leaf shape or in resistance to disease, while others differ in the character and quality of the coffee that can be obtained from them. *Arabica* coffee has a number of varieties—Mundo Novo, Bourbon Vermelho, Caturra, and so on—some of which are dwarf varieties, others differ in the color of the fruit, and some, such as the Maragogipe, produce quite large fruits and seeds. These varieties and their subvarieties are of interest primarily to the botanist and the planter. The coffee trade divides the world's coffees into a simpler scheme: *arabicas* and *robustas,* subdividing *arabicas* into "milds" and "Brazils." "Mild" in the coffee trade does not mean that such coffees taste mild; it simply means the coffee does not have harsh, hard taste characteristics. As a practical matter, all the world's *arabica* coffees outside Brazil are milds; this constitutes about one-third of the world coffee supply. Brazils are considered separately in the trade for two main reasons: although they are all *arabicas,* they range widely in quality from very poor and harsh to fine; Brazilian varieties make up 25 percent of the world coffee supply.

In the cultivation of coffee the grower's initial consideration is the species to be planted. *Robusta* tolerates higher heat better than *arabica* and does best at elevations up to two thousand feet. It also tolerates disease better, which is why, for example, the low-elevation coffee plantations of Java were replanted to *robusta* after the *arabica* plantings were wiped out by leaf-rust disease. In a given region, *robusta* might be the only economically viable coffee to plant. Presuming that it is possible to grow *arabica* and that the goal is fine coffee, high elevations might be chosen for the cooler temperatures (consequently slowing growth) and the frequency of cloud cover. This last is important, for coffee does not tolerate full sun well and in many coffee districts is traditionally grown under shade trees. A. E. Haarer states that the ideal conditions for growing fine *arabica* coffee include temperatures between 60° and 70°F (and never higher than 75°); even rainfall of seventy-five inches annually with a peak wet season; loamy, fertile, well-drained soil; high humidity; plenty of mist and cloud; diffused light; and moderate winds. Geographically speaking, these conditions are almost never encountered except at high elevations in certain jungly regions. Needless to say, much of the *arabica* coffee in the world is not grown under such conditions, but with almost no exceptions, the finest coffees produced in the world are cultivated in conditions close to the ideal.

COFFEE TREE

COFFEE FRUIT

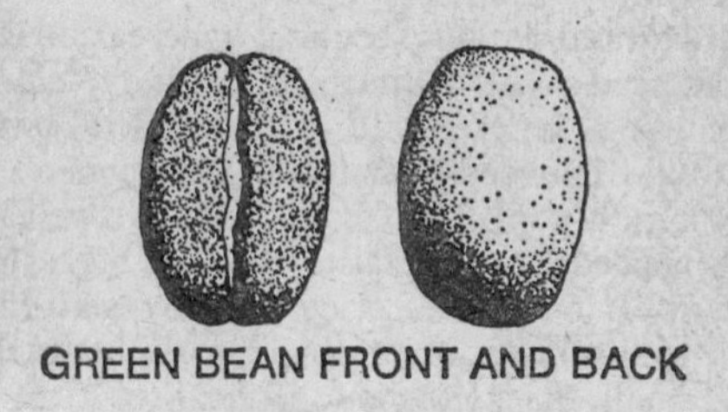

GREEN BEAN FRONT AND BACK

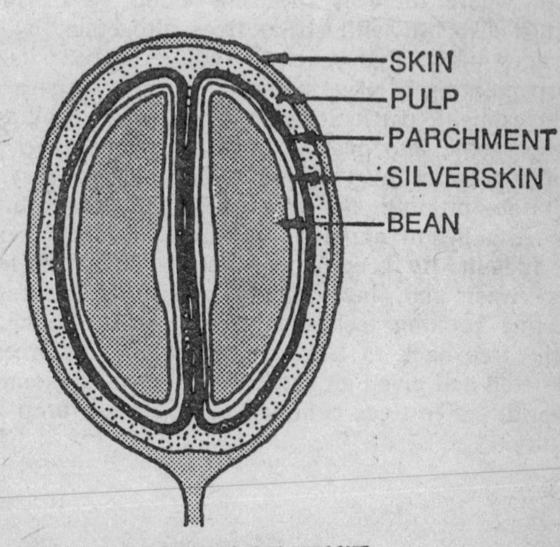

CROSS SECTION OF FRUIT

Coffee is grown almost entirely from seeds. Although it is possible to propagate it by cuttings or grafts and this permits the planter to grow trees identical in character and quality to the trees selected as the source of cuttings, this is a laborious process and in many cases is not an economical proposition. Instead, efforts are made to select carefully the seeds produced by vigorous trees from long-planted estates. These seeds are essentially green coffee beans, usually cleaned and prepared by hand but left in the parchment (the tough outer skin of the seed). They are sown in nursery beds, carefully watered, and partially shaded from sunlight. Seedlings are planted in fields at about six months of age, or when they have produced about a half-dozen leaves. In some areas it is common to wait and transplant a much older and larger seedling, whereas in Brazil simply sowing the seed right in the field is the typical practice. Nursery planting is preferred because it allows the planter more latitude in weeding out weak specimens. *Arabica* coffee is commonly planted from nine to twelve feet apart in similarly spaced rows (*robusta,* a much bigger plant, is planted so there is a space sixteen feet by sixteen feet around it). It is common to plant shade trees between the rows, and many small farmers plant bananas or fruit trees to get an alternative crop. In Brazil coffee trees are usually planted close enough together to enable them to be self-shaded; where there is sufficient cloud cover, many new plantings dispense with shade trees altogether.

It takes up to five years for coffee to bear its first full crop so planting a large stand of coffee trees is a considerable investment, particularly in labor. While waiting for the coffee to come into bearing, mulching, fertilizing, pest control, and pruning the young trees are all necessary. Without appropriate pruning, the tree would grow to fourteen feet or more, a height at which picking would be considerably more difficult. By keeping the tree to about six feet, picking is easier and, in addition, yields are increased. One interesting pruning technique is that of stumping, or cutting the tree back to a stump, by which old trees can be rejuvenated and given an extended life-span. In some parts of the world, coffee trees continue to produce a crop for up to a century.

The Processing of Coffee

In order to understand the nature of coffee-processing, it is necessary to know something about the structure of the coffee berry. The oval fruit grows in small clusters on the branch, and a single one can be plucked off easily. A ripe coffee berry (cherry) resembles a cranberry in size, shape, and color. It contains—normally—two oval seeds, each with a rounded side and a flat side with a lengthwise crease. (Inside the fruit, the seeds are found with their flat, creased sides together.) Between the outer skin of the cherry and the seeds is a thin layer of sweet, sticky, gelatinous juice called the pulp. This layer is quite thin, but slick enough so that if the fruit is given a hard squeeze, the seeds will shoot out. The seeds themselves are white and each is covered in two skins of its own: the stiff, shell-like outer one is called the parchment and the thin, delicate inner membrane covering each green bean, or seed, is known as the silverskin (see page 39).

The object of processing is simply to remove the green beans from the pulp, parchment, and silverskin, and to sort them according to size. To prevent spoilage after picking, coffee must be processed through to the green-coffee stage promptly, at which point it is relatively stable and can be stored for many months without significant flavor loss. Coffee is almost always shipped "in the green" and roasted in the country of consumption, because, once roasted, coffee loses its flavor within weeks.

Harvesting

In the third or fourth year after its planting, the coffee tree puts forth small clusters of white flowers resembling jasmine or orange blossoms in shape and scent. This blossoming (or flowering) lasts only a few days at its peak, filling the air of a large plantation with a soft, sweet fragrance. After the blossoms wither and fall, barring damage during flowering from heavy rains or winds, small green coffee berries appear and slowly begin ripening. The coffee fruit is fully ripe some six to nine months after the blossoming, at which time the fruit—the cherry, as it is called then—typically has a deep red color. In some coffee-growing areas of the

world, there may be three successive crops from each tree in a given year; in other areas where growth is much slower there may be only one harvest, or a major crop and an additional smaller crop.

What complicates the harvesting of coffee is that flowering and ripening usually do not happen in neat stages. Instead, there may be three or four flowerings—each from different buds maturing at different times—and consequently the fruit will be ripening at different times. A coffee crop rarely ripens all at once: It takes as little as three weeks or, more often, as much as three or four months or longer for all the fruit of a given crop to mature. Blossoms, unripe green berries, and the ripe fruit may appear at the same time on the same tree and even on the same branch! Harvesting is therefore a selective process, necessitating berry-by-berry handpicking so that only ripe fruit is picked. But this has two advantages. If all the coffee fruit turned ripe simultaneously, it would be extremely difficult to harvest it all at once, a requisite for producing fine coffee. In addition, a relatively small picking crew is needed; they can simply harvest the coffee continuously as it ripens. Nonetheless, the sheer laboriousness called for in coffee-picking can be appreciated when one realizes that it takes some two thousand handpicked coffee cherries to produce one pound of roasted coffee, which, interestingly enough, is also the average yield of a mature coffee tree. An acre of coffee trees produces from four hundred to six hundred pounds of green coffee per year. Recently, however, intensive cultivation methods developed in Hawaii in the 1950s have made it possible to achieve dramatic increases in yields—three thousand to six thousand pounds per acre—by judicious combinations of severe pruning, extremely close planting to allow self-shading, abundant water, and heavy fertilizing. (Whether the coffee produced by these methods is of equal quality to coffee produced by more traditional methods does not seem to be a settled question as yet.)

The principal reason why coffee must be picked only when ripe is that only mature fruit will yield high-quality coffee. Green, unripe fruit, besides being difficult to process, lacks the flavor fully ripened fruit gives to its seeds (the beans); overripe fruit, on the other hand, results in strong, harsh coffee flavors. Nonetheless, in Brazil a good deal of coffee is harvested by simply stripping the trees of all their fruit—ripe, unripe, and overripe—at one particular time. Leaves, twigs, and fruit are simply pulled or knocked off the branches

and thrown under the trees; they are collected, the fruit sieved, and then simply sun-dried. This method of collection, as well as its subsequent processing, results in poor-quality coffee. But since it is considerably more economical to produce coffee this way, it finds a market and a use in blends.

The Dry Method and Natural Coffees

The simplest method of coffee-processing is the dry, or natural, method. The whole berry is simply allowed to dry on the tree, or is picked and dried. The green beans are then removed from the dried, leathery fruit skins by grinding between stones, or hulled in more up-to-date equipment. It takes about three weeks to a month to sun-dry picked coffee, and the problems inherent in processing such coffee uniformly—given weather variations and the possibility of taints arising from microorganisms growing in the pulp—make high-quality natural processed coffees difficult to produce. Consequently most of the world's fine coffees are rapidly processed by what is called the wet method, and coffees treated in such a manner are called washed coffees. As M. Sivetz and H. E. Foote point out, however, the *best* natural coffees are equal to the best washed coffees. In spite of the risk of getting poor-quality coffee by this method, it is the only one feasible in many areas where the large supply of water necessary for the wet process is not available. High-quality natural coffees are made from carefully picked ripe berries (as in the best Ethiopian and Indonesian coffees); the lowest-quality naturals are made from strip-picked fruit of varying degrees of ripeness (as in Brazils).

The Wet Method and Washed Coffees

Since virtually all the mild coffees of the world are processed by the wet method, let's follow the typical route a fine coffee would take from the tree to the ready-to-ship stage. As mentioned before, pickers take only the ripe fruit from the tree, which means that each day during the weeks or months of the ripening season all the trees in the orchard or field are visited, and whatever fruit has matured is picked and dropped into baskets or sacks carried by the harvesters, who may be a small farmer's family or the labor force of a large estate hired for the picking. If payment is made by the basketful, the fruit is weighed in the field and dumped in sacks for transport to the nearest processing station. Pick-

ing as well as transporting the coffee can be extremely difficult in many of the better coffee-producing regions, particularly those that have rugged, mountainous terrain. In some cases, vehicular traffic may be impossible and only mules can be used to transport the picked fruit up or down steep hillsides. (In some more fortunate areas the coffee can simply be washed down to the factory in a flume of running water.) To prevent possible spoilage of the fruit, it is, if possible, brought to the central factory or pulping station the same day it is picked.

Receiving and Pulping

At the processing station, which may be a simple shed or a large complex, the fruit is tipped into receiving tanks. These vary in design from boxes filled with water to elaborate concrete funnel-bottomed tanks equipped with running water. This initial step allows separation of cherries that float from those that sink. "Floaters" are often empty inside or just immature fruit. The use of receiving tanks also allows the removal of stones, twigs, leaves, and other unwanted material. In a large factory setup, the fruit may be taken through several succeeding tanks, but a small grower will simply take the fruit directly to the pulping machine, which passes the cherries into narrow slots with water and squishes out the seeds by means of a drum or disc. The grower then pushes the seeds along by hand (or in a large factory by moving water in troughs) and reprocesses small unpulped cherries that slipped through the pulper the first time.

The parchment coffee, as it is now called, is carried along in channels to separators, which, whether simple or elaborate, serve to separate different sizes of the parchment coffee, so that they can be given the fermentation period suitable for their size.

Fermentation and Washing

The gummy remnants of pulp that cling to the parchment coffee (called the mucilage) create a particularly slippery, sticky coating that can encourage the growth of micro-organisms that might spoil the coffee. Producers of high-quality coffee waste little time between picking and fermentation in order to reduce the possibility of spoilage to a minimum. Fermentation amounts to holding the wet parch-

ment coffee in tanks or troughs for twenty-four to forty-eight hours to let the enzymes in the mucilage dissolve themselves. Not all biochemical activity during fermentation is undesirable, however; according to Wellman, research indicates that yeast and bacterial growth during fermentation is partly responsible for the body and acidity found in coffee. In any event, timing of fermentation is considered highly important; too much or too little and the quality of the coffee suffers.

Fermentation is considered complete when a handful of the coffee feels sloppy and gooey, but washes as clean as pebbles under a stream of water. At that point, all the coffee is promptly washed—rinsed, as it were—in clean water, often in large sluices or washing channels where it is pushed back and forth with long paddles. Recent research has shown that it is possible to speed up fermentation by the addition of chemicals, or by fermenting the coffee in warm water, or even by scrubbing the coffee in special machines, but these methods are so far not in common use.

Drying in the Parchment

The next step is drying the washed coffee, and in many countries this stage of the process consists in spreading out the parchment coffee on a clean mat in the sun. Larger quantities are dried at large estates and cooperative factories on giant concrete and cement patios (called *barbeques*), where workers rake, push, heap, and respread the mounds of coffee to see that it dries uniformly. (These days one man on a small tractor takes the place of dozens armed with brooms.) In large factories, the coffee is half-dried for a day or two in the sun, and then dried to 12.5-percent-moisture content (considered the ideal for stability of quality) in giant rotary driers that slowly tumble the coffee in hot air for eight hours or more. By this time, almost half the moisture of the bean has been taken out. Once coffee is dry, it is considered relatively safe from additional deterioration in quality, and only improper handling—letting the coffee get wet, moldy, come into contact with kerosene fumes, and so forth—will cause damage.

Curing Coffee (Hulling and Polishing)

After drying, coffee is ready to be "cured," a term used to cover the processing of the dried bean. This is apt to suggest,

falsely, that some improvement in quality takes place at this time, in the same way curing affects a ham. Actually, although there is an *occasional* enhancement of flavor in a very few natural coffees due to their long drying in contact with the pulp, the steps in the coffee process are intended merely to conserve the quality of the coffee when picked.

A natural coffee that has been sun-dried for a month will have a moisture content equal to that of the machine-dried, rapidly but elaborately processed washed coffee. The natural coffee is fed into a huller (a kind of milling machine) in order to remove the dried skin and parchment; the washed coffee in its dried parchment state goes into a huller (or a machine specifically used for parchment removal, known as a peeler or a sheller). By now, the coffee bean inside has shrunk away somewhat from the parchment, which can be peeled away in the hand. Hulling machines typically have two wheels that rub the bean between them, after which it is effectively winnowed from the parchment skin by a blower. Passing the hulled coffee through a screening machine or another blower ensures that no bean-sized pebble or sand is allowed to go any further in the process. (In some systems the coffee is destoned before hulling.)

In other machines, the coffee is polished—that is, the delicate silverskin is removed (some machines hull and polish at the same time). At this point the coffee is in a form ready for roasting: the green bean under the silverskin is light olive-green to bluish-gray to brownish shades, depending on its origin and whether the wet or dry method of preparation was used.

The Grading of Coffees

The grading of coffee, like the grading of tea, is usually misunderstood by consumers—if, in fact, they know anything about the process at all. Essentially, it is the *sorting* of the beans by size, shape, and the number of imperfections (and bits of extraneous material) that can be found in a given sample of green coffee beans. Consequently, coffee grades are not indicative of cup quality per se. What they do signify is that the beans of a given grade are similar in appearance and have been cleaned to a certain standard. In a large factory, pneumatic machines move the coffee by air blasts from the polishing machine to a spiral plate or an in-

clined rotating sieve perforated with holes (or a drum of bars a certain width apart) that allows beans of a certain size to fall through into separate compartments. The result: beans from a given lot being processed are separated into certain standard sizes, from very large to very small. While grading systems differ from country to country, a typical one might use A, B, C for sizes of normally shaped beans, A being the largest and C the smallest. A-grade beans usually amount to half the crop, B 20 percent, and C 10 percent. There are always beans broken in processing (called triage); these comprise about 13 percent of the production. Unusually shaped but good beans amount to about 7 percent.

The variety of the tree and its particular conditions of growth affect the size and shape of the bean. Even in the most unvarying conditions, beans from one picking will vary considerably—some are twice the size and weight of others. Maragogipe, as mentioned before, is a variety of *arabica* that normally produces very large beans; the Bourbon variety grown in Brazil characteristically has quite small, curly beans as does the Mocha coffee from which the Bourbon variety comes. Most of the other coffees in the world fall somewhere in between these two sizes; some are fatter than others, some have flattened tips; some have wide irregular creases, others tight creases; and so on. Regardless of the characteristic appearance of the bean from a given region or tree variety, however, beans will still vary in size, and these size differences are the basis of grading by appearance. There are two unusual malformed or freak bean types that occur in small percentages in every crop: the peaberry (about 4 percent) and the elephant berry (about 3 percent). On occasion, one of the flat-sided beans fails to grow, which allows the other seed to assume a rounded shape. The fruit is smaller, and the single small seed is called peaberry (in Central America it is called *caracol*—Spanish for snail). Elephant beans occur when two seeds are found joined into one large irregular seed.

There is no relationship between the size of the bean and the cup quality of the beverage made from it. Some of the best coffees are made from the medium-sized, not the largest grades, of a coffee crop. Peaberries, however, are said to roast particularly well, because of their shape, and consequently command a slight premium. In fact, the primary reason for sorting beans by size is to ensure that a given lot of coffee will roast uniformly, and in this sense, careful grading—not what the grade is—is important to cup quality.

If beans of all different sizes were roasted together, the smallest ones would burn while the largest would be under-roasted. The beverage made from such a roast would have a green-burnt flavor.

While the uniformity of the beans in any given grade is a significant quality factor, equally important is the number of imperfections that can be found in any given sample of the beans. How clean a coffee is has an indirect but significant bearing on the quality of the beverage. A stinker (a bean fermented by accident) roasted, ground, and brewed with clean beans will add a strong taint to the beverage.

Today electronic sorting machines supplement (or supplant) hand-sorting methods for weeding out imperfect beans, discolored beans, spotted, nicked, or otherwise abnormal beans, as well as foreign material that has not been removed thus far in the coffee process. These tireless machines, in use in many producing countries, are programmed to remove all beans not falling within a permitted range of color, shape, size, weight, and other factors. Nonetheless, a great deal of hand-sorting still goes on, sorting out undesirable beans in a box or on a moving belt. The grading system used for Brazilian coffees illustrates grading for imperfections as well as by bean size. Brazilian beans are classified by size from 20 (very large bean) to 8 (smallest peaberry), but in addition are given type numbers according to how many imperfections appear in a pound of green beans. A blackened, discolored bean is considered an imperfection, and other undesirable beans or material (shells, broken beans, pods, stones, and so on) are considered equivalent to one black bean or a fraction thereof. Thus, type No. 1 is considered to have no black beans or equivalents. (Since this is near-perfect in terms of uniform cleanliness, it is rare.) Other grades are as follows:

No. 2 No more than 6 black beans or equivalent per lb.
No. 3 ″ ″ ″ 13 ″ ″ ″ ″ ″ ″
No. 4 ″ ″ ″ 29 ″ ″ ″ ″ ″ ″
No. 5 ″ ″ ″ 60 ″ ″ ″ ″ ″ ″
No. 6 ″ ″ ″ 115 ″ ″ ″ ″ ″ ″
No. 7 or 8
More than 115

While something like the Brazil system could be used to grade other coffees produced in the world, standards of maximum imperfections (or defect allowance) are usually incorporated into the size grades, or else given grades are

simply described as handpicked. Washed, mild coffees are presumed to be relatively free from imperfection. Since many markets have high standards of appearance, producers commonly grade and pick their coffees to meet these various requirements. Some European markets, particularly West Germany, demand coffee not only polished and uniformly sized, but also free from blemishes and cracks, and of uniform color. Further electronic sorting may even be done in the importing country. It is true that uniformity and cleanliness of appearance is an encouraging sign of *uniform* cup quality, but it is by no means a guide to the character or quality of the coffee. Beans of excellent color and appearance may carry taints or simply lack flavor. A coffee with a highly attractive appearance may have nowhere near the aroma, body, and flavor of a coffee of nondescript appearance. Despite the fact that one doesn't drink the appearance, a handsome appearance itself has become a desirable aspect of coffee for some buyers, although this has never been the case in the United States, where coffees are bought solely on cup qualities, blending characteristics, or price.

The final step in grading the coffee consists in sampling it in the cup. A small amount of each batch of coffee is roasted, brewed, and tasted to analyze its cup quality or flavor. The coffee beverage is called the liquor of the coffee, and coffee tasters are called liquorers. How coffee is analyzed, tasted, and judged is discussed in detail in Chapter Four. Here it is only important to note that cup qualities are *not* taken into consideration in the grading systems of most coffee-producing countries. Brazil grades its coffees by broad taste categories, but most countries simply incorporate a certain flavor standard into their grading system, so that coffees with a very poor taste are not exported or are eliminated from the usual grades. Cup-quality analysis may also be used to set prices to growers to encourage quality production, but its most immediate use is as a means of quality control over the processing, since defects such as underfermenting or overfermenting, use of brackish water for washing, and so on can be discovered by taste. In brief, cup qualities in the world's coffees are for the buyer to discover by cup sampling; it is the buyer's demand for coffees of certain types, characters, qualities, and prices that shapes the cultivation and production of various coffees.

The Marketing of Coffee

Coffee is among the five most important agricultural commodities in international world trade (the others are wheat, sugar, wool, and cotton). It is the principal commercial crop of some dozen countries, half of them earning 25 to 50 percent of their foreign exchange revenues from coffee exports. Over 125 countries consume coffee produced in seventy of them. During the 1950s world export trade in coffee was exceeded only by world exports in petroleum; although today coffee is farther down the list of important commodities of world trade, it is still a multibillion-dollar industry and of enormous importance to the principal producing and consuming countries. World exportable production of coffee over the past twenty years has waxed and waned from highs of about sixty-five million bags (for the purpose of statistics, a bag is understood to weigh sixty kilograms, or about 132 pounds) to occasional lows of about forty million bags. In recent years exports and imports have been around fifty-five million bags, of which the United States, traditionally the world's biggest coffee customer, takes about a third. The rest of the coffee-consuming countries of the world take 10 percent or less of world production.

Production is as lopsided as consumption. Latin America as a whole exports about three-fifths of the world total. Brazil, at one time the source of most of the world's coffee, still supplies one-quarter of world exports. Colombia is next in importance, supplying about 12 percent. Africa now supplies about 25 percent, and Asia and Oceania supply about a tenth of the world's beans.

The sheer size of the international coffee market and the traditional dependence of the economies of many countries on the sale of their coffee crop has long meant that rising and falling prices for coffee have had a disproportionate effect on the production of coffee, not to mention the producing countries' economies. These days, fewer of the producing countries are the one-crop economies they often were in the past, when overproduction caused falling prices and a falloff in production, to be followed by shortages, sharply rising prices, and another boom-and-bust cycle of overproduction.

Ups and downs in coffee exports are not caused solely by

economic factors, however, but are, like any of the world's crops, also brought about by weather. Brazil's production, in particular, is much affected by frosts, which not only reduce the harvest for the year, but can damage trees and thus affect production in future years. The International Coffee Agreement, begun in the 1960s and renewed sporadically since then, helped stabilize the world coffee trade by adjusting export quotas for producing countries when it was operative, but has yet to become an effective answer to the problems of the coffee trade.

As might be expected in an international market of such size, there are any number of ways in which coffee makes its way from the trees of the coffee regions to cups of consumers. Basically, coffee goes from the farmer or planter to various marketing centers (usually port cities) and then to an exporter who in turn sells it to an importer or agent; in countries where the coffee industry is controlled by the government, it sells directly to importers, sometimes by auction. Buyers in consuming countries obtain coffee from importers who purchase coffee themselves or through agents or brokers who purchase coffee for them; the largest coffee customers, the giant roasting and packing firms that produce the major blends, may import directly from the producing countries and maintain their own buying organizations. In addition, there are importers, agents, and brokers who import and reexport a considerable amount of coffee from trading centers like Amsterdam, Hamburg, and London, which also have auctions. The volume of imports into the United States is large enough to sustain a secondary market of considerable size called the spot market, which consists of coffee already imported and warehoused being traded among importers, brokers, agents, and large roasters. Coffee futures are traded, just as futures are traded for other commodities. Such transactions are concerned not with the actual transfer of coffee but with buying and selling contracts for the future delivery of the beans, which in some cases may still be on the trees. This aspect of the trade has to do primarily with financing by hedging against actual and future coffees and their prices, though like all commodity trading it has its share of speculators.

The coffee industry in a consuming country is concerned with either the green coffee or the roasted product, and sometimes both. Green coffee is handled primarily by importers, brokers, and agents who in turn sell the beans to a "roaster." A roaster, naturally, is anyone who roasts coffee,

but in the coffee trade a roaster is any business engaged in buying green coffee, roasting it, often grinding and packing it as well; it may even produce soluble coffee. Some, such as the big chain grocers or national firms with their own blends, are packers; other, smaller wholesale roasters may supply coffee to local restaurants, specialty shops, hotels, and other institutions, whereas trade roasters roast and pack coffees for retailers and chains to sell under their own name. There are hundreds of businesses in the United States engaged in one or another of these aspects of the coffee trade.

Although the coffee may change hands many times as it makes its way from producing country to retail shelf, much of this trading is on paper. Most commonly, the coffee, after grading and cleaning, is packed in heavy jute or fiber bags and sent by ship to the consuming countries. Just as in the tea trade, samples of various coffees are flown by exporters in producing countries to interested buyers, who roast, grind, brew, and sample the resulting beverage to make their decision. Later samplings are made after the ordered shipment arrives to see that the coffee is in good condition and to prepare blends (the method of sampling is covered in Chapter Four). As mentioned before, virtually all coffee is shipped to consuming countries in green form, since it becomes stale far more quickly after roasting. Ninety-seven percent of the coffee brought into the United States is in the form of green beans, and these must be roasted before they become the product familiar to consumers.

The Roasting of Coffee

The coffee bean in its green state exhibits not a hint of the attractive, aromatic character that it does when roasted. Tea is fragrant even in the field; many wine grapes are delicious right off the vine. But the coffee bean has nothing to say for itself until it has been turned deep brown, whether over the flames of a Bedouin campfire or in the penetrating heat of a modern roaster. Only after passing through the fire, so to speak, does coffee release its heady aroma, its depths of flavor; the potential qualities locked in the green bean can be drawn out only by the chemical transformation brought about by the absorption of a certain amount of heat in a certain amount of time. Up to the mid-nineteenth century,

most coffee was given a more or less imprecise scorching at home over a wood or charcoal fire. Now virtually all coffee is roasted before it reaches the customer, and is better roasted as a result.

Roasting machines vary from small shop models that roast twenty-five pounds at a time to huge automated continuous roasters. The smaller the roasting setup, the more hand operations are still used in the process; the largest firms, who roast several hundred thousand pounds per day, have computerized plants where enormous quantities of green beans are transferred from stage to stage by sophisticated "airveyers" and turned into cans of roasted and ground coffee in one continuous operation. Typically, the coffee is cleaned again before roasting, often by air blasts, to remove dirt, dust, nails, pebbles, and other foreign matter that may have accumulated during shipment. If it isn't immediately roasted, it is stored, sometimes in elaborate bins with bucket elevators that lift the coffee to mixing machines. (Virtually all coffee that reaches the consumer is blended, and as a practical matter most is mixed before roasting.) From the mixers, it goes into the roasters.

The transformation of the green bean to brown is called its development, and a considerable amount of research has gone into exactly what sort of roasting brings out the maximum flavor and aroma of the bean. Early roasting machines tumbled the beans in a perforated cylinder over gas flames, sometimes subjecting the coffee to 2000°F temperatures for up to twenty minutes. This tended to char the outer portion of the bean, did not always roast it uniformly, and drove off much of the coffee's flavor oils and waxes in the form of fumes. Later it was discovered that beans develop equally at the center and the surface, and far fewer flavor elements were dissipated if their temperatures were kept at about 500°F. Newer roasters were developed to roast quickly at lower temperatures by rapidly circulating the beans and the heat. The largest roasters now require a mere five minutes to transform the beans to the desired shade of development, with far more even roasting.

Many coffees are still roasted in batch roasters, particularly unblended specialty coffees. While it is possible to roast by the book, so to speak—so much temperature for such-and-such time for X amount of coffee—only a skilled eye can judge if a given batch of coffee has attained the desired level of development, and this is done by sliding out a

few of the smoking tumbling beans through a peephole in the roaster with what looks like a long skinny trowel.

Roasters commonly recognize about a half-dozen distinct shades of coffee roasts. From the lightest to the darkest, they are cinnamon, medium high, city, full-city, French, and Italian. Although local taste and custom dictate what sort of roast is preferable, there are distinct differences between coffees roasted to different degrees. The darker the coffee is roasted, the more acidity is lost. Since acidity in coffee is a desirable taste characteristic, roasters in areas with alkaline water (which counteracts coffee acidity) tend to give their coffees a light roast to retain acidity in the bean, so that brews made with local water will not taste overly flat. The ideal roast in terms of fully developing the character and quality inherent in the coffee is what is called a full-city roast. If the coffee is roasted any darker than that, the oils, waxes, and other flavor elements are driven to the surface and are partially dissipated in roasting. (This is why dark-roasted beans have an oily gleam, while full-city roast is an even chestnut color without shine.) The burnt-taste nuance introduced by the dark roasting effectively masks shortcomings in flavor that a light roast would reveal. Hence, it is traditional in countries where a great deal of poorer-quality coffees are imported—as in France, which imports almost exclusively *robusta* coffee from her former colonies—to give coffee a heavy (*i.e.*, dark) roast. Incidentally, dark-roasted coffee is not stronger than lighter-roasted coffee; it merely has a more aggressive flavor. Caffeine content is nearly identical in all shades of roasts and, in fact, is slightly less in the very darkest roasts.

During roasting, beans expand in size. Although the change is not as dramatic as popcorn, it is quite noticeable if one compares the green bean with the roasted bean. This swelling is related to the moisture lost from the green bean when roasted, called shrinkage in the trade. Shrinkage refers to weight loss, not loss in bulk. About 15 percent of the weight of the green beans is lost after roasting, which means, in practical terms, that it takes about 118 pounds of green coffee to make 100 pounds of roasted coffee. Light, cinnamon roasts lose only 10- to 12-percent weight, while the darkest, almost black Italian roasts lose 20 percent. (This is why a pound of espresso is noticeably bulkier than a pound of light-roasted coffee.)

Loss of coffee through shrinkage has led some processors to soak coffee in water before roasting, but today most overly

price-conscious roasters would be more likely simply to use cheaper coffees. One perfectly legitimate use of water on beans is to cool them after roasting to prevent further development, although this is not easy to monitor, and consequently most beans are air-cooled in large drumlike machines (cooling pans) immediately after roasting. Since the beans are now lighter than they were when green, they are often passed by blasts of air up a chute to storage bins, a step (destoning) that is used to remove any last bits of stone, string, coins, and so forth.

It is worth talking about whether coffee-roasting can be done effectively at home. Actually there is no reason why it couldn't be, except that, to my knowledge, there exists no satisfactory home roasting device. Considering the enormous number of coffee-making devices available, one would think some enterprising manufacturer would offer a small electric roaster. That way, coffee lovers could have the ultimate: fresh-roasted, fresh-ground coffee right in their kitchen. The only vaguely suitable roasters are the one-pound sample roasters, usually found in banks of four or more, used by coffee buyers to roast green samples for cup-tasting. These are too cumbersome for kitchen countertop use, and the only alternative is the primitive method of frying the beans in a heavy, covered pan. Regulating the heat and agitating the pan so that the beans are evenly roasted without burning is a difficult task, so much so that all that really can be attempted are dark roasts. A kitchen thermometer is a help—try not to exceed 500°F—and when the beans are fully brown, begin taking out a bean every so often to crack. When one cracks easily (compare with a commercially roasted bean) and is brown all the way through, it is done. Experimentation and patience are necessary for the task. Until a good home roaster comes on the market, coffee lovers will find it hard to achieve coffee superior to reasonably fresh commercially roasted beans.

Instant, Canned, or Bean Coffee

From the storage bins the roasted coffee is handled in a number of ways, depending on its quality and ultimate destination. Obviously, coffee can be sold to retail customers in bean form right after roasting—which is, in fact, exactly what is done in specialty shops, who obtain various bean coffees from small roasters, although a few do their own

roasting. But the form of coffee most familiar to most Americans is roasted and ground vacuum-packed coffee—in other words, coffee in a can. Canned coffees are produced mainly by a handful of large nationwide firms who heavily advertise their blends. These blends are identified as brand-name products by consumers and bought on the same basis. The firms, each of whom may package coffee under several well-known labels, do roughly half the coffee business in the United States; the rest of the coffee trade is divided up among small roasters and packers, local brands (canned or bagged), and specialty shops.

The grinding and packing operations are performed reasonably soon after roasting, since, once roasted, the coffee begins fading in flavor and is considered stale within three weeks. Naturally, it makes little sense to pay more for good coffee simply to lose the extra quality by letting it go stale, so roast coffee is quickly ground and packed. In particular, once the roast coffee is ground, the oils and other flavor elements are directly exposed to air and begin staling within hours and the coffee is completely stale in a week; hence most coffee, once ground, is packed within a day. Grinding is performed by crushing the beans to a uniform size between specially grooved rollers, the particular size depending on the intended use for the coffee—vacuum grind is fine, percolator grind is coarse, and so forth. The reason why there are different grinds offered on the market has to do with the relationship between the particle size of the grind and the length of time of the brewing cycle of the particular coffee-making method. (This somewhat technical topic is discussed in Chapter Seven.)

A small roaster might simply pack his ground coffee in bags for delivery to local restaurants or retail outlets that need a fresh supply every few days. The major brands are all vacuum-packed, a method invented in Chicago in 1900 and used for 90 percent of ground coffee today; it delays staling for one to six months. Coffee drinkers are usually astounded to hear that figure, since their presumption is almost always that coffee in a can will stay fresh indefinitely. What they don't realize is that there is no packaging technique that can remove all the air from the can; consequently, what air remains begins to react with the aroma and flavor factors of the ground coffee, albeit at a reduced rate. Customers who wonder why canned coffee always smells wonderful the moment the lid is pierced but rarely so good afterward will probably be somewhat dis-

enchanted to hear that the aromatic *pfffft* sniffed on opening most likely contained a good deal of the aroma the coffee had.

The quality of coffees available in cans varies enormously. Most of the major brands are quite middling; always clean, typically underroasted, they offer little of the seductive aroma and dramatic flavor found in the finest coffees. This really isn't so surprising, any more so than the fact that *vin ordinaire* or jug wine doesn't have the superlative qualities of the world's finest wines. After all, to most people, coffee is simply a hot beverage, not a gourmet experience. Most significantly of all, the average coffee-buying consumer always buys the cheapest coffee. This has a profound effect on the quality of the blends offered, since the best coffees are considerably more expensive than the cheapest, poorest-quality coffees. When low cost is the critical factor, quality necessarily suffers. Today the typical standard brand of canned coffee is about equal parts mild, Brazil, and *robusta* coffee. This cost-conscious mix has been brought about primarily because of market pressures to keep coffee cheap, and these days the only way to keep prices from rising is to cut quality. Actually, the average price of a pound of coffee in the United States has remained roughly the same for years. In order to keep costs low, the major brands have, at one time or another, added fillers and stretchers from chicory to chick peas and pearl barley, suggested more cups per pound could be made with their blend (the unbiased consensus has long been that forty cups is all you'll get without wateriness), and lately, simply turned to *robustas*. It's no secret that the amount of *robustas* imported into the United States has been increasing substantially, and the proportion used in brands that once were mostly milds or Brazils has increased too.

This isn't to say that all the advertised brands are put together to achieve a salable product for the lowest cost; after all, there are markets and there are markets. Many national packers have higher-price blends that are all mild coffees—for example, the various blends of 100-percent Colombian put out by a number of roasters, most of which offer good coffee quality for not much more than you'd pay for a disappointing cheap blend.

It is obvious that there is no reason why the finest coffees cannot be ground and packed in cans. However, the demands of the marketplace make this impractical. The finest coffees are not always available, and it would be

difficult to offer a coffee with consistent quality and taste unless it were a blend. Part of the interest in fine coffees are their differences, and these can be enjoyed only if they are tasted unblended. To do so, one has to obtain them in bean form, and this means buying them at one of the ever-growing number of specialty stores that offer bean coffees. How to buy coffee wisely from such outlets is the subject of Chapter Six.

Most coffee drinkers buy cheap coffee because they have no idea how to brew a pot of coffee properly. Since the methods used by most Americans would turn the finest high-grown *arabica* into a cup of mud, many customers end up buying cheap coffee because it all tastes the same after they get through with it. The faint flavor apparent in the bitter, watery brews most Americans make is a letdown of the magnitude that drives people to instant. If it's going to be lousy coffee, a lot of people seem to think, it might as well be instant lousy.

It is certainly true that a well-prepared cup of the best instant coffee is superior to a poorly prepared brew of even fine coffee, even though instant coffees don't offer a very high level of quality. Soluble coffees (this includes instants and freeze-drieds) are prepared by dehydration from concentrates of brewed coffee. The technology is complicated, expensive, and appropriate for the space age: gas foamers, vacuum chambers, extraction batteries, vibrating coolers, and so on. The product is certainly the ultimate in convenience, and it may be true that some people cannot tell the difference between the best instants and regular coffee (personally I think this says a great deal about the regular coffee they've been drinking), but I have never had a soluble coffee that could be described as better than a passably pleasant hot drink. This isn't to say there aren't differences among them; there are. There are also differences among TV dinners. To my way of thinking, soluble coffees are useful for backpackers, mountain climbers, and the lazy. All others ought to give regular coffee a chance first.

While on the subject of modern improvements in coffee, I should mention that there is such a thing as decaffeinated coffee beans. The process does not rob as much flavor out of the coffee as one would think, and the flavor loss is particularly negligible in dark-roasted coffees. Those who like good coffee but for medical reasons cannot tolerate caffeine can still have all the fun of those who grind their own, and much of the same taste enjoyment in their breakfast mug.

CHAPTER FOUR

How to Taste Coffee

While a wine lover who is not an expert does not think it strange to be told how to taste wine, a coffee lover is apt to say, "I know a good cup when I taste it!" Actually, few of the millions who drink coffee do, and fewer still can tell one cup of coffee from another. With a little application to the rudiments of coffee-sampling, however, they could improve their tasting ability, enhancing their enjoyment of the beverage by learning to recognize the basic virtues of a good cup and the basic faults of poor ones. Coffee advertisements have done the idea of coffee-tasting a disservice by fostering the notion that coffee expertise consists in wearing a big sombrero and alternately frowning and swooning over steaming cups of *café* in the plazas of sleepy mountain villages.

Coffee-sampling by experts goes on at a number of stages as coffee is grown, processed, bought, shipped, resold, and so on for the purposes of quality control and to determine the effect of field and factory methods on coffee quality, but the type of sampling done by buyers is closest to the kind of sampling a coffee lover can conduct at home to increase his or her own appreciation of the beverage. Buyers are interested not only in whether the product has been tainted or spoiled through improper preparation and handling, but also in what kind of character and quality it has so they can decide how much it is worth. Buyers first examine small samples of the green coffee from each lot of beans under consideration; then the beans are roasted, ground, and brewed in small cups. The buyer taste-tests them, sampling them against each other, and assesses the beverage made from each sample.

How Coffee Experts Taste Coffee

Over a hundred different kinds of coffee are imported into the United States each year, and there are different grades, origins, growth elevations, market names, styles of preparation, even differing amounts of storage time for each kind. Since each kind varies from lot to lot as the world's overlapping coffee seasons progress, there are considerable differences in taste between one shipment of, say, Colombian coffee and the next. Nonetheless, according to Ukers, practically all the coffees brought into the United States before the twentieth century were simply judged on the appearance of the bean. Today, no competent buyer would consider purchasing coffee without first cup-sampling it, and to facilitate this need, airmail samples of particular lots ("chops," or invoices) of coffees are flown from producing countries by exporters to interested buyers or importers, and samples are sent in turn by importers to interested roasters.

While samples are sometimes sent in both green and roasted form, most often they are sent green so that the taster can roast the beans. Tasters, who may sample up to hundreds of cups a day, usually have well-equipped tasting rooms. The typical coffee-tasting outfit consists of a battery of miniature roasters (called sample roasters), a heavy-duty grinder for the roasted samples, a round table about 3½ feet across with a revolving top, a laboratory scale for weighing out the coffee, a source of water and one or more kettles, a source of heat to boil the water, and stools, trays, cups, spoons, and a waist-high cuspidor.

The first thing the professional taster (called a "liquorer" or "cupper" or "cup tester") does is examine the coffee in its raw state—that is, the green bean. To the well-trained eye, the beans reveal a good deal. They may be compared with a sample of green beans of known character and quality from the same origin (some buyers keep whole reference libraries of such beans) or simply compared mentally with the green coffees from that particular corner of the globe he or she has seen previously. The taster notes the size of the bean —large (bold), medium, small, or mixed sizes—and its shape (flat, curly, etc.). The color (bluish, grayish-blue, greenish, brownish, pale, etc.), the type of preparation (washed or

natural), and the care taken in cleaning it (the number of defective beans noticeable) are noted as well. High-grown beans are harder, smaller, and typically have a tight crease or center cut on the flat side; some buyers heft them in the hand, claiming that dense, high-grown coffees have a characteristic flinty feel, like little pebbles. Low-grown coffees are typically lighter, often larger, less firm, and show a more open crease. While this examination settles nothing, it gives the buyer familiar with a wide range of coffees some clues as to what quality brew to expect. A simple tasting session might involve examining a half-dozen to a dozen coffees at once, perhaps a survey of a number of different coffees recently arrived or a careful comparison of different lots of the same kind of coffee available from different sources.

Next the samples are roasted. About six ounces of each green sample is placed in its own small sample roaster (these hold about eight ounces of coffee each and operate just like larger roasters). As the beans develop in the heat, the taster can pull out a few beans at a time with a trowel-like metal tryer, poked through the front end of the revolving cylinder of the roaster. For the first three or four minutes there is no apparent change because most of the moisture in the raw bean is being driven off as steam. Then, over several more minutes, the beans go through a rapid series of color changes, turning from straw to light brown, to golden brown, to a full chestnut color—but no darker. A cracking or popping sound announces the roasting is nearly complete; the expert eye watches the color closely, and a short time later the small cylinders of the roasters are swung forward to dump the beans into a cooling pan where further development is checked by air drafts. Each sample is then dumped into a shallow metal pan, placed on the revolving table, and labeled with a small card showing its lot number.

Now the appearance or style of the roasted bean is scrutinized. Is the roast dull or bright? Are there a great many "quakers" or "stinkers"? (These underdeveloped or blighted beans that roast lighter than the other beans can affect the taste of the coffee.) Is the roast color even? All these factors give an indication of the uniformity of the coffee and hence the uniformity of the cup quality it will yield. The crease may be white, brownish, or irregular. Some tasters sniff the beans as they cool. One bit of coffee lore—a rule of thumbnail, so to speak—has it that high-grown coffees are tough to crack with the fingers after roasting, while low-grown coffees can be broken with relative ease.

Certainly it is true that high-grown coffees, due to a denser makeup, make a chattering noise as they are ground —the next step—while low-grown coffees make a softer racket. After each coffee sample is ground to a standard fineness, water is put on to boil in the kettles.

The water used may be local water from the tap, or local water that has been filtered to remove most of the objectionable off-tastes that would impair objectivity in sampling, or even bottled water. While waiting for the water to boil, china cups or Pyrex custard cups with a five- to six-ounce capacity are arranged around the slightly depressed edge of the revolving tasting table, one in front of each sample of the coffee, sometimes arranged in three trays, one containing the green bean, one the roasted bean, and one the ground coffee.

A small amount of the ground coffee (about ten grams, roughly the weight of a nickel or a penny and a dime) is weighed out in the scale and dumped into the cup in front of the sample trays. (Some tasters note the aroma of the ground coffee at this point.) Each sample is weighed instead of measured with a scoop because different coffees have different densities, thus only weighing ensures accuracy.

When the water has come to a full boil, it is carefully poured on the grounds in the bottom of each cup or bowl. Each is filled nearly to the brim, and care is taken to make sure the temperature of the water is constant as it is poured into each cup. This ensures the strength of the brews will be equal (a large copper kettle holds the water at about 200°F for the time it takes to fill most of the cups).

At this point, the taster sits on a stool, positions the spittoon between his or her legs, rinses the tasting spoon (typically a round-bowled tablespoon), and revolves the table as he or she begins examining the coffees in order. Within a few moments the grounds of the coffee float evenly along the surface, forming a frothlike "crust." The taster bends over each cup, bringing his or her nose close to the surface, and "breaks the crust" with a few slow, back-and-forth motions with the edge of the spoon, wafting what is called the "wet-smell" toward his or her nose. This scent is the first indication of the potential quality of the coffee, and one sniff reveals most of what the coffee has to offer in aroma. Having broken the crusts in order, the taster waits a few moments for the grounds to sink to the bottom of the cup and for the liquor (as the liquid or brew is called) to

cool to about 110°F. (Tasting liquors much hotter than that may scald the taste buds.) The small amount of grounds that have been put in the cups results in a weak brew, but coffee tasted full-strength would soon coat the palate and make the coffees taste alike. A cup of warm water may be kept at hand to rinse the mouth after a number of samples.

Coffees are tasted in the order they were poured out, so that they are all sampled at approximately the same temperature and length of brewing time. The taster dips the tasting spoon into the cup, takes up about half a spoonful of liquor, and sucks off the liquid with a loud slurping noise. The noise is made for a reason: the object is to spray the liquor mixed with air directly over the entire tongue where it is savored, rolled, or swished once, and then spat out. (Swallowing adds nothing to the analysis and would soon bloat the taster.) By spraying the coffee from the spoon to the back of the mouth, the aroma reaches the nasal passages again, and the complete structure of fragrance and flavor can be assessed. The back part of the tongue is sensitive to bitter nuances and reveals the liveliness of the coffee; the sides of the tongue detect staleness; the tip of the tongue reveals specific flavors. Each coffee is tasted in turn, the first spoonful from a different coffee often used simply to remove the taste of the previous coffee, the actual analysis done with the second slurp. Of course, the coffees must be tasted again as they cool to see if any change in character emerges, or specific samples may be set aside for further comparisons or analyses.

The cup test is the final criterion of quality. A coffee may have an excellent appearance, but a poor aroma and a tainted flavor; on the other hand, a nondescript coffee may have an exquisite fragrance and superb flavor. Despite all the research into coffee in recent years, no chemical tests exist that could replace this taste-testing by an experienced palate. The subtleties of fine coffee do not have any simple, direct correlations to the specific chemical constituents that have so far been identified as contributing to coffee flavor; coffee quality is analyzed and described by cup-testing terms used by coffee tasters, of which the most basic are acidity, flavor, and body.

Acidity is the most difficult term to describe to coffee enthusiasts who do not have an example of an "acidy" coffee in front of them. They are liable to think of it as bitterness or some other undesirable taste when they hear acidity explained as a kind of sharpness. It is that, but it is a very

pleasing sharpness, a kind of piquant quality or bright note that points up and accents the flavor of the particular coffee. Acidity is not a flavor in itself, but a quality of all high-grown coffees; it gives "snap," "verve," and an "alive" quality to the liquor. (Sivetz states that an acid coffee has a bite about equal to that of a raw carrot.) A coffee can be attractive in spite of low acidity—such coffees are described as "soft" or "mellow"—but without some acidity, a coffee tastes flat, dull, lifeless, or even "dead" in the cup. In short, acidity in coffee, unless excessive, is a highly desirable characteristic.

Flavor has two meanings. One is a broad, complimentary use of the word; when one describes a coffee as flavorful, this means that the total impression of aroma, acidity, and body is distinctive, rich, fine, exquisite, and so on. The second meaning of flavor is that of specific tastes: chocolate, nuts, spices, or something less pleasant—straw, grass, earth, rubber, and so forth.

Body is the impression of the liquor's weight and texture in the mouth. Coffees range from watery, slight, thin, light to medium, to full, heavy, thick, or even syrupy in body. It is easiest to detect in full-strength coffee, though it should not be confused with the impression coffees made too strong give, or the aggressive taste of dark-roasted coffees; it is a distinct (though not actual) tactile sensation of viscosity on the palate when the liquor is "worked" or swished in the mouth.

Acidity, flavor, and body are sometimes merely described on a scale ranging from none, slight, medium, to good, very good, fine, and very fine. Although there is no standard vocabulary of coffee-tasting terms, the following list covers most of the terms in common use in the trade. In drawing up the list, I have drawn upon the terms used by Sivetz, Ukers, Wellman, Haarer, and others. In some cases, however, the definitions are not simply the technical ones usually given, but also include my attempt to explain these in a nontechnical fashion.

Note: Italicized words appear elsewhere in this list.

A Coffee Taster's Glossary

Acidity High acid (or acidy) coffees have a sharp, pleasing, piquant quality that points up their *flavor* and gives them

snap, verve, liveliness in the cup. Acidity may be high, medium, light, low, or lacking altogether in coffees, in which case the coffee tastes *flat* and dull. Acidity is characteristic of high-grown coffees. See *sour*.

Aroma Refers to the odor of the prepared coffee beverage. It may be lacking, faint, delicate, moderate, strong, or fragrant (also called aromatic), and distinctive as to character.

Baked A taste description given to underroasted coffee, or coffee roasted too slowly at too low a temperature, so that the flavor is underdeveloped. See *green*.

Bitter A harsh, unpleasant taste detected on the back of the tongue. Found in overextracted brews as well as in overroasted coffees and those with various taste defects.

Body The tactile impression of weight and texture in the mouth. Coffees may be watery, *thin*, slight, light, medium, full, heavy, thick, or even syrupy in body, as well as *buttery*, oily, *rich*, smooth, chewy, etc., in texture. Easiest to detect in full-strength coffee.

Burnt A *bitter*, burnt flavor characteristic of dark-roasted coffees.

Buttery Said of an oily *body* or *texture* in the mouth. Denotes full flavor and richness. Not a common description.

Cinnamon Underlying spicy accent sometimes detected in the *aroma* of fine coffee, a *flavor* nuance. Not a common description. (Also a term describing a very light roast.)

Clean Opposite of *dirty*. Characteristic of all fine coffees. Does not necessarily imply clarity of flavor impression (see *natural coffee* and *wild*). Associated with washed coffees.

Cocoa Characteristic sweetish smell of completely *stale* roasted coffee. See *stale*.

Dirty An undesirable unclean smell and taste, slight to pronounced. Dirty implies a defect, such as sourness, earthiness, or mustiness. See *natural coffee* and *wild*.

Earthy A highly undesirable dirt odor and flavor taint picked up by coffee when dried on the ground; also called groundy. See *musty*.

Flat A dull lifeless quality due to lack of *acidity*.

Flavor (a) The total impression of *aroma, acidity*, and *body;* if the impression is strong, fine, and pleasant, the coffee is described as flavory or flavorful or ranked on a scale from poor, fair, good, to fine-flavored. (b) Specific taste flavors may suggest spices, chocolate, nuts, or something less complimentary—straw, grass, earth, rubber, etc.

Fresh Opposite of *stale.* Applies to roasted coffees.

Fruity A *flavor* taint said to come from overripe fruit pulp.

Grassy A *flavor* taint from use of swamp water for washing, or from improper drying. Also used as synonym for *green* and *past-croppish.*

Green (a) A *flavor* taint found in coffee harvested before fully ripe. (b) Characteristic taste of underroasted coffee; pasty.

Hard Opposite of *sweet* or mild; *harsh.* Description of Brazils between *soft* and *Rio-y.*

Harsh Crude raw taste; used to describe certain Brazils and *robustas.*

Hidy Smell of hides or leather from improper storage.

Light Used to qualify *aroma, acidity,* or *body;* a light coffee would be delicate in flavor.

Mellow Full, well-balanced, satisfying coffee; implies low or medium *acidity.* See *winy.*

Musty A smell and taste taint caused by mildew; similar to *earthy.*

Natural coffee *Aroma* and *flavor* characteristics of coffees processed by the dry method. They are often blander than washed coffees and may lack clarity of *flavor* and pointed *acidity;* some may have intense, complex flavors and full, thick body. See *wild.*

Neutral A characterless, flavorless coffee, inoffensive to insipid; without virtue (save for economical blending) but without defect. A desirable character in *robusta* and otherwise undistinguished Brazils.

Nutty (a) Said of coffees that lack coffee *flavor;* also peanutty. (b) A specific *flavor* nuance, suggesting almonds, and so on.

Past-croppish Not to be confused with *stale.* Said of coffees that have deteriorated in the green state before roasting, and thus taste as if from a past crop. See *strawy* and *woody.*

Rancid Extremely *sour* and very unpleasant.

Rich Indicates depth and complexity of *flavor* and full, *buttery body;* overused.

Rio-y A *harsh,* heavy medicinal or iodine *flavor* typical of the poorest grades of Brazils but encountered in other coffees as well. Said to be caused by allowing berries to dry on the tree.

Rubbery Burnt-rubber odor characteristic of *robusta.*

Soft Low-acid coffees are described as soft, *mellow, sweet.*

Sour Not to be confused with *acidity.* A distinctly *sour,* rank,

or *rancid* taste is a defect, often due to improper processing. See *wild*.

Spicy Said of fine *aroma* or *flavor* suggestive of spices.

Stale Roasted coffee that has faded in quality after excessive exposure to air. Aroma of stale coffee changes from *flat* to *rancid* and finally to cocoalike; the flavor of stale coffee changes from *bitter* to *rancid* and tastes cardboardy. Not to be confused with *past-croppish*.

Strawy Characteristic scent of *past-croppish* coffees; haylike. See *woody*.

Strong Term used to indicate intensity of either defects or virtues (as in "a strong, sour taste" or "a strong, fine aroma"). A strong-flavored coffee is therefore not necessarily a fine-flavored coffee.

Sweet Said of a smooth, palatable coffee, free from taints or harshness. Also *soft*.

Thin Said of coffees with watery body and lack of *flavor;* typical of low-grown coffee.

Wild Coffees with extreme *flavor* characteristics, or odd, racy, tangy nuances in *aroma* and taste. Usually applied to *natural coffees*. These characteristics may be intriguing or undesirable. See *dirty*.

Winy Sometimes used to indicate thick *body* and mellow quality, but also used to denote a sappy, vinous *acidity*. Characteristic of certain fine coffees.

Woody A flavor taint caused by overlengthy storage in warm wood sheds; also characteristic scent and taste of old, *past-croppish* coffees.

On Coffee-tasting Expertise

It is possible to achieve a degree of skill in tasting coffee scarcely credible to the layman: for example, expert liquorers are said to be able to tell the altitude, within a few hundred feet, at which two otherwise identical coffees were grown. Of course, what is not generally realized when such tasting feats are described is that the taster probably spends all day tasting nothing but coffees grown in a particular region; it would be surprising if he or she did not develop a very detailed familiarity with them. A buyer who samples coffees from all over the world on a daily basis probably never has enough samples from a given region with enough frequency to have more than a general acquaintance

with them. It is the same with wine; there are experts who can identify dozens of the great châteaux wines of Bordeaux tasted blind, but that does not mean the same expert could do the same with the wines of the Rhine. It is all a matter of familiarity.

The amateur taster also rarely realizes that these feats of expertise are only a by-product, as it were, of the real function of having an expert palate. Coffee tasters, like tea tasters or wine tasters, are skilled in the analysis of their chosen beverages, but although they may be able to make a number of identifications blind, that has little to do with, and is not a test of, their ability to detect subtle nuances in the unfamiliar sample before the nose. Only the finest examples of coffee, tea, or wine exhibit a distinct enough character that they can often, but not always, be identified. Run-of-the-mill examples of these beverages can taste very much alike.

The range of tastes found among the world's coffees constitute a much narrower spectrum than that of wines or teas. Wines are red or white, sparkling or still, dry or sweet, but what really gives them an enormous range of tastes is that they are made from hundreds of different grape varieties, of which at least a dozen can be easily distinguished from one another. Add to this the differences imposed by soil, climate, and wine-making methods, and one has an enormous spectrum of distinct tastes. Teas are made from two varieties of the tea plant and their hybrids, grown in a vast range of geographical and climatic conditions, and are processed by a great variety of manufacturing methods that impose further distinctive characteristics on them. Coffees—at least coffees that could be described as fine coffees—are, on the other hand, all made from one coffee species, *Coffea arabica,* and processed in only two ways: wet or dry. Although there are differences in character attributable to different *arabica* varieties, geographical and climatic conditions impose the most significant differences in character found among these coffees. Consequently, the spectrum of distinct tastes found in the world's fine coffees overlap and share certain characteristics with one another. There are not the night-and-day differences between different coffees the way there can be between teas or wines.

Positive identifications of country or district of origin are thus even harder to make for coffees than they are for teas or wines—that is, on the basis of a mere sniff and sip. Coffee beans differ considerably in appearance, particularly

when examined in the green, but apart from obvious differences—the big flat bean of Java *arabica* would never be mistaken for the small curly mottled beans of Brazil—it is no easy matter for the nonexpert to distinguish, say, Costa Rican beans from Venezuelan beans. Then, too, just as it is not always possible to say with certainty where in the world a given wine from a given grape variety was grown, so too it is not always easy to say where a fine *arabica* comes from, with nothing more than a taste to go on. High-grown East African coffees have a characteristic sappy, bright-flavored quality, but certain lots of them might be mistaken for certain lots of Central American coffees. Experienced tasters can often distinguish Brazilian, Ethiopian, East African, Central American, and Indonesian coffees from one another when ranged on the sampling table, but not in every case. In short, a coffee does not *always* have unique characteristics that would mark it as unmistakably from a particular district. This doesn't mean that there is no difference in coffees, any more than the fact that Burgundian winegrowers have trouble telling the difference between some California Chardonnays and Meursault means that there is no difference in the wines. Even an amateur can detect rather subtle differences between coffees tasted side by side. But as in wine-tasting, analysis is one thing; positive identification is another. It is the ability to analyze objectively any cup of coffee that experts seek to develop—and so should enthusiastic coffee lovers who want to know their beans.

Coffee tasters put their tasting powers to the ultimate test in creating a blend, for here they need art as well as skill. As was explained in Chapter Three, almost all coffees are sold as blends. There are very few coffees that can't be improved by judicious blending, and because coffee is a variable agricultural product, blending is necessary for any coffee firm trying to supply a consistent quality product with a particular character. Of course, all commercial blends are put together within a certain price range, depending on the market for which the coffee is intended. Some price ranges are quite a bit lower than others. The lowest-priced coffees, as I have mentioned, necessarily contain a good deal of *robusta* coffees or neutral Brazilian coffees. For a high-grade blend, coffee tasters experiment with mixing samples of sharp-flavored, aromatic, but light-bodied high-grown *arabicas* with heavy-bodied, mellow, low-grown *arabicas*. Only the most expensive blends are assembled from the best mild

coffees, and even these fall short of the quality that can be obtained from occasional lots of outstanding unblended (or "straight") coffees available from time to time. Probably the best of these could not be improved by blending. The average commercial blend is mostly neutral, inexpensive "filler" coffee enlivened by a small amount of moderately expensive "flavory" coffee. Unfortunately, the resulting cup may be less enlivened by the amount of better coffee in the blend than one might expect. On this subject, Sivetz states with some emphasis that mixing a good coffee half and half with a poor coffee downgrades the blend closer to the level of the poor product. It is true enough that even a small portion of Brazilian coffee, with its all too common straw-like flavor nuance, will be quite noticeable when mixed in with a good mild coffee.

To create a blend, a taster develops a mix of several different coffees that will yield an attractive cup with harmonious aroma, flavor, and body. To maintain the consistency of the blend's character and quality, the taster has to be prepared to substitute one kind of coffee for another as the availability of coffees of a certain character from a certain area changes. A blend of Kenyan, Guatemalan, and Brazilian coffee may have to be changed to Costa Rican, El Salvadoran, and Brazilian in six months' time to produce a closely similar coffee taste. The coffee that was used to provide the precise acidy note that the blend needed may no longer exhibit the needed quality as the season wears on; in this case the taster looks elsewhere among the milds for the acidy nuance that he or she needs—and that will be compatible with the other coffees in the blend.

Just because one coffee is heavy-bodied and lacks aroma, and another has wonderful aroma and a thin body, does not necessarily mean that they will make up each other's defect in a harmonious fashion. Their cup chemistries may clash and cancel out their best qualities. No coffee can be blended simply by recipe. What goes into a good blend varies and the proportions vary; what goes into a poor blend varies, not to maintain taste so much as to maintain price. In each instance the blend may have to be reassembled each week from the palette of flavors the currently available coffees have.

Coffee-tasting at Home

Tasting coffees against one another is the best way to develop a critical coffee palate, discover your personal preferences, and find the best coffees for the price. It is also easy to do at home, right in the kitchen. It requires no special equipment, apart from what most coffee lovers have on hand: cups, spoons, a kettle, and a grinder. The method is the same, whether you are simply exploring the world of coffees or doing a careful comparison of the same type of coffee from different retail outlets.

Plan to taste no more than a half-dozen coffees at the same time and to have, preferably, no more than two people tasting at once; more coffees and too many tasters gets confusing. Simply line up six plain white six-ounce coffee cups—or six small five- to six-ounce glass custard dishes—on the counter next to the kitchen sink (that way you can rinse your spoon and spit out the samples easily). Behind each cup place the bag or sample of coffee to be tasted, and from the first bag take a heaping tablespoonful of beans. Grind the beans to a standard fineness (say, about fifteen seconds), and place a carefully measured level teaspoonful of the ground coffee in the bottom of the cup in front of the bag. Discard the rest of the grounds and give the grinder bowl a quick wipe to clear it out for the next coffee. Repeat for each coffee. (Admittedly, since different coffees fluff up differently due to different densities, it would be more accurate to weigh the samples—ten grams or a nickel's worth to a cup. But this requires a scale, something only the perfectionist will want to invest in. Careful measuring will give reasonable accuracy.) If you use preground coffees, try to see that they are the same grind—drip is best.

Bring a little over a quart of freshly drawn cold water to a boil in a kettle and immediately pour it on the samples, touching the kettle back down on the burner briefly between cups if it starts cooling rapidly. Fill the cups to just under the brim (to ensure that each gets the same amount of water). Pour in order. On a pad of paper, write down the names of the coffees in the same order they were poured. When the coffees cool enough so that you can place your nose close to the crust—usually a minute or two—gently break the crust that the grounds have formed on the sur-

face by giving a few slow sweeps with the edge of a spoon, closely sniffing as you do so. Don't overagitate the crust; try to concentrate on the impression of the first couple of sniffs. (Excessive sniffing simply exhausts the olfactory nerve.) Note your impression on the pad in one or two specific concrete terms, such as "faint," "strong," "spicy," and so on, rather than in abstract impressions like "terrible," "wonderful," and so forth. Note any off-odors ("dirty," "strawlike," and so on). Do this to one cup at a time, giving the spoon a shake or rinse between cups. After reviewing them all, return to any you like, but refrain from stirring up the surface, since the grounds are now in the process of settling and you want the strength of the brews to be equal.

As the grounds settle (some will remain on the surface, but don't let that bother you), the coffees will cool to the point where the liquor can be held on the tongue with comfort and not scald the taste buds. This will be slightly hotter than lukewarm, but below the temperature at which coffee is normally enjoyed. Taste by slurping the liquor from the edge of your spoon, letting it spray over the tongue. Spit out the samples in the sink (despite your instinct that you have to swallow it to tell what it tastes like, this is not true). Note your impression from one or two slurps in terms of flavor, acidity, and body. Is the flavor full? neutral? rich? attractive? harsh? Is it acidy (lively, sappy, sharp) or medium-acidy, or does it lack acid (soft, mellow, lifeless)? Is the body thin, full, or heavy? Body is best detected in full-strength coffee, and those who want to experiment further can try making another set of comparisons, this time using two level tablespoons of coffee in individual filter cones over the cups to make full-strength brews. When comparing full-strength cups, try comparing them hot, then lukewarm, then nearly cool. A fine coffee is still tolerable when cool. You will also notice that many coffees change character in the cup as they cool, just as fine wines evolve in the glass as they are exposed to air.

The first thing one notices with such tastings is that relatively small differences in coffees are readily apparent in direct comparisons. No one but an expert with an extremely detailed memory can assess a cup of coffee accurately on its own, and even experts make no final judgments except by direct comparisons.

Exploring the world of coffees through tastings gives one a quick overview of the range of tastes to be encountered

in fine coffee. Natural coffees, such as Ethiopians and Brazils, can be distinguished from washed coffees such as Central Americans without a great deal of experience, and the differences between acidy, high-grown coffees and full, mellow low-grown coffees are easily detected by amateurs. It takes much more familiarity with coffee, of course, to be able to recognize when a coffee is characteristic of its type or not (see Chapter Five).

Much of the time, the most useful purpose of comparative tastings is to aid in comparative shopping, where one is looking for the best coffee for the price. It is, of course, difficult to put a value on the opportunity of tasting a rare coffee, but for everyday breakfast coffee, it is well worth cup-sampling to discover that such-and-such blend is a better coffee than the exotic and expensive beans offered in a specialty shop.

For these sorts of tests, it is better to taste blind—that is, with the bags of coffee hidden, so that expectations and prejudices do not affect one's assessment of what's in the cup. You can simply number the bottoms of the cups with a china marker after putting the ground coffees in, make a list of the coffee types by number, put the bags away, and either shuffle the cups yourself or have someone else do it. Then make a new list of the cups—A, B, C, and so on, from left to right—and after the tasting, simply lift the cups to find out which number cup was A, and so on. Compare lists to find out your impressions of the coffees tested. For tests to discover how much value a given coffee offers for the money, assign a point system for acidity, body, flavor, aroma (say 1 point for low, 2 for medium, 3 for strong, and for off-flavors and scents minus 1 or 2 points). Divide the price of the coffee by the score it rates to discover how much it costs per point of value for each coffee.

Amateurs who wish to hone their palates may want to have others prepare delta tests—that is, prepare two identical cups of coffee and one different cup of coffee, numbering the odd cup on the bottom. The object is to see if one can pick out the odd cup. Start out with very distinct coffees and then try more similar coffees. A variant of this is to pick out a sample of a coffee from a series of other coffees that matches a given cup sample (retasting is permitted). These sorts of tests can be quite difficult, particularly with certain groups of mild coffees such as Central American.

Creating Your Own Blends

Most coffee enthusiasts will be more interested in developing their own blends than putting their newfound talents to use in parlor games. The key to creating a good blend is to remember that coffee blends are developed in comparative samplings, not by recipe, in spite of what some merchants will tell you (see Chapter Six). Sample a series of coffees either by the cup-sampling method or by making a series of full-strength cups. After noting flavors, isolate the coffees into full-bodied, aromatic, acidic, and flavorful according to their most prominent characteristic. (Some may combine these features.) In a separate cup, add some of the acidy coffee, tablespoon by tablespoon, keeping count. This is your key coffee, the one that carries the "flavor note." Then add, tablespoon by tablespoon, the full-bodied coffee, tasting as you do until you achieve a well-balanced cup. The proportion will depend on their compatibility. Some coffees simply won't mix well. At first, try blends of two or three coffees; this is often all that is necessary and easier to handle than a mash of a dozen. Keep track of the proportions, tablespoon to tablespoon, and you have the proportions of your blend. Remember that this blend will retain this character only if the coffees you use are the same coffees you composed the blend with. A few months later the Ethiopian coffee you used to add that high, exotic note to your blend may be from a different lot and might add an unpleasant earthy note instead. A blend that is often quite successful and takes little fussing simply consists of a certain proportion—a fifth to a half—of darker-roasted coffee to lighter-roasted coffee of the same type. This is particularly successful with many mild coffees. Classic blends such as one-half Mocha and one-half Java are first rate if one can find suitable Mochas and Javas, something not easy to do these days. Experiment with heavy-bodied but rather flat, aged coffees such as "old crop" Colombian, strongly acidic coffees such as Tanzanian peaberry, exotically flavored types such as Ethiopian Djimma, aromatic Konas, and so on, to achieve your own version of the ultimate cup.

CHAPTER FIVE

A Guide to the World's Coffees

The principal coffee-producing countries are the nations of Central and South America, East and West Africa, and to a lesser extent Asia, the East and West Indies, and Oceania. These parts of the world are sufficiently close to the equator to have the warmth of climate, amount of rainfall, and jungle soils necessary to grow coffee successfully. Many of them include subregions where geography and local climatic conditions bring out the best qualities of the fruit and in addition stamp a distinct and sometimes individual character on the coffee.

Coffees are known by species—the principal ones are *arabica* and *robusta*—and by countries of origin. They are further subdivided by method of processing—wet (resulting in washed coffees) or dry (resulting in natural, or unwashed, coffees), by market or district names (usually the region, political subdivision, principal city of the area or port city through which they are shipped), indicating, in most cases, specific districts of origin, and often by the elevation at which they are grown.

Among the countries that produce mild coffees—*arabicas* of good to fine quality—there is often a greater range of quality and character to be found among a single country's coffees than between the better coffees of most of these coffee lands. This is only to be expected from crops that are sometimes measured in the millions of bags and have been grown in a variety of conditions and variously processed. Nonetheless, there are broad distinctions in character between coffees of various countries and geographical areas. The fine coffees of the East Indies are not like the fine coffees of East Africa; the fine coffees of Ethiopia and Yemen are not like the fine coffees of Central America; and so on. The care taken in cultivation, harvesting, processing, and preparation of the bean differs, too, from country to country, and this enhances or detracts from the characteristics climate and geography give the coffee.

PRINCIPAL COFFEE EXPORTING AND COFFEE IMPORTING COUNTRIES

PRINCIPAL COFFEE EXPORTING COUNTRIES (MILLIONS OF 132-LB. BAGS EXPORTED ANNUALLY)

(ALL FIGURES APPROXIMATE)

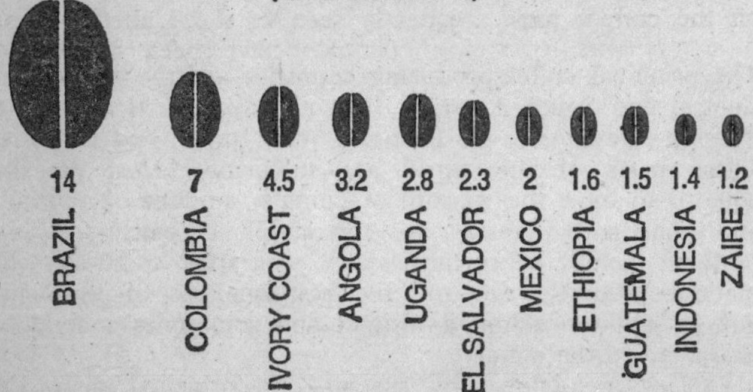

PRINCIPAL COFFEE IMPORTING COUNTRIES (MILLIONS OF 132-LB. BAGS IMPORTED ANNUALLY)

(ALL FIGURES APPROXIMATE)

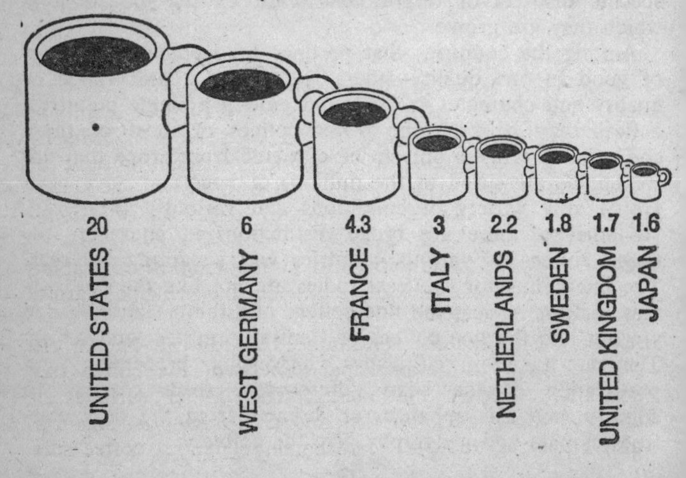

Whether or not such-and-such a coffee land produces a superb coffee is often as much a matter of whether or not and to where the best coffees are exported as it is a question of whether the right growing conditions are present. While the United States is the world's biggest coffee customer, it is not safe to assume that country X has no first-rate coffees just because none or very few are imported here. However, the following brief guide naturally puts emphasis on the coffees most frequently seen in the United States. A number of producing countries have been omitted—Equatorial Guinea, Timor, Paraguay, Togo, Cape Verde Islands, among others—because their coffees are either of no commercial importance or of no gustatory interest to a coffee lover. But some infrequently seen names that may be seen more frequently in the future are included, and for the convenience of the coffee novice, some common coffee terms as well.

Unless otherwise noted, all coffees discussed are *arabica* coffees. Italicized words appear elsewhere in this list.

Abyssinia See *Ethiopia.*

Aged coffee Aged coffees are those that have been stored in the green for a number of years, usually in cooler high altitudes. Also called "old crop" or "plantation" coffees, they come from Venezuela, Colombia, India, and elsewhere. They are typically yellowish in color before roasting and are very heavy-flavored and heavy-bodied in the cup. They usually lack acid and thus are also rather lifeless, even "dead," in taste. Some can be successfully blended.

Altura Term for high-grown coffees of *Mexico.*

American roast See *Full-city roast.*

Angola This West African country has well over a million acres planted to coffee, of which 96 percent is *robusta.* Angola is fourth in world exports. A small amount of *arabica* is grown in the south of the country.

Antigua A high-altitude coffee-growing district of *Guatemala.*

Arabian coffee Refers either to coffee from the Arabian Peninsula (see *Yemen*) or to *arabica,* the principal variety of coffee (see below).

Arabica *Coffea arabica* (pronounced ah-rah-bee′-kah or ah-rah′-bee-kah) is the principal variety of the coffee tree and the source of the finest coffees. Other varieties of coffee (including *C. liberica* and *C. canephora*—this last also known as *robusta)* yield harsh to neutral coffee suit-

able for some blending purposes and the manufacture of soluble coffees (instants and freeze-drieds).

Arabic coffee See *Turkish coffee.*

Armenia Market name for certain coffees of *Colombia.*

Armenian coffee See *Turkish coffee.*

Blue Mountain Coffee-growing district of *Jamaica.*

Bolivia Bolivia has some thirty thousand acres planted to coffee and exports about half her small crop; the rest is for domestic consumption. Cultivation is by commercial plantations at about three thousand feet that produce washed coffees.

Bourbon Santos "Bourbon" indicates the flat bean (as opposed to the *Peaberry)* grown in São Paulo and shipped through the port of Santos.

Brazil Until recent decades, Brazil dominated world trade in coffee; today, she produces one-quarter of the world's exportable production. This represents less than three-quarters of her annual crop of over twenty million bags from about six million acres. (Brazil has a sizable per-capita consumption of coffee.)

The quality of coffee produced in Brazil is not high. While virtually all of it is *arabica* coffee (save for some *robusta* shipped out of Rio de Janeiro), much of it is cultivated, harvested, and processed by relatively crude methods (see Chapter Three). Over 95 percent of Brazilian coffee is unwashed or natural coffee. "Brazils," as they are called in the coffee trade to distinguish them from "milds" (*arabicas* produced elsewhere), are consequently less expensive (though more expensive than *robustas*) and in demand as neutral coffees for blending with more flavorful, expensive coffees.

Brazils are elaborately classified by district of origin, type, size, and color of beans and by broad taste categories: "strictly soft" (mild and sweet), "soft" (mild), "hard" (harsh), and "Rio-y" (an especially harsh taste associated with the coffees produced in the Rio de Janeiro district of Brazil; reminiscent of iodine, it is found in other Brazils as well, and sometimes in other coffees; according to Wellman, it is caused by allowing the coffee fruit to dry on the tree). The best coffee produced in Brazil is considered to be Santos (sometimes called Bourbon Santos), named for the port through which these coffees pass (Santos) and the variant of the coffee grown there (*v. bourbon).* Its small, curly beans yield a low-acid, light-bodied brew, of which the best examples have a

pleasant aroma and a smooth, attractive flavor. It is an excellent choice for those who like a very mild coffee. The most common fault found in otherwise palatable Brazils is a strawy scent and flat flavor, indicating the coffee was past its prime even before roasting.

Burundi This small East African country has about 125,000 acres in coffee, grown mainly by small farmers on the high plateau. About 95 percent of the country's production is washed *arabica*, of which the best are equal to the finest East African *arabicas*.

Cameroon Coffee production in this West African nation is about evenly divided between *robustas* and washed *arabicas*, the latter being grown in the more mountainous regions. Production and exports are increasing rapidly.

Cappuccino A serving variation of *Espresso* that is topped up with steamed hot milk and/or whipped cream and cinnamon.

Central African Republic All of this nation's coffee crop is *robusta*, most of which goes to France.

Chicory The dried, roasted, and ground root of this plant (it is related to the dandelion and resembles a parsnip) has long been used to stretch coffee or as an outright coffee substitute. The bittersweet tang it lends to coffee is enjoyed in some parts of Europe and the southern United States. See *New Orleans coffee*.

Coatepec A coffee-producing district of *Mexico*.

Coban A market name for certain coffees of *Guatemala*.

Colombia Colombia is second only to Brazil in importance as a coffee producer, supplying about 12 percent of world coffee exports. Her normal annual crop is 9.5 million bags of washed *arabica*, grown at various elevations and produced mainly by thirty thousand small farms. Colombian coffees are considered high-quality milds by the coffee trade and are widely used in blends. The crop is harvested all year round, most of it gathered from October to March.

The most common Colombian grades seen are Supremo (large beans, best quality), and Excelso (medium and mixed beans, standard quality). While there are a great many market names and districts of origin (Bucaramanga, Cúcuta, Santa Marta, and so on), the principal ones seen these days are Medellín and Armenian. These names have become somewhat generalized and are not indicative of any substantial distinctions in character or quality. Colombian coffee is widely regarded by the public as syn-

onymous with quality, but it is a mistake to suppose they are invariably superior to other milds; at best, they are simply comparable to other fine coffees. The heady aroma, rich flavor, winy acidity, and almost buttery body that distinguishes outstanding examples are not found in the vast majority of Colombian coffees, which nevertheless often possess an attractive balance between good acidity, mellow body, and excellent flavor.

Continental roast See *Dark-roasted coffees.*

Costa Rica This small Central American country produces about 1.3 million bags of washed *arabica* coffee from over thirty thousand farms, ranging from a few acres to several thousand in size. The top grade—roughly 40 percent of the crop—is Strictly Hard Bean, produced on the Pacific slopes at elevations from 3,900 to 5,400 feet. These typically bluish, well-polished large flat beans yield aromatic brews with excellent acidity and very good body and taste. While the best examples are superb on their own, Costa Ricans are most popular for blending purposes. Much of the crop goes to Europe.

Cuba Cuba's annual crop in recent years has been about half a million bags of coffee now that her industry has recovered from the hurricane damage of the mid '60s. Most of the crop goes to meet considerable domestic consumption; a small amount is exported to Europe. Cuban coffee has no great reputation, but is considered typical of much of the Caribbean region—rather heavy and flat, and best suited for dark roasts.

Dark-roasted coffees Dark-roasted coffees are those that are roasted past the point at which the full flavor of the beans are brought out (see *Full-city roast*) in order to introduce a burnt nuance to the flavor. Depending on the degree of further roasting, this flavor element is slight or completely dominant. Dark roasts have no standard nomenclature. The lighter dark-roasted coffees are dark brown, and the surface of the bean is shiny with flavor oils. Some names for this degree of roast are Vienna roast, Continental roast, French roast, New Orleans roast, and so on. The darkest roasts are nearly black and the surface of the bean glistens with flavor oils. Some names for this degree of roast are Espresso, Italian roast, and in some roasting nomenclatures, French roast.

Decaffeinated coffee Coffee contains about 2-percent caffeine, a nitrogenous plant product with a marked physiological effect. A cup of coffee contains about one

hundred milligrams of caffeine (roughly half again as much as a cup of tea), an amount sufficient to act as a mild stimulant. Some people are more sensitive to caffeine than others; hence the popularity of decaffeinated coffee since the chemical process of removing the alkaloid from the bean was developed in Germany in the early 1900s. Decaffeinated coffee is available in all forms—whole bean, ground, and instant. The process can give a caramel-sweet flavor to coffee, but when carefully used with good beans, has little effect on coffee flavor.

Dominican Republic Some 700,000 bags of coffee are produced on this Caribbean island nation, primarily on small farms, of which about half is exported to the United States. Quality varies widely; the high-grown coffee is said to be quite good.

Ecuador Most of Ecuador's coffees are grown in low altitudes to about 1,300 feet, but some coffee is grown in Cumbaya at 9,000 feet. Nevertheless, the quality of the washed *arabica* is considered typically poor and is usually described as mildly woody in flavor with slight acidity and thin body.

Elephant bean A freak bean that occurs when the two seeds (beans) of the coffee fruit grow as one large irregular bean. About 3 percent of the normal *arabica* crop is elephant bean. It is liable to break apart during roasting and has no special qualities. Not to be confused with *Maragogipe.*

El Salvador El Salvador ranks sixth in world exports of coffee and is surpassed only by Colombia as a producer of milds. Her two-million-bag annual crop is grown primarily on the slopes of the central range at altitudes from 2,300 to 5,000 feet. About 15 percent of the crop is "Strictly Highgrown" (4,000 to 5,000 feet) and is noted for medium acidity, body, and mild, sweet taste. Most of the Salvadors brought into the United States are round, full-bodied coffees used for blending.

Espresso A very dark-roasted coffee; also a method of rapid coffee brewing in which steam is forced through the grounds by a special machine that prepares one cup at a time. See *Dark-roasted coffees.*

Ethiopia *Arabica* coffee is native to Ethiopia, and it is from there that coffee was taken to the Arabian Peninsula about the ninth century. Much of Ethiopia's several-million-bag annual crop is still gathered from coffee trees growing wild in the high plateaus at 5,000 to 6,000 feet.

Most of the country's product is unwashed, natural coffee. The most commonly seen district names are Jimma (or Djimma), Sidamo, and Harar. Ethiopian coffees are distinctive, "wild" coffees, not only in origin, but also in taste. Highly exotic, the best are sharply acidic, with racy, tangy flavors, and can be very thick-bodied. The beans are small, mottled, and do not always yield a uniform brew, so that the same coffee may differ from pot to pot. Flavors are complex, suggesting vegetative, sometimes earthy nuances, while the usually penetrating aroma may have high, strange notes. Ethiopian coffees are not always rich, winy, and dramatic; many lack acid and have dirty scents and sour flavors. Their character differs from region to region, but Harar coffees are considered the best and are divided into "Longberry" or "Shortberry" in accordance with bean size. Ethiopians are close in style to Mochas, and consequently a good many are sold as such. See *Yemen.*

Excelso A grade of Colombian coffee indicating mixed bean sizes and standard quality. See *Colombia.*

French roast See *Dark-roasted coffees.*

Full-city roast A degree of roast darker than that typically found in canned coffees; it is the point at which the maximum flavor (or development) inherent in the bean is brought out. It is roughly a full chestnut color. The surface of the bean, while bright, should not gleam with flavor oils.

Greek coffee See *Turkish coffee.*

Guatemala This Central American country has over half a million acres devoted to coffee cultivation. The United States is its biggest customer, and of the roughly one million bags of Guatemalan coffee imported each year, the long, bluish beans of the "Strictly Hard Bean" grade (produced above 4,500 feet) exhibit qualities that are hard to find these days among other Latin-American imports. The best can be superbly aromatic, lively, and acidy, yet soft and mild in flavor, and very heavy-bodied; in short, perfectly balanced and probably what most people would find an ideal cup of coffee. One sometimes sees district names (such as Antigua or Cobán) or sometimes even *Maragogipe,* an extralarge bean coffee variety (see *Maragogipe*).

Haiti Haiti, which shares its island with the Dominican Republic, produces about half a million bags of coffee annually, both washed and unwashed. Quality varies from

musty and poor in the low-grown unwashed coffees to full-bodied and flavorful in the high-grown (to 1,500 feet) washed coffees. Haitians are used in blends and dark roasts.

Harar Coffee-producing district of *Ethiopia.*

Hawaii The only coffee cultivated in the United States is grown in the Kona districts on the island of Hawaii. Seeds were first introduced in 1829, and while today production is small—less than twenty thousand bags a year —methods of cultivation are modern and intensive, and yields are very high. Most of the coffee is grown on the steep, rocky western slopes of the Hualalai and Mauna Loa volcanoes at 800- to 2,400-feet elevation. Cloud cover and mountain shadows contribute to ideal growing conditions for *arabica,* and the best grades of this rare growth command high prices. At best the large, wide, flat beans make one of the world's finest coffees—superbly aromatic and highly distinctive. It is a striking coffee, with a clear, high, bell-like note of flavor; its medium acidity gives it a perky tang, while its fine, smooth body and clarity of taste make it a particularly refreshing cup. Unfortunately, Kona is rarely this good; most of what is available resembles ordinary milds in taste.

High-grown coffees Other things being equal, coffees grown at higher elevations exhibit finer qualities than coffees grown at lower elevations. Unique climatic and geographical conditions can modify this general rule. See *Low-grown coffees.*

Honduras Some 250,000 acres are planted to coffee in this Central American country, mainly on small farms in the mountainous areas in the west at 2,000 to 6,000 feet. Most of the coffee is washed. Honduras exports about half a million bags of coffee, the best of which has good acidity and mild taste but rather slight body. It is used widely in blending.

India India has about 350,000 acres planted to coffee in the southwestern part of the country (particularly in Mysore state) of which 60 percent is *arabica* and the rest *robusta.* Both washed and natural coffees are produced. Plantation *arabicas* are washed; Malabar and Monsoon *arabicas* are unwashed. The best Indian *arabicas* are well-balanced, strong-flavored, and intriguing.

Indonesia Indonesia, which today includes the islands of Java and Sumatra, has been known for its coffees since 1696, when the Dutch brought shoots from the Malabar

coast to plant in the fertile lands of their newly acquired Indonesian empire, particularly Java. The experiment was more than successful, and for a long time thereafter Java coffee was the standard by which coffee quality was measured. In this country, "java" even became a synonym for coffee. The ravages of leaf-rust disease in the late nineteenth century soon put an end to *arabica* coffee grown at low elevations, and today the great majority of Indonesia's 900,000 acres of coffee are planted in *robusta.* Washed *arabicas* grown at high elevations—the plantation coffees—still come from Java and command high prices due to their scarcity. Outstanding examples are hard to come by, but at their best have an unmatched aromatic spiciness, strong, vibrant flavor, low acidity, and a rich, smooth, full-bodied character. Unlike the bright flavors of many *arabicas,* Javas have an attractive muted tone or texture all their own. Sumatra *arabicas* are generally unwashed, natural coffees. Mandheling in particular is (at its infrequent best) a low-acid, uniquely heavy-bodied coffee, almost syrupy, with a concentrated, exotic flavor. Ankola is a similar Sumatran coffee, also highly regarded. Fine Indonesian coffees have something of a family resemblance, and Kalossi from Sulawesi (Celebes) is rather close to Java in character. *Arabicas* come from Bali as well. The poor examples of Indonesian coffees—and they are many—are sourish, thin, and have the strawy character of so-so Brazils and a dirty undertone to boot.

Irish coffee Irish coffee is hot, strong, sweetened coffee with Irish whiskey added and topped with whipped cream.

Italian roast See *Dark-roasted coffees.*

Italian coffee Another term for *Espresso.*

Ivory Coast This West African nation is third in world exports of coffee, shipping some four and a half million bags of *robusta* a year, of which a good proportion is brought into the United States.

Jamaica The island nation of Jamaica contributes a minute fraction to the world's total coffee production, exporting about twelve thousand bags a year, a little more than half its annual crop. Its coffees are grown on small holdings at varying elevations in the mountains that traverse the island from east to west. Its most famous coffee, grown in the unusual climate of the jungly, cloud-covered Blue Mountain district, has a reputation all out of proportion to its tiny production—about a thousand bags a year, traditionally shipped in barrels under several

marks designating subdistricts (Mavis Bank, Wallenford Estate, Silver Hill, and so on). At one time its superlative qualities were thought to be due to a particular strain of *arabica,* but cuttings from the trees grown elsewhere do not yield the same quality. At its best, Blue Mountain is highly aromatic, acidy, rich, and full-bodied, with a lingering, savory, almost bouillonlike flavor. It is easily one of the great coffees of the world, and because of its scarcity, commands two to three times the price of other milds. As a consequence, many coffees sold as Blue Mountain are nothing of the sort (see the discussion under Coffee Labeling and Authenticity in Chapter Six). Two other coffees are exported: High Mountain Supreme, a designation used for fine-quality, high-grown coffee other than Blue Mountain, and Prime Washed, a low-grown coffee of no special distinction.

Java Name applied only to the *arabica* coffees grown on the island of Java. See *Indonesia.*

Kenya Kenya has a modern coffee industry begun in this century and today produces washed *arabica* coffees equal to the best of Latin America. Recent crops have reached one million bags, virtually all of which is exported. Much of the crop is grown at high elevations and the small, gray-blue beans of the best grades yield sharply acid coffees with a penetrating flavor. Fine Kenyas have a clean, bright-flavored style and a solid body and taste that sometimes approaches a most attractive sappy or winy character. Poor Kenyas can be sour.

Kona See *Hawaii.*

Low-grown coffees Other conditions being equal, coffees grown at low elevations typically lack the fine qualities of *High-grown coffees.*

Malagasy Republic About one million bags of primarily *robusta* coffees are produced each year on this island nation off the African coast. Some *arabica* coffees are grown in the central highlands.

Malawi Malawi grows a small amount of *arabica,* said to be of fine quality, in the highlands at 4,000 to 6,000 feet.

Mandheling A Sumatran coffee. See *Indonesia.*

Maracaibo Market name for certain Venezuelan coffees shipped through the port of that name. See *Venezuela.*

Maragogipe Maragogipe is a variety of *Coffea arabica* that produces extremely large beans. It was discovered in Baía, Brazil, where it is called *Coffea indigena.* It is grown in Brazil, Colombia, Guatemala, and elsewhere. It has the

same character as the other coffees produced where it is grown. Not to be confused with *Elephant bean.*

Medellin Market name for certain coffees of *Colombia.*

Mexico Mexico produces three and a half million bags annually from nearly 800,000 acres of coffee plantings, mainly on the slopes of the Sierra Madre. All washed *arabica,* Mexican coffee is classified by origin, such as Coatepec and Orizaba from Veracruz, Tapachula from Chiapas, and Pluma Oaxaca from Oaxaca. It is also classified by altitude ("Altura" is high-grown coffee from over 4,000 feet). Mexican beans make a handsome roast, due to their large size and distinct center cut. Coatepecs are considered particularly outstanding, but other fine Mexicans have medium acidity, an attractive aroma, and the sweet, smooth round body and satisfying flavor that make them popular for blending and excellent drinking unblended, if a well-balanced example can be found.

Milds "Milds," as the term is used in the coffee trade, are all *arabica* coffees with the exception of Brazils. All fine coffees are milds and virtually all of them are *washed.*

Mocha The name is used loosely. Only coffees grown on the Arabian Peninsula are properly labeled Mocha. See *Yemen.*

Mocha-Java Traditionally, a blend of Mocha and Java coffee. Its quality varies with the character, quality, and compatibility of the Mocha and the Java used in the blend. There are other coffee blends of equal or greater interest.

Mysore Mysore state in southwest India produces most Indian coffee. See *India.*

Natural coffees Natural coffees are processed by the dry as opposed to the wet method, which is used for *Washed coffees.* Fine coffees are produced by both methods, but the wet method is preferred for milds as it yields more reliable and uniform results. (See The Processing of Coffee in Chapter Three.)

New Orleans coffee New Orleans coffee is traditionally roasted dark and has *Chicory* added. Hence, it is also a name for a certain degree of *Dark-roasted coffee.* Rio-y Brazils are widely used in New Orleans coffee. At its best, it is a strong, flavorful beverage.

Nicaragua The half-million bags of coffee exported annually from this Central American country are grown mainly on the slopes of the Pacific Cordillera at elevations of 1,500 to 2,500 feet, as well as in the Matagalpa and Jinotega regions at 2,000 to 4,500 feet. All exported cof-

fees are washed, and although the average Nicaraguan coffee is neutral and useful only for blending, the high-grown coffees have good acidity and mild flavor.

Panama Panama grows coffee principally for domestic consumption, but exports fifteen thousand to twenty thousand bags of washed *arabica,* mostly to Europe. The "Strictly Hard Bean" grade, grown in the highlands at 4,800 feet, has good acidity, fine heavy body, and mild flavor.

Papua and New Guinea Started in 1950, the coffee industry on the island now produces about 500,000 bags, of which most is *arabica* and the rest *robusta.* The washed *arabicas,* grown in the highlands, are said to be of good quality.

Peaberry A freak bean that occurs when one of the two flat-sided beans in the coffee fruit fails to grow; the remaining small bean assumes a rounded shape. About 4 percent of the normal *arabica* crop is peaberry. Some feel it has a more concentrated flavor, but others feel it is simply another bean size and shares the character and quality of the crop as a whole.

Peru Peru now exports some 600,000 bags of coffee each year. The high-grown coffees are noted for excellent body, good acidity, and mild flavor.

Puerto Rico Puerto Rico produces coffee for domestic use; her exports in recent years have been dwindling and green coffee exports stopped altogether in 1972. The quality of the best coffee is said to be good.

Regular roast See *Full-city roast.*

Rio or Rio-y coffees See *Brazil.*

Robusta *Coffea canephora* is commonly referred to as *robusta* coffee. It grows wild in the forests of West Africa, *Zaire,* and *Uganda.* It is a prolific species of coffee grown for use in manufacturing soluble coffees and as an inexpensive blender. It has none of the characteristics or quality of *arabica.*

Rwanda Some 200,000 bags of washed *arabicas* are exported from this small East African nation. Much of it is grown in the high plateaus in the interior and the best is considered equal to the best East African *arabicas.*

Salvador See *El Salvador.*

Santos See *Bourbon Santos* and *Brazil.*

Sumatra See *Indonesia.*

Supremo Grade size indicating large bean and best quality of Colombian coffee. See *Colombia.*

Tanzania Tanzania produces almost one million bags of *arabica,* from mountainous districts in the north and south of the country. *Arabica* was first planted here in 1900 on the slopes of Mt. Kilimanjaro, today an important coffee district. Almost one-third of Tanzania's production is *robusta,* grown in the northwest. The best Tanzanian *arabicas,* while possessing the acidity, intense flavor, full body, and aroma characteristic of fine East African coffees, are often better balanced than Kenyas.

Turkish coffee Not a bean, but a type of coffee-brewing common in Turkey, Greece, Armenia, Egypt, and the Eastern Mediterranean in general. Dark-roasted coffees are stone-ground to a powder and mixed with sweetened water in a long-handled tapering pot called an *ibrik.* Brought to a boil thrice, it is served in tiny cups. (See Chapter Seven for a more complete description.)

Uganda Uganda exports some three million bags of coffee annually, making her fifth in world exports. Almost all the coffee is *robusta,* although some washed *arabica* from the Bugisu district, considered good quality, is exported as well.

Venezuela Venezuela's annual coffee crop hovers around one million bags. Since domestic consumption is increasing, only a third of the crop is exported. Coffee is grown at altitudes ranging from 1,000 to 5,000 feet, much of it in the mountainous Tachira, Mérida, and Trujillo regions. The main port for Venezuelan coffee is Maracaibo, hence many of the coffees shipped from there are known by that name. Some Venezuelans are light-bodied with a delicate flavor and acidity; others are very mellow, full-bodied, and soft. District names do not denote specific qualities. Venezuelan coffees are widely used in blends.

Vienna roast See *Dark-roasted coffees.*

Viennese coffee Coffee served with a dollop of whipped cream.

Washed coffees Washed coffees are processed by the wet method, which involves pulping, fermentation, washing, drying, and hulling, as opposed to the dry method, which eliminates the first three steps and results in *Natural coffees.* Most milds are washed (see Chapter Three).

Yemen Yemen has probably the oldest coffee industry in the world, and although its geography and climate are not considered ideal for coffee, its stands of *arabica* cultivated on terraced mountain slopes at 3,000 to 7,000 feet yield coffees highly regarded on the world market. The

coffee is natural, with a small, round, irregular, olive-green to yellow bean, and has been famous for centuries as Mocha, since it was through that former port (long closed by a sandbar) that coffee was first shipped to the West. Mochas are now shipped from Hodeida and Aden, and exports have long been around sixty thousand bags a year. (Only a small amount is imported into the United States.) "Mocha" is associated in the public mind with a chocolaty taste, which is perhaps why many Mochas are held in higher esteem than they deserve to be, since they are often no more attractive than the duller Djimmas from Ethiopia. The finest grade of Mocha is Matari, which can approach—somewhat—the uniquely acidic, fragrant, syrupy-bodied, bitter-chocolate-flavored cup that Mocha at its best is known for.

Zaire This large African country exports well over a million bags of coffee annually, primarily *robusta,* although some *arabica* is produced and exported as well. These latter coffees are grown at an altitude of around 5,000 feet near Lakes Albert, Edward, and Kivu. At their best, properly picked and processed "Kivus," as they are called in the trade, are regarded as among the finest coffees of the world, having a superb balance of flavor, acidity, and body.

CHAPTER SIX

How to Buy Coffee

Coffee—at least in its canned and instant forms—is one of the most commonly available grocery items in the United States. Before the invention of vacuum-packing, virtually all coffee was sold in beans to be ground at home by hand, but because of the greater convenience of canned preground coffee, both for the retailer and the customer, it soon dominated the market. Now bean coffee is appearing with more and more frequency in specialty stores, delicatessens, and even chain grocery stores and supermarkets. The resurgence of bean coffees today is undoubtedly related to consumer interest in fine cooking and the small but steadily growing demand for connoisseur-quality foodstuffs. The giant national brands of coffee, highly aware of this trend, are offering more expensive canned blends and even "gourmet instants."

The retail operations of most interest to would-be coffee connoisseurs are those specialty shops devoted, sometimes exclusively, to bean coffees that are opening up to meet the public's demand for a better cup of coffee. These shops, keenly aware of modern merchandising, often make good use of an "old-fashioned" look and the attractiveness of a variety of exotically named beans spilling out of burlap bags. The coffee lover who makes his or her way into a specialty shop offering a dozen coffees from all over the world, with names such as Tanzania Peaberry, Mocha-Java, Guatemalan Antigua, Burundi Elephant Bean, Colombian Supremo, a variety of roasts—New Orleans, Italian Espresso, Viennese; an assortment of drip coffee makers; and perhaps a "custom blending service" is unfortunately likely to be so thankful for the sight of real coffee after years of looking at cans on shelves, that he or she is liable not to be very critical of the quality of the coffee offered at this newfound oasis.

Behind the enticing sight of beans in burlap and the heady, appetizing odor of fresh-ground coffee are some unhappy facts: you may not always be buying what you think

you're buying, and despite the higher prices, the beans may not make better coffee than what you can get from a can. The coffee business is a highly competitive business and has its share of sharp merchants, including some who aren't above fleecing the unsuspecting coffee enthusiast. Fortunately, you don't have to be a coffee expert to protect yourself from overpriced, lousy coffee. All you need is a modest amount of accurate information about coffee and its appreciation, and a willingness to do some comparison shopping. I don't mean to suggest there are no trustworthy retail coffee merchants; on the contrary, a growing number are enthusiastic coffee lovers who are pleased to steer customers to coffees they'll enjoy that represent good value. But since many are more enthusiastic than knowledgeable, there is no substitute for knowing something about coffee yourself, if you want to get the most for your money, or for that matter, the most in appreciation for the coffee in your cup. When it comes to buying coffee, it helps to know your beans.

Coffee Labeling and Authenticity

The mislabeling of coffees and the loose use of coffee names is as old as the coffee trade. Although deliberate mislabeling of coffee probably happens no more often than, say, the mislabeling of wine occurs in the wine trade, there are a number of misleading labeling practices coffee lovers should know about. They should be aware, for example, that the name under which beans are sold does not always mean the coffee is pure unblended coffee from that particular region or district. Many coffees sold as specific coffee types contain a substantial amount of some other bean. Not that there is anything wrong with blends per se—on the contrary, only the finest coffees reach a level of quality that couldn't be enhanced by careful blending. But regardless of whether or not blending makes for a better cup of coffee, it's misleading to sell blended coffee without identifying it as such, since you'll assume, naturally, that "Guatemalan" means straight, 100-percent Guatemalan, not half Guatemalan and half Costa Rican or something else. With this kind of labeling, you have no way of knowing if you're be-

coming acquainted with the coffee type you thought you bought or not.

Another labeling problem: some coffee names, such as Mocha and Java, have become rather elastic. The first coffee name familiar to the West was Mocha, the name traditionally given to Arabian coffees shipped from the port city of that name on the Yemen coast. (Arabian coffees are no longer shipped from there; see Yemen in Chapter Five.) As Mocha became associated with high-quality coffee of a particular character, the name became one used rather loosely. "Mocha" is now regularly tacked on to Ethiopian coffees somewhat similar to coffees from the Arabian Peninsula. Some merchants whose customers ask for Mocha will tag these non-Arabian coffees "Mocha-style"; others, far less exact, will sell and tag as "Mocha," coffees that bear no resemblance whatever to what a fine Mocha should taste like. Most customers probably won't find this information unsettling, because most people now think of Mocha as a flavor name given to everything from ice cream to soda pop, not a district or regional name.

The other widely known coffee name is Java, which, at least in the grittier movies of the thirties and forties, became a synonym for coffee ("Gimme a cuppa java and make it fast"). Obviously genuine Java can come only from the island of Java, but since fine-quality *arabicas* from there aren't easy to obtain these days, the name is now loosely applied to any coffee from Indonesia, from the Celebes to Sumatra. Despite the basic similarities these coffees may have to Java, a consumer might justifiably wonder how loose such a label can be without being both meaningless and misleading. Since a good many customers will expect to find Mocha and Java coffees at any store purporting to offer a good selection of the world's finest coffees, however, most proprietors will offer coffees under those names. Rather than explain that little Java worthy of the name is obtainable and that it wouldn't be as good as, say, the Colombian the store offers, some merchants are tempted to do some blending to bring a poor Java up to snuff, or simply sell a Java-style coffee (even if it's Central American) under the name "Java."

Besides the misleading practices of not identifying blended coffees as such and using coffee names loosely, another problem is the downright fraudulent practice of selling completely mislabeled coffee—coffee containing not one bean of the coffee type it's sold as. Coffees sold as Jamaican are the prime example of this: most of them are completely phony.

Jamaica produces a very small amount of coffee, including Prime Washed, High Mountain Supreme, and Blue Mountain. Jamaica Blue Mountain in particular has a well-deserved reputation for being, at its best, one of the world's finest coffees, and the demand for this scarce item has pushed the price up sharply. The genuine beans retail at prices from four to eight dollars a pound in the United States. With the exception of a small amount of Blue Mountain and High Mountain Supreme sent to the United States, *all* of Jamaica's export coffees are shipped to its best customer, Japan, where the Blue Mountain retails for the equivalent of ten dollars a pound. No Jamaican coffees are sent to Europe. A tiny amount of Blue Mountain coffee is imported by two firms in the United States: B. C. Ireland, a San Francisco importer, and Zabar's Gourmet Foods in New York City. An equally tiny amount of the High Mountain Supreme is shipped only to Zabar's. Thus, in the United States, authentic Blue Mountain is sold only in a few West Coast shops and Zabar's, which sells all its Jamaican coffees right in its own store on upper Broadway in Manhattan. The implausibility of merchants obtaining any of these coffees from elsewhere (say, having them reexported from Japan at enormous expense) makes it a virtual certainty there's not a single Jamaican bean in all the bags of "Blue Mountain" and "High Mountain Supreme" displayed in stores across the United States.

Even without knowing who the importers for the United States are, one would have to conclude that there was something strange about the amount of Jamaican coffee on sale after looking at the coffee import and export figures released by the U.S. Department of Commerce and published by the Pan-American Coffee Bureau and in coffee trade annuals and directories. Why? In 1975, less than two hundred bags' worth (Jamaican coffee is traditionally shipped in barrels) of genuine Jamaican coffee, shipped by the Jamaican Coffee Industry Board, were imported into the United States.

Some retailers purporting to sell Jamaican coffees in the United States claim to have bought theirs from some mysterious source in Europe. European dealers purporting to sell Jamaican coffees claim to have bought theirs from some mysterious source in the United States. But no Jamaican coffees have ever been reexported from Japan or the United States. Nonetheless, the high prices that genuine Jamaican coffee commands makes the sale of bogus

beans attractive to unscrupulous merchants. Creative merchandisers usually give the would-be "Jamaicas" the ring of authenticity by asking about four to six dollars per pound for them. Considering that at the best you're getting coffee consisting of beans that would normally retail at about three dollars per pound, it's obvious there are fat profits in funny coffees. Now it may be true, as coffee people say, that hardly anyone could tell the difference between Jamaica Blue Mountain and High Mountain Supreme and a fine Central American coffee, but it's just a plain rip-off to sell Central American coffees as Jamaican and ask dollars extra a pound for them.

The fact that there's a lot of hocus-pocus going on with some coffees makes one wonder how many other exotic coffees are created out of fresh burlap, a stencil set, and a steady supply of Central American beans. Particularly suspicious are other coffees known to be in short supply. Less than twenty thousand bags of the fine, distinctive Hawaiian Kona, for example, are produced each year. That amount of Kona is not much to go around when you subtract local use, exports to Europe, what goes into canned Kona, and what disappears into blended coffees. That's not to say there isn't any genuine unblended Kona around, but for an extremely scarce coffee, there's a peculiar abundance.

Just how widespread *deliberate* mislabeling is, it's hard to say, but many in the coffee business privately acknowledge that it's common enough to give the knowledgeable customer pause—and they'll also point out that it's impossible to prevent this practice. There are endless opportunities for rebagging and imaginative stencil work at every level of the trade, from the countries and ports of origin to trade centers in Europe to importers, wholesalers, roasters, and finally retailers. Undoubtedly some bogus coffee is being sold by people who don't know any better (even if they ought to), just as it's obvious that a good deal of it is sold by those who certainly know what they're doing. People sometimes dupe each other all the way down the line, but all too often it's just the retailer simply duping the last and least knowledgeable link in the chain, the customer.

Is there any way, then, a coffee lover can tell by looking at a sack of beans, or tasting the coffee, that it is what it purports to be? Considering the nature of coffee appearance and taste (discussed in Chapters Four and Five), it isn't easy to determine by sight, smell, or taste that any given bag is full of bogus beans. Frankly, the average customer

has simply no way of knowing whether two dozen coffees listed in a shop are actually twenty-four distinct kinds or a half-dozen types artfully blended and rebagged twenty-four different ways. In addition, over a hundred different kinds of coffee are imported into the country from hundreds of different sources, so that, with the exception of Jamaican coffees, it's very difficult to say a merchant couldn't have a genuine example of practically any given coffee produced in the world.

All the coffee lover has to go on is "cup quality," and whether the coffee exhibits anything like the character that kind of coffee is supposed to have. Actually, that tells you most of what you need to know, because, quite apart from the question of mislabeling, there are considerable differences in quality among the same kinds of coffee offered by different retailers. Just because you see Colombian Supremo in two stores doesn't mean both will taste the same (even if they're both 100-percent Colombian Supremo), because many of the coffees on the wholesale market are available in a wide range of quality. Even the next batch of that coffee at a particular retail outlet may taste different in a few weeks' time: coffees are a variable agricultural product and can differ considerably from lot to lot and month to month.

In other words, if being sure of getting the best matters to you, comparative shopping is important. Labels are easy to fake; it's impossible to fake quality.

Roasts

Many people shopping for coffee are confused by the variety of roasts available in specialty stores. In order to bring out all the quality and flavor inherent in a fine coffee bean, it must be roasted to an optimum degree (see Chapter Three for a more detailed discussion). This level of roast is called a full-city roast, or American roast, or regular roast, or breakfast roast, and so forth, and should be slightly darker than the roast typically given most canned coffee. It is the roast most of the bean coffees available will be given. Depending on the area of the country, the next darkest roast is called French, Continental, or Vienna, or perhaps New Orleans roast. Italian roast usually means espresso or the very darkest roast possible, almost black. (Confusingly, the very darkest roast is sometimes called

French roast.) Don't let the terminology bother you; whatever the various roasts are called, the lightest roast given the majority of the coffees sold will be the regular roast. Most outlets offer in addition only two or three darker roasts, of which one is usually an espresso type, while the others fall somewhere between the dark and light roasts.

Many coffee drinkers are great fans of dark-roasted coffees, having been attracted to them because they make a cup with a strong, distinct taste, which seems an improvement over the thin, flavorless brews most canned coffees produce. But a burnt, dark taste is no substitute for a lack of genuine flavor, nor should it be confused with richness merely because the effect on the palate is one of aggressive strength. Roasting the bean darker than regular roast disguises the individual character of the coffee-bean type because it introduces a burnt nuance, which becomes more pronounced the darker the roast, and dominant in espresso. Thus if one wants to experience the distinct aroma and flavor nuances found in the world's coffees, they must be tasted when given a full-city roast and no darker.

Of course, darker-roasted coffees can be enjoyable in their own right, and there are significant differences in the qualities of dark roasts sold. Bad espresso roasts taste like chewing on the end of a pencil; at its best it makes an attractive bitter-burnt cup. But if good beans are used and the coffee is given proper roasting, handling, and reasonable storage, one shop's espresso tastes pretty much like another's. Although using beans of good quality is important, it is pointless to use a very fine coffee for making the darkest roasts, because practically any decent coffee roasted that dark will taste just the same—or just as burnt. It's equally pointless to pay more for espresso made with fancy beans. The lighter dark roasts do not completely disguise coffee character, so that here the quality of the bean is more important, but not so important that it is worthwhile to roast the top qualities of fine coffees such a shade —or for the customer to pay extra for what in effect is scorched coffee with a fancy name. Mexican coffee is often used for darker roasts, not so much for taste as appearance, since its large fat beans make a handsome Continental roast.

Rating Your Retailer

Very few coffee shops selling bean coffees do their own roasting. Of the ones that do, some roast in small (sometimes antique) twenty-five- to fifty-pound-capacity roasters on the premises, while others take their coffees to what is called a trade roaster—much as a farmer would take his wheat to a mill to be ground—and have it roasted to order. Roasting coffees properly is not a simple job; it requires experience to judge the precise moment when all the character of the bean has been brought out. There is no necessary reason why shops that do their own roasting should have an edge in coffee quality over shops that buy roasted beans from wholesale roasters, but this often seems to be the case. Proprietors that roast their own or have their coffees roasted to their specifications have greater control over their product. Since they are not dependent on wholesale roasters (who in some cases may not take great care in handling and roasting coffees) for supplies, they are in a position to do their own importing or at least to select and obtain green coffees from a number of importers. Of course, any merchant who expects to do a good job of selecting the best coffees from the vast number available at any given time has to spend a great deal of time cup-sampling. Most shops simply cannot afford the time or expense of doing their own roasting and are not equipped to cup-sample. Instead, many simply rely on a single supplier, often a restaurant or wholesale roaster, for all their needs, and may not even bother to sample what they sell. They may not really know what kind of coffee they are getting, or be able to offer any meaningful advice about their coffees to customers.

This means that the customer has to do his or her own comparative sampling and selecting of coffees. Bean coffees from the same outlet may vary from sour to superb in quality and reasonable to ridiculous in price. Even in the retail outlets that make an effort to carry consistently high-quality coffees, there will be significant variations simply because not all the best qualities of all the world's coffees are available at all times. Coffee, after all, is a crop, and is subject to the vagaries of weather in addition to the vagaries of the marketplace.

Comparative shopping and sampling not only ensures that you're getting your money's worth, but that you'll have a bright, clean, aromatic coffee in your morning mug—no small achievement. Comparative tastings (see Chapter Four) needn't be a weekly chore; as long as you have access to a freezer, you can lay in a three-month supply of the best coffee you come across, a method of storage that will be described shortly.

First, are there any guidelines for what sorts of coffees might be good bets to try? Unfortunately, it's difficult to generalize, since particular types of coffee differ in their availability across the country. I would first try the house blend of any specialty shop, on the ground that although the quality of the exotic imports will necessarily vary, any coffee outlet worth patronizing ought to be able to supply a consistently good blend from week to week. There is no reason why the shop can't vary the coffees that go into the blend if that should be necessary (as it often is) to keep up the character and quality. Then start exploring the more exotic growths, first by trying different kinds of coffee against each other to bring out their differences, and then by comparing several coffees of the same type from different sources. Just because you happen not to like a particular coffee, don't write it off; you may not have had a good representative example.

Second, I would always include in my comparative tastings a good standard example of a local or national coffee blend. Some grocery chains, such as the well-known A & P stores, offer inexpensive, good-quality bean coffees, and these provide some standard by which to judge more expensive "gourmet" coffees. If the quality isn't markedly better, it is hardly worth paying a substantial premium merely because the gourmet coffee is sold under a fancy name in a fancy outlet. In fact, you may well find that many of the gourmet coffees sold are not a bit superior to coffees like A & P's Bokar blend, or the several brands of 100-percent Colombian coffees offered in cans.

Storing Coffee at Home

Although green coffee is considered relatively stable and under certain conditions can last for years, once coffee is roasted it retains its best flavor for only three weeks (it has

the very best flavor during the first week); it begins to slide into stale condition after a month has passed. One notices the drop-off in quality much more readily with fine coffee—it has much more to lose. Espresso and other dark roasts seem to last longer, probably because their burnt character dominates the taste anyway.

Once roasted coffee is ground, it lasts a week at the most, and is better within four or five days. Actually, it begins fading toward staleness within hours if exposed to air, which is one of the reasons why grinding your own is highly recommended for those who want to get the most out of their beans. Many stores supplying bean coffees get their supplies of roasted coffee weekly, so that having your coffee ground on the spot presents no particular problem if you don't buy more than a week's supply at a given time. If you do buy ground coffee, keep it in a closed and preferably airtight container in the refrigerator. Some claim this is a bad idea, since moisture will inevitably condense inside when the container is opened, thereby speeding the coffee flavor's demise.

A far better solution is to invest in a grinder, buy bean coffee, and grind your own. (Chapter Seven discusses some of the types available; a perfectly serviceable no-fuss electric model costs about fifteen dollars.) Keep the beans you buy in an airtight canister at room temperature (or the refrigerator), but do not let the cold container sit out on the counter so that moisture condenses on the beans. Remember, too, that coffee picks up smells; it should not be stored near strong-smelling foodstuffs like onions. (For that reason it is best stored in closed bins, not open bags, at the retail level, preferably plastic bins which can be cleaned thoroughly to prevent the buildup of rancid coffee oils.) The principal advantage of grinding your own beans (besides better-tasting coffee) is the convenience of long-range storage. Since coffee beans retain their flavor up to three or four months if frozen—particularly if the temperature is below zero—you can dispense with weekly trips by simply laying in a number of pounds of a particularly fine coffee you come across. The beans must be carefully stored in moisture-proof containers; glass jars with rubber seals are excellent. Simply take whatever beans you need for immediate use out of the freezer at any time and grind them at once. The best way to prevent flavor deterioration from moisture condensation is to divide your freezer supply into small containers so that you needn't take the entire amount in and out of the freezer

each time you need coffee. Keep what you need for daily use in the refrigerator.

Readers who do not live near a source of bean coffees should consult the appendix on Shopping for Fine Coffees and Teas by Mail.

Blending to Order

Virtually all coffee sold at retail is blended, but that does not mean that all coffees blend well with each other, as was pointed out in Chapter Four. Yet because the idea of coffee-blending is so much ingrained in the public mind as the sine qua non of fine coffee, many coffee drinkers think (wrongly) that no unblended coffee could be superior to blended coffee. This isn't the case, and coffee drinkers who always insist on blended coffees miss the opportunity to appreciate the spectrum of aromas and flavors found among the world's fine coffees. Then, too, coffee merchants are well aware of the great appeal of personalized blends—that is, blends created for customers who can then take home their own individual, private blends to serve as something special to their friends.

Some coffee customers take this to ludicrous lengths, thinking to achieve the *ne plus ultra* by imaginative alchemy: "I'd like three ounces of American-roast Peruvian Chanchamayo, two ounces of French-roast Yemen Mocha, six ounces of regular-roast Sumatra Mandheling, three ounces Colombian Armenia Supremo Italian roast, about a dozen Tanzanian peaberries, a couple of Burundi elephant beans, and a pinch of chicory, please." Some merchants will play along with these fantasy orders, using the excuse that the customer is always right; others will try to explain that indiscriminate mixing is a good way to end up with a cup of expensive mud, and that if they want something a little different, why not try a blend of a little French-roast house blend in the regular-roast house blend? Unfortunately, many customers would rather think they have something special than be sure they have something good.

There is nothing that difficult in trying to create your own blend, provided it is realized that successful blending requires making up cup samples of individual coffees first, and then combining their liquors to see if the cup chemistry works. Coffees cannot be successfully blended by recipe; sometimes it works, sometimes it doesn't, again because

coffees differ significantly from lot to lot, and two fine coffees, instead of complementing each other, may simply cancel out each other's best qualities. (Blending at home is discussed in more detail in Chapter Four.)

CHAPTER SEVEN

How to Make Good Coffee

There's little point in going to the trouble of tracking down a superb coffee just to kill it in the pot. Just as processing, at its best, tries to preserve the quality inherent in the bean, so too the purpose of careful preparation of the beverage is to preserve the quality locked up in the roasted bean. The achievement of a decent cup of coffee requires, first, good coffee; the most painstaking preparation won't make a good cup from lousy beans. How to recognize and find good (or better) coffee has been covered in detail. The second requirement, how to get a good cup from those beans, is the subject of this chapter. Neither skill nor experience is required to make superb coffee, merely the ability to follow a few simple directions and use a few simple pieces of kitchen equipment. In fact, I'd say that compared with making coffee, boiling an egg properly is *haute cuisine.*

In centuries past, coffee used to be ground and then simply cooked or boiled, a method still used to prepare Turkish coffee. The modern way is basically infusion—the ground coffee is brought into contact with very hot to boiling water for a certain length of time in order to extract the coffee flavor, so that the resulting brew will be attractive and satisfying and exhibit the character and quality of the coffee used. This seems a simple enough task, but whereas the best method of tea preparation has been established for centuries and is subject to very little disagreement, the best method for making an excellent beverage from coffee has been a vexing question practically since the discovery of the beverage, and certainly since its introduction to the West. This unsettled state of affairs is undoubtedly responsible for the enormous number of coffee-making devices that have been invented in the last several centuries. Today one can find scores of coffee makers, from simple to extremely elaborate machines. Most of them, however, can be categorized by method of preparation into percolator, vacuum, drip, and, for lack of a better word, "steeped infu-

sion" coffee makers. Fortunately, enough is now known about the chemical structure of the coffee beverage to provide a means of narrowing the number of coffee makers and methods to those that prepare an acceptable cup of coffee.

Grinding Coffee at Home

In order to be able to extract any flavor from the roasted coffee bean, it must be ground. Even if one buys freshly ground coffee every few days, the quality of the beverage it produces can never be as high as coffee made from beans ground immediately before making the brew, because, once the bean is ground, its flavor constituents are exposed to and evaporate into the air (which is why coffee smells so attractive as it's ground, and why the ground coffee starts to fade and stale soon afterward). The sooner the brew can be made after grinding, the more flavor constituents can be captured in the cup rather than lost to the air.

Proper grinding is not just a simple matter of smashing up the bean. In order to get the best possible extraction of flavor from the ground coffee, it is important that the grind consist of evenly sized particles (for reasons explained shortly). Frankly, the giant rollers used by large roasters and packers (described in Chapter Three) do this best, crunching, cracking, and slicing the bean into particles of the desired size with great precision. The next-best grinding mechanisms are chopping plates, spiked or coglike wheels that oppose each other and grind the beans between them by having one plate turn while the other remains stationary. These produce more even particles in the fine grinds than the coarser grinds. Two home-sized electric grinders that use such plate mechanisms are the KitchenAid Electric Coffee Mill (Model KCM) and the Braun (Model KMM 1); both have grind selectors and run about thirty-five to forty-five dollars.

There is no lack of inexpensive little electric grinders on the current market. These generally have a clean, space-age design, usually consisting of an upright cylinder with a half-cup-capacity cup to hold the beans and a removable plastic top. These grinders actually chop the beans rather than grind them, using what looks like a little propeller that whirls at great speed at the bottom of the cup where the

beans are held. The drawback to this method is that the particles are uneven in size, which causes uneven extraction rates during brewing. However, the inexpensive propeller-type grinders create a more even-particled fine grind than they do a coarse grind, because it takes up to thirty seconds to chop the beans to a very fine grind. (Fortunately, fine grinds are required for some of the best methods of coffee brewing.) The large increase in quality one gets using fresh-ground coffee makes the small inexpensive electric grinders understandably popular, and they are easy to clean.

Most of them have a safety feature that won't permit operation until the cap is put on, thus preventing the possibility of lost fingertips should you have to pry loose the occasional bean that wedges under the grinder blade. Braun, SEB, Moulinex, Peugeot, Mitey-Mill, and Salton offer models along this line, and doubtless there are or will be other manufacturers offering versions as well. The cost ranges from about ten to twenty dollars.

It's perfectly possible to grind beans in a mortar and pestle (a method advocated by Brillat-Savarin), but this is a laborious task, particularly with hard high-grown beans. The squat wooden coffee mills common in every kitchen a generation or so ago actually do a fairly good job of grinding beans, depending on the model. Most simply have a large crank and a burrlike mechanism that crunches the beans, and a small drawer below to catch the grinds. Still, the job of cranking out enough coffee from a coffee mill held between the knees every time you want a pot of coffee would be regarded by most Americans as something of a chore, particularly by those who like electric toothbrushes and other time- and labor-saving gadgets.

It is also possible to grind coffee in a blender. Many blenders come with a small baby-food-sized glass cover to use for grinding nuts, and this can be used for coffee beans as well. Unfortunately, control of times and fineness of grind is something that has to be worked out for each blender, since most models have several different speeds, blade designs are different, and so forth. Very fine grinds would probably be the most successful ones to attempt.

In selecting any grinder, one should be concerned not only with the method and ease of grinding and the safety features, but also how easily the grinder can be cleaned, particularly the grinding prop plate itself. The coffee lover who wants to experiment with different coffee tastes needs a

grinder that can be wiped clean of the previous coffee with reasonable ease.

Few coffee lovers understand why the nature of the grind is so important to the cup quality of the brew. Many are aware that the *fineness* of the grind is related to the type of method one uses to make the coffee, if only because most coffees come in several different grinds: fine or vacuum grind, drip or medium grind, and coarse, percolator, or regular grind. This variation in grinds has to do with the nature of extraction of solubles from the grounds. In nontechnical language, the degree of extraction indicates the amount of flavor removed from a given amount of grounds. If too little is removed, the cup flavor is underdeveloped; if too much is extracted, the flavor is bitter (ideally, no less than 18 percent and no more than 22 percent of solubles should be extracted from the coffee grounds during brewing). The degree of extraction depends on the fineness of the grind and how long the grounds remain in contact with the water. After about five minutes in contact with 200°F water, about 20 percent of the solubles have been extracted from drip or medium-grind coffee. Longer contact with water simply extracts bitterness. More coarsely ground coffee takes longer contact with water at the same temperature to extract the same flavor. Based on this research, the coffee industry has generally adopted the following standards: fine grinds are suitable for methods in which the grounds are in contact with the water from one to four minutes, drip grinds are suitable for methods taking from four to six minutes, and coarse grinds are best for methods taking from six to eight minutes of contact with water. This research, then, is the source of the recommendation that you should always match the grind to the method to derive the maximum flavor from the bean. If a coarse grind is used in fast-method coffee makers, a flavorless brew is made; if a fine grind is used in a slow-method coffee maker, a bitter cup results. And, as mentioned before, the evenness of the ground particles is related to the uniformity of the extraction. The reason why uneven particles are not ideal is that they give under- and over-extraction at the same time.

The average amount of time necessary to produce given fineness of grinds for different coffee-making methods in the simpler electric grinders is as follows:

Coarse (percolator method)	6 seconds
Medium (drip method)	10 seconds

Fine (vacuum method)	15 seconds
Very Fine (filter-cone method)	30 seconds

Naturally, there is some variation in this, depending on the particular coffee maker used and the particular grinder used. While these times are a reasonably accurate guide, don't hesitate to experiment with different amounts of grinding time.

Water for Coffee

Since 99 percent of a cup of coffee is water, the effect of water quality on coffee quality can hardly be ignored. If you don't like the taste of the water that comes out of your tap, it makes no sense to think making coffee with that water will produce a palatable beverage. Merely because water is *safe* to drink is no indication that it is *pleasant* to drink. Chlorination, excessive hardness, alkalinity, brackishness, organic content, and other factors affecting water quality found in local water supplies can downgrade brewed-coffee quality. Sivetz states that at least half the coffee brewed in the United States will be downgraded by the quality of the water available, and in some areas a good brew quality is impossible to achieve. The best water for coffee is free of off-tastes, odors, and impurities, not overly soft or alkaline, and possessing a mild mineral content, or slightly hard. On this basis the Northeast, the Pacific Northwest, and parts of the South have the best general water conditions, though of course local conditions—or even the individual conditions found in your basement water pipes—are just as important. Artificially softened water, for example, makes poor coffee.

What can you do if your local water supply is poor? Considering that most coffee drinkers do not drink a great many cups per day, using filtered or bottled water may provide the answer without a great deal of additional expense. Steam distilled water, in addition to being de-aerated (and therefore somewhat flat-tasting), yields somewhat sourish coffee, perhaps because of excessive extraction. Some bottled "spring" waters have too much mineral content and fail to extract enough flavor from the grounds. You may have to experiment with coffee made from various bottled waters or filtered tap water to find an appropriate substi-

tute for poor local water. If excessive chlorination is the problem, simply letting water stand in a large pot for a few hours to a day may bring about a marked improvement in the water, and thus your coffee.

Even in areas with high-quality water, be sure to use only cold, freshly drawn water. Letting the tap run for a few moments before filling the kettle ensures that the stale, flat, de-aerated water that has been left standing in the pipes has run off. Do not use water from the hot-water tap; this is certainly quite stale and flat from sitting in the boiler.

One of the principal causes of poor coffee made in most United States homes (and restaurants, too) is that too much water is used in proportion to the amount of ground coffee used. In spite of efforts by industry trade organizations, some coffee firms still make excessive claims for how many cups of coffee can be made from a pound of their blend. At one time in the United States it was a common claim that up to seventy-five cups could be made from one pound of coffee, even though it is hardly in the industry's interest to claim that more servings can be made from less coffee. No one in the centuries of coffee use has ever been able to show how more than about forty servings can be made from a pound of beans without a diminution in beverage quality. What is more, this "serving" or "cup" is a six-ounce cup, not an eight- or ten-ounce mug.

The ideal proportion of coffee is one standard coffee measure (two level tablespoons of ground coffee) per six ounces of water. This relationship holds true regardless of the method used. The only exceptions to this rule are double-strength coffees. These include French *café filtre,* and other coffees made in a Moka-type pot or an Italian machinetta. (Since these double-strength coffees are traditionally served in small demitasse cups, for convenience I'll refer to them as demitasse coffees.) These coffees require *two* standard coffee measures (or four level tablespoons) per six-ounce serving. Other coffees requiring a higher-than-normal proportion of coffee to water are espresso and Turkish coffee.

The proportion of two level tablespoons per six-ounce serving is considered ideal because it yields a brew with excellent strength: not weak, but not too strong. The strength of a cup of coffee can actually be measured by the concentration of solubles found in the beverage (this is easy enough to determine with a hydrometer, which tells you how many solids are dissolved in the liquid), and this

strength is directly related to the proportion of coffee used in a given amount of water. Using a recommended measure of coffee to water, one gets forty servings per pound, of which each serving has from 1.15- to 1.35-percent soluble solids. Trying to get more servings from a pound—making the coffee weaker—will result in less than 1.15-percent soluble solids in the beverage and a brew that will appear weak and thin. Making the coffee too strong—getting much less than forty cups per pound from it—will result in far more than 1.35-percent soluble solids, and a brew that will be excessively strong for most tastes. The exceptions here again are the demitasse coffees, whose extra strength is tolerable because they are served in small amounts.

Excessive extraction (causing bitterness) is not the same as excessive strength; it is possible to make a weak (low-strength) but bitter cup by grinding coffee excessively fine, using less than the recommended proportion, and boiling it for ten minutes on the stove. The result will be thin, watery, and bitter. It is also possible to make an excessively strong, but underdeveloped (flavorless) cup by using a very coarse grind in twice the recommended amount through a filter cone. The coffee will be strong, but lack coffee character. Probably one of the reasons Americans often make coffee too weak is that the methods they use often result in over-extraction. To avoid the resulting bitterness, many use less coffee. Many people think they don't like full-strength coffee, when in fact they have simply never had a properly brewed cup made in the proper proportion. In order to brew coffee properly, it should be made full-strength, and then, some claim, if it is still too strong, it can be diluted with hot water in the cup. While this is certainly preferable to brewing it weak, I find that dilution degrades the coffee's character. Before resorting to dilution, try simply switching to a milder coffee—a lightly roasted Brazilian Santos, for example.

In short, proper measuring of the coffee and the water is a must. Many coffeepots and coffee makers do not have accurate cup markings, so check these first before relying on them. Although few people will be willing to go to such lengths, it is true that coffee is more accurately measured by weighing than by cubic measure, because coffees "bulk" differently according to roasts and origin. For those who are interested in pursuing the ultimate in coffee perfection, the weight equivalent of the recommended proportion is ten to eleven grams per six ounces of water. For those making

large amounts of coffee, this is 1 pound of coffee to 2 1/8 gallons of water. Some useful measurements in between are: for 3 cups of coffee use 1 ounce of coffee to 16–20 ounces of water; for 8 cups (48 ounces) of coffee use 2.4–3 ounces of coffee; for 10 cups (60 ounces) use 3–3.75 ounces of coffee. My personal preference is for coffee made at the upper-strength limits.

The temperature of the water used is another important factor in proper coffee-brewing. The ideal temperature for water when it comes into contact with the ground coffee is 200°F: in fact, the temperature of the water should vary no more than plus or minus 5° from this norm. Fortunately, achieving this sort of precision does not require anything fancy in equipment, since it is the range of temperature that a pot of boiling water falls to the moment it is removed from the heat. In a number of coffee-making methods—drip, filter cone, vacuum, and so on—water must first be brought to a boil and then added to the ground coffee, often by simply pouring the water on the grounds. Water brought to a boil in a kettle will fall to the required temperature as the kettle is lifted from the heat and the water is poured. Bring the water to a full boil, but do not let it boil any length of time, as this will drive off the air in the water and deaden the taste.

In order not to impart any foreign flavor to the water, I recommend using a stainless-steel kettle, rather than any old saucepan, although a porcelain pot would seem unproblematic. Many people use whistling kettles, but these have one considerable drawback: the narrow neck makes it impossible to clean the kettle. If you've ever had occasion to look inside a kettle used for a year or two you're liable to be startled by the extraordinary buildup of mineral and other deposits left as accumulated residue from the boiling of hundreds of gallons of tap water. Needless to say, these formations don't help the character of the freshly drawn water, since it is being boiled in their presence—not to mention that most of this material does not look like the sort of thing most people would care to imbibe purposely along with their coffee. I happen to use the stainless-steel bottom half of a vacuum coffeepot; with the lid on, it boils as fast as the usual kettle and can easily be cleaned, since its wide mouth will admit an entire hand. Any similar-design kettle would doubtless work as well. I have been told that it may be something of a possible health hazard to scour the inside of such a kettle with an abrasive pad, since scouring the surface may

allow small amounts of chromium to be leeched into the water, depending on the alloy of the metal. A swipe or two every once in a while with the sort of plastic scrubbing pad that is recommended for use with Teflon products is all that I've found necessary to clean my kettle, at least if it's not used for anything else. I find no inconvenience in not having a whistle, since I almost always first put the water on to boil, and then select and grind the coffee, prepare the pot, ready cups and the like, after which time the water is often at a boil.

Coffee-making Methods

Percolation

Technically speaking, percolation refers to the method allowing hot water to pass once through the ground coffee and into a waiting pot below through small holes in the coffee container—a method that sounds exactly like a description of what we think of today as a drip pot. What we think of today as a percolator is, strictly speaking, a *pumping percolator,* invented in the early nineteenth century by Nicholas Felix Durant, a Parisian. He took the drip pots of his day one step further by utilizing steam pressure to raise hot water up through a central tube in the pot to spray continuously over the ground coffee held in a perforated basket. Given a good design and the proper grind—coarse—such a method, properly used, *can* yield an acceptable cup of coffee. Unfortunately, thc designs of many modern electric percolators violate a number of the known requirements for making good coffee. Some models attempt to extract the coffee's flavor at far too low a temperature, while others practically boil the coffee for periods of up to twenty minutes, a method guaranteed to turn the most exquisite high-grown *arabica* into what Brillat-Savarin called a beverage "fit only to rasp the throat of a Cossack."

Until recently well over half the coffee prepared in American homes was prepared by percolation, though there are signs that many are now turning to other methods. Considering what electric percolators do to coffee, it is a wonder that they have held sway so long in United States kitchens! Claims have been made that the average coffee drinker cannot tell the difference between electric-perked

coffee and coffee made by superior drip methods, but since there certainly is a quite noticeable loss of quality when properly prepared fine coffee is compared with the same coffee parboiled in a percolator, I think the claims have more to do with the generally poor-quality blends of coffee most Americans use than with method.

The attraction Americans have for percolators is probably based on the facts that (1) they are automatic and electric, allowing sleepy-eyed morning risers simply to stab the plug of a ready-to-go pot into an outlet and think no more about it until they're ready for a cup, and (2) they give off a nice aroma while perking away. Unfortunately, what that nice "coffee's on" smell signals is that the coffee parboiled in a percolator, I think the claims have more save the aroma for where it belongs—in the cup.

In all fairness, it must be said that there is one type of percolator that escapes the general condemnation the electric perks deserve: the stove-top percolator. Admittedly, there are not many of these around anymore, but they produce good coffee if the following method is used:

1. Remove the coffee basket and stem from the coffeepot. Fill the basket with a measured amount of regular—coarse or "perc"—grind coffee.
2. Bring a measured amount of freshly drawn cold water to a boil in the percolator pot. (Be sure that the water level will not touch the bottom of the basket when it is inserted.)
3. Remove pot from heat, insert basket and stem, cover, and return to gentle heat.
4. Percolate slowly six to eight minutes maximum. Remove basket and stem before serving.

It is possible to get a decent cup of coffee by this method, but it is time-consuming, requires careful attention and timing, and is messy, particularly when it comes to removing the hot basket and grounds. It is also quite difficult to get the proper grind for such a method from a home grinder, which all too often creates fine particles that clog the pores of the basket. The coffee varies according to the amount of heat used, and in addition, it is all too easy to let the coffee perk far longer than eight minutes, in which case all that is being extracted from the grounds is bitterness.

Vacuum

The vacuum pot is an ingenious way to make coffee and, done properly, yields a fine cup. The coffee maker consists of two parts, a lower bowl or pot that has a wide opening to hold a fitted upper bowl with a short stem and filter. In this method, the grounds are placed in the top and wetted by boiling water that passes from the lower bowl to the upper by steam pressure. Removal from heat creates a vacuum in the lower bowl, which then sucks the brew through the filter into the lower bowl. The principle behind the method is simple, although the process is difficult to describe and somewhat complicated to use. The steps are as follows:

1. Remove the upper bowl and insert the filter through the stem and attach. Measure the correct amount of fine-grind coffee on top of the filter.
2. Bring freshly drawn cold water to a boil in the lower bowl; remove from heat and insert upper bowl, giving it a slight twist to ensure a proper seal, and return to moderate heat.
3. As the water starts to rise into the upper bowl and begins mixing with the grounds, begin timing, and lightly stir the mixture with a zigzag motion for about twenty seconds to facilitate extraction. Remove from heat after one minute has elapsed.
4. When brew has been pulled into lower bowl (it may take two minutes), remove the upper bowl and serve.

Some vacuum coffee makers have adjustable filters that permit selection of very strong or light filtering of the brew; either way, a clear, clean cup is easy to produce if the steps are followed with care. Its drawbacks as a method are considerable, however; it requires careful timing and attention; the upper bowl has to be inserted tightly in the lower bowl to ensure a vacuum will be created, and consequently is often enormously difficult (depending on design) to remove when the coffee is ready to serve; the beverage varies according to the heat used; and it's messy—the upper bowl won't stand up on its stem (as one discovers when adding coffee to it), and it's difficult to handle a hot bowl full of grounds.

Drip

The first drip pot seems to have been invented by Jean Baptiste de Belloy, Archbishop of Paris, and frequenter of the coffee houses of his time; his invention came into use about 1800 and consisted of a perforated metal container to hold ground coffee inside a larger pot. Since hot water was intended to be poured on top to pass once through the grounds, this was essentially the modern drip pot.

Drip pots today come in several forms—simple pots, filter-cone methods, and electric drip machines. The drip pot is probably most familiar, so I'll discuss that first. The drip pot comes in a variety of shapes and styles, but always consists of a lower section with spout and handle, middle section that holds the coffee in a perforated basket above the lower pot, and an upper section that fits on top, perforated with tiny holes so that when boiling water is added, it drips through the basket holding the grounds and the brew can drip through the basket to the bottom. The method is quite simple:

1. Preheat the lower half of pot by rinsing in hot water. Add the basket.
2. Put a measured amount of drip-grind (medium grind) coffee into the middle section of the drip pot. Add the upper section.
3. Pour a measured amount of freshly drawn cold water that has been brought to a boil into the upper section. Cover.
4. When dripping is complete (four to six minutes), remove upper section, give brew a stir, and serve.

In many models of drip pots it is not necessary to measure the amount of water brought to a boil, since the upper section is marked and the boiling water is added rapidly enough to measure with reasonable accuracy. Nevertheless, I recommend measuring the water.

The advantage of the method is that it makes superior coffee, chiefly because the water is passed through the coffee in a single downward draw in a relatively short time. The method is also nearly foolproof, since it requires no timing (although the upper section and the basket with the spent grounds should be removed promptly when finished) and little fuss. It is slightly less messy than percolators and vacuum pots. A note: Many drip pots are made of alu-

minum, which may slightly affect coffee taste; stainless steel or even porcelain is preferable.

Filter cones are a variation of drip pots that utilize a glass or ceramic pot for the lower half, and an inverted plastic, ceramic, or glass cone for the upper that holds a folded (or molded) paper filter. The method is identical to that of the drip pot, save that very finely ground coffee is placed in the cone lined with filter paper, which, having considerable porosity, passes the water through rapidly. In order to get a first-rate cup with the filter-cone method, water cannot simply be dumped in the upper section onto the grounds. This creates a mixture of froth and lumps and causes uneven extraction. For best results:

1. Put cone on top of pot and insert and smooth paper filter.
2. Put measured amount of coffee in filter.
3. Pour about one-half the amount of boiling water in the cone first, wetting the grounds thoroughly in a circular motion.
4. Lightly stir the mixture with a spoon in a zigzag motion (do not dig or paw at the bottom of the cone as this is liable to tear the filter), and then let the water drip completely through.
5. At this point, add the rest of the water, pouring in a slow circular motion onto the grounds. (The kettle need not be kept boiling while waiting.)
6. After the water is dripped through, remove the upper section and, before serving, give the brew a stir to ensure the even distribution of flavor.

The advantages of the filter-cone method are considerable. It is rapid and nearly foolproof; little variation occurs from cup to cup; it allows full control over the coffee being made, produces a clean, clear, delicious cup, and makes as good a cup when the pot is not used to full capacity (something not true of other methods). Filter-cone pots are easily the unmessiest method to use—when the coffee has dripped through, the filter cone is simply removed and thrown away, and the upper half need only be rinsed in hot water. Their greatest disadvantage is that they require filter papers. If desperate, one can fold up a piece of paper toweling to make a filter cone, but this makes a poor substitute for the filter papers designed to be used in the pot. These cost about two to three cents apiece, which adds on the average about a half-cent to the price of each serving

of coffee. Not an overwhelming expense, and one that to many will seem small compared with the convenience of their use. I am familiar with three makes of filter-cone pots (there may well be other designs): Melitta, Chemex, and Tricolette. It is important to use the filter paper designed for the pot (as well as the correct size), because a good fit in the upper half is necessary for proper filtration. Some experimentation with grind may be necessary, since the porosity of the filter papers varies.

The newest, and to judge by the sales, the most popular kind of drip coffee maker is the electric drip coffee maker. To date, over a dozen manufacturers (Braun, Melitta, Norelco, West Bend, Sunbeam, General Electric, and so on) are producing a variety of models. These machines run about thirty to sixty dollars—but the best of them produce excellent coffee in a matter of minutes and keep it at serving temperature, all automatically, a welcome advantage in busy home kitchens and in offices. Cold water is kept in a reservoir in the coffee maker, where it is heated and released in a spray at about 200°F over the coffee grounds, which are held in a basket or filter over a carafe, which in turn sits on a warming element. In short, coffee makers of this design are simply the drip method gone automatic. Their chief disadvantages (outside of initial expense) are bulkiness (they take up some counter space), the need for filter papers (most models require them), and difficulties in cleaning. Mineral scale can build up in hard-water areas in inaccessible parts of the machine, which may call for cleaning with vinegar. While you should follow the manufacturer's instructions, ignore any advice which suggests you can use less than the normal amount of coffee per serving. In addition, most do not make small amounts of coffee satisfactorily. In sum, the beverage produced by these machines is at best the equal to that produced by more conventional drip methods; in order to avoid paying attention to the brewing cycle, one takes on higher initial expenses and the chore of cleaning and maintenance. In spite of these drawbacks, the electric drip share of the coffeepot market seems on the verge of overtaking the percolator, surely a welcome sign. Anyone contemplating purchasing one of these machines should compare various models first, feature by feature.

Other Methods

Some additional coffee makers and methods worth noting

include the plunger pot, cold-water methods, espresso, and older traditional methods, such as camp coffee and Turkish coffee.

The plunger pot, a French invention, consists of a tall cylindrical glass (or plastic) pot into which fine-grind coffee is measured and covered with boiling water. After three to five minutes, a mechanism with a close-fitting metal filter is pushed down to the bottom of the pot, trapping the grounds. The brew can then be poured off. A certain amount of sediment remains in the coffee, but many coffee drinkers like this character in their cup. Unless poured out at once, the brew sits on the grounds; removing the grounds in cleaning the pot is a messy proposition. It makes excellent coffee, however, and does not require the use of filters. Whether it is an advantage over the ordinary drip pot is a moot point. The models I have seen are the French Melior and the American Insta-Brewer.

Cold-water methods involve steeping a pound of ground coffee in a small amount (one quart) of cold water for about half a day to produce a coffee concentrate, which can be kept refrigerated for weeks, To make hot coffee, one adds about an ounce of the concentrate to a cup and fills it up with hot water. Unfortunately, the coffee lacks the flavor oils, acids, and other slightly bitter nuances that are characteristic, in small amounts, of fine coffee, because the cold water fails to extract these. This is an advantage, however, for diet-restricted patients who can tolerate caffeine but are not able to drink normal coffee. The two cold-water coffee makers I am aware of are the Filtron Instant Coffeemaker and the Toddy Coffee Maker.

The simplest method of making coffee is simply to bring water to a boil in a pot or saucepan, remove from heat, dump in an appropriate amount of coarse ground coffee, stir, and return to heat to simmer lightly for, say, three to five minutes, and strain into cups. This is often known as "camp" coffee, and its quality varies with the grind used, timing, and care taken in measuring. One interesting variation of camp coffee is the "sock method," used by both Scandinavians and Brazilians. Simply bring a measured amount of water to a boil in a pan, and then lower a sock filled with a measured amount of coarse ground coffee into it, letting the pan sit off the heat (or at a minimal simmer) until a good-colored brew is achieved. This method produces a good cup, though experimentation with grind, timing, and type of sock is necessary.

Turkish coffee (or Armenian or Greek or Egyptian) is traditionally prepared by boiling, a method long abandoned elsewhere. It calls for twice the normal amount of coffee per serving. Basically, cold water is added to extremely fine-grind dark-roast coffee (fifty seconds in an electric grinder) along with one teaspoon sugar or honey per three-ounce serving, and brought to a foaming boil in an *ibrik* (a tall tapered copper pot with a long handle), then allowed to subside, then brought to a boil twice more and served in tiny cups. Prepared this way, the coffee, good as it can be, is a different kind of beverage altogether from the coffee prepared in the West. A reasonable facsimile can be made using a saucepan.

Espresso is the closest form of coffee to it in taste. Today, prepared by modern machines invented in the late 1940s, it is a unique and attractive coffee beverage. A combination of steam and boiling water is forced through a small amount of finely ground, very dark-roasted coffee. About twice the normal ratio of coffee to water is used, and only one cup at a time is prepared. Since an espresso machine takes about ten seconds to prepare a cup, this is not as slow a method as it might seem. The rapidity of the process makes an attractive, unusual beverage from the generally uninteresting quality coffee typically used. While home-sized espresso machines are available, they are quite expensive.

A reasonably good approximation of true *caffè espresso* can be made at home with a Moka-type pot, which forces hot water through the grounds by steam pressure, somewhat like a vacuum pot. To approximate espresso, you should use very finely ground espresso or Italian-roast coffee, and use twice the usual amount of coffee per serving (four tablespoons per six ounces of water). You can also make double-strength espresso roast coffee in a *machinetta,* an Italian version of the drip pot. The design of these pots varies slightly, but the principle is the same: a lower pot holds the water, a two-part perforated basket that holds the ground coffee is placed on that, and an upper pot with a spout (the serving pot) is placed upside-down on top of the basket. When the water boils (the pot steams and hisses) the entire machine is inverted, and the water quickly drips through the coffee into the serving pot. Use twice the normal proportion of drip or medium-grind coffee (four tablespoons for each six ounces of water). The resulting demitasse coffee is excellent, though not as enticing as that from an espresso machine. The *machinetta* is really the same device as that used for French *café filtre*, and of course,

roasts lighter than espresso can be used with it or the Moka-type pot to produce a less bitter but still strong after-dinner brew.

The Essentials of Good Coffee-making

There are a number of dos and don'ts connected with good coffee-making that are common to all methods, worth summarizing briefly here.

1. Use high-quality coffee, preferably recently roasted and ground just before serving.
2. Always use the correct grind for the method. If your coffee is too bitter and muddy, the grind is too fine; if the brew lacks flavor, the grind is too coarse.
3. Always use freshly drawn cold water.
4. Never guess amounts. Use the correct proportion of coffee and water (two level tablespoons per six ounces cold water for regular-strength coffee), preferably measuring both. If coffee is too strong or weak, change grind and/or blend, not proportion of coffee to water.
5. Make sure the coffee maker is scrupulously clean and thoroughly rinsed. Coffee quickly picks up off-flavors during the brewing process.
6. For best results, always brew at least three-fourths of the coffee maker's capacity. Most large coffee makers do not make one or two cups satisfactorily.
7. Never guess when timing. Use the clock.
8. Remove the grounds from the brew as soon as the brewing cycle is completed to prevent bitterness. Also for that reason, never rewet grounds.
9. Serve coffee immediately after brewing. (With drip methods, stir the brew before serving.) Coffee is at its best when just brewed.
10. If coffee must be kept warm, try to hold it at 180° to 190°F. Brewed coffee stays palatable for twenty minutes, drinkable for one hour maximum. The longer it is held, the less desirable it becomes.
11. Never reheat cooled coffee; it breaks down in flavor. Never allow the brew to boil; its flavor turns bitter.

A Note on Good Coffee at Work

Since coffee does not stay palatable for more than an hour, even if kept warm, taking your breakfast coffee to work in a vacuum bottle is not the answer to getting good coffee on the job. Even if the only coffee available where you work is vending-machine instant, you can have superb coffee as long as you have access to fresh, cold water and an electrical outlet. All you need for boiling the water is one of those small electric pots used to heat a can of soup, a single cup filter-cone holder that sits on top of a coffee mug, a supply of filters, a spoon that can be used to measure coffee, and a mug. Simply bring fresh-ground coffee to work in a small airtight plastic container or jar every few days (or every morning). Measure out two level tablespoonfuls into the filter cone, place on mug, bring six ounces of freshly drawn water to a boil in the pot, unplug pot, and pour on the grounds as per instructions given under drip methods above. Remove holder, discard filter, and you have a decent cup of coffee with no more fuss than having instant would require. The filter holder is easily rinsed right along with your cup.

Serving Coffee

To appreciate properly made fine coffee, you have to tackle it black. If it's fine, this isn't a grim prospect. Sugar, lemon rind, cream, cinnamon sticks, bruised cardamom seeds, and all the other traditional accompaniments and spicy helpers have been developed primarily to make so-so coffee palatable. Bitter coffee is helped by the addition of cream; lemon rind adds acidity to dark-roasted coffees (which is why it is popular in demitasse and espresso). Cream seems to complement coffee better than milk, which has a tendency to make coffee look gray. However, *café au lait*, popular in many countries, consists of equal parts hot coffee and hot milk poured simultaneously into a cup. Neither cream nor milk is traditionally added to demitasse, espresso (except for *cappuccino*), or Turkish coffee, but sugar is often added to every kind of brew. The British are fond of adding

"coffee sugar" to theirs—brown crystals of pure cane sugar. Brazilians add chocolate to their cups, while Swedes add cardamom seeds, the Viennese a dollop of whipped cream, and so on. All this is a matter of taste, although it is true enough that a really exquisite high-grown *arabica* is best appreciated on its own.

Except for espresso, demitasse, and Turkish coffee—all traditionally served in very small cups—coffee should be served in reasonably good-sized (six-ounce), not too delicate cups. Mugs have their place, but fine coffee is not out of place in fine china either.

While it is the custom in many countries to have coffee with breakfast, it is overdoing it to drink coffee through lunch and evening meals. Coffee is not intended to be used to wash down food but is best with desserts or after meals, when it can be savored. As to what type of coffee to serve when, I find clear, clean-flavored growths best in the morning and midday, and the heavy, exotic, and dark-roasted coffees best in the evening. With breakfast and after lunch I prefer Kona, Colombian, Brazilian Santos, East African, and Central American coffees; in the evening I enjoy Ethiopian and Indonesian growths, Mochas, and all dark-roasted coffees. Part of the enjoyment of fine coffee lies in discovering these preferences, trying your own blends (see Chapter Four) out on guests, and seeing which coffees best complement the desserts they accompany.

Coffee Variations

Iced Coffee

Something like 97 percent of all the coffee drunk in the United States is served hot. Iced coffee, unlike iced tea, has never been popular, probably because it is rather strong-flavored to use simply as a thirst-quencher, and lacks the clean astringency of iced tea. Nonetheless, many enjoy it from time to time, particularly with cream and sugar:

1. Make coffee double strength (use four tablespoons of coffee for each six ounces of water).
2. Pour immediately into tall glasses with ice cubes.

Or

1. Make full-strength coffee as usual.

2. Cool for no more than three hours in a glass or earthenware pot.
3. Serve over ice cubes in a tall glass.

Coffee with Liqueurs

There is something about dark-roasted coffee—particularly demitasse and espresso—that lends itself to serving with liqueurs. Either add them to the coffee (a small dollop will do) or serve on the side in a small glass. Some combinations you might enjoy are coffee with:

Anisette
Crème de Cacao
Curaçao
Cointreau
Dark Rum
Grand Marnier
Kahlúa
Kümmel
Strega
Tía María
White Crème de Menthe

PART II

Tea

CHAPTER EIGHT

A Brief History of Tea

Legendary Beginnings

The early history of China, where tea-drinking began several millennia ago, is primarily legendary, and so too is the history of the discovery of tea. Despite the efforts of historians, it will doubtless never be known just how and when it was discovered that steeping the leaves of the tea bush in boiling water results in a beverage that banishes drowsiness or when and how the actual cultivation of tea plants began.

Ancient Chinese texts attribute the discovery to one of China's legendary emperors, Shen Nung, said to have ruled about 2737 B.C. The "Divine Husbandman," as his name is usually translated, supposedly invented the plow, taught the people husbandry, and discovered the curative value of plants. For this reason, the discovery of tea was also ascribed to him, since tea was first drunk as a medicinal beverage. As the story goes, Shen Nung was sipping hot, boiled water in his garden one day when a leaf from a tea bush nearby fell into his cup. The emperor tasted and smelled the infusion, and decided it was a considerable improvement over plain hot water. Thus, tea-drinking began. There are several references to tea in the *Pen ts'ao* (Medical Book) —a work attributed to Shen Nung but actually written in the Han dynasty (A.D. 25–220)—which have often been offered as proof of tea's antiquity. However, the references to tea seem to have been added even later than the actual writing of the text, some 3,400 years after the legendary reign of Shen Nung.*

Besides the difficulty of tracing the actual history of tea in early accounts, another problem in dating the first ref-

*Whatever their historical status, they make amusing reading. Among the tea recipes for health in the book is this "Receipt for a Noise in the Head: Take white ants of the largest sort dry'd, with some Seed of Tea, reduce them to a Powder and blow them up the nostrils. This Remedy has a good effect."

erences to tea accurately concerns the word or character used to represent "tea." Not until the T'ang dynasty (A.D. 618–907) did tea have its own character, one by which it was known generally. Prior to that time, the names of several other shrubs were sometimes used for tea; thus, it is nearly impossible to be certain whether a particular reference means tea, or whether it means sow-thistle or mere grass.

Tea in China

Early History

In spite of the lack of historically accurate information on the beginnings of tea-drinking and cultivation, the extensive references to customs of tea-drinking and planting in later Chinese texts suggest tea had been drunk and cultivated in China for centuries at the least, and so China is quite probably correctly credited with its discovery.

The first historically reliable reference to tea is Chinese. A definition of it is found in the annotated version of an ancient Chinese dictionary, *Erh Ya.* Although the dictionary itself is attributed to the Duke of Chou, famous for his role in consolidating the Chinese empire in the twelfth century B.C., it seems probable that the annotator, a scholar named Kuo P'o, inserted the definition for tea in about A.D. 350. According to his account, tea was primarily a medicinal beverage, prepared by boiling raw green tea leaves in kettles with water, a method employed by aboriginal tribesmen of southwestern China hill districts. Since boiling the water before drinking killed harmful bacteria, the recommendations of tea as a healthful drink responsible for longevity probably had some basis in fact. At the time of Kuo P'o tea was probably a bitter, rather unpleasant drink, although there are accounts of its lovely fragrance. It seems likely, too, that tea leaves were being sold locally in parts of Szechuan at that time and that the Chinese had begun to cultivate the tea plant, rather than simply chopping it down to strip it of leaves as had been done previously.

With time, refinements in the preparation of this beverage were established: a fifth-century dictionary, the *Kuang Ya,* describes a method of infusing tea leaves that had been processed. The leaves were pressed into cakes; the cakes were

roasted, and then pounded into pieces and put in a chinaware pot. Boiling water was poured over them, and, probably to improve the flavor, ginger, onion, and orange were added. The chinaware pot was not the teapot known today, but a tall, vase-shaped earthenware ewer with a slender spout, originally used in serving wine. From there it was poured into teacups with no handles or saucers, although the hands were protected from the hot cup by a wooden cup holder. Tea was also infused directly in each cup, a method some considered preferable to using the pot.

By the end of the fifth century, special teas were being reserved for the emperor, and tea had become an article of trade. Legend has it that by this time Turkish traders bartered for it on the Mongolian border.

Until the end of the sixth century, however, tea continued to be drunk primarily as a remedy for illnesses as diverse as headaches, kidney trouble, poor digestion, and ulcers, and to guard against "the noxious gases of the body and lethargy."

T'ang Dynasty and the Ch'a Ching

Gradually tea propagation spread, and methods of tea manufacture established in the T'ang dynasty (A.D. 618–907) made possible the transport of tea throughout China. Tea became a common beverage, prized for its flavor as well as for its medicinal properties. About 725, tea was of sufficient importance in daily Chinese life to be given its own character, *ch'a,* and by 780 of sufficient economic significance for the first tax to be levied on it. In 780, too, the first work exclusively about tea was published, the *Ch'a Ching* (The Classic of Tea), written by the poet-scholar Lu Yu at the request of a group of tea merchants. The *Ch'a Ching,* which became extremely important in the development of tea's cultural significance in China, codified contemporary tea knowledge, and included a section on references to tea in Chinese texts prior to that time. Lu Yu formulated in the *Ch'a Ching* a code of tea in harmony with the Taoist spirit of the times; each step in the taking and making of tea was imbued with a sense of order and ritual, since attention to every detail would make beauty and harmony possible. Not surprisingly, Lu Yu became the patron saint of tea, and even in the beginning of the twentieth century, small images of him, thought to bring good luck, could be found in Chinese tea-processing establishments.

The ten parts of the three slim volumes of the *Ch'a Ching* include information and elaborate instructions for every aspect of tea growing, harvesting, manufacture, brewing, and drinking. In setting standards for the critical evaluation of tea, however, Lu Yu reminded connoisseurs that "its goodness is a decision for the mouth to make."* Many foreigners as well as the Chinese learned from it much about the nature of the tea plant, its soil requirements, the plucking of tea leaves, quality standards for the appearance of the leaves, and the utensils and method used in manufacturing the tea bricks common in the T'ang dynasty. Essential facts are mixed with rules that now seem amusing, such as the one requiring tea pickers, mostly women and girls, to refrain from eating pungent fish and meat and to bathe before picking in order that their breath and body odors not affect the fragrance of the leaves.

The tea-manufacturing method in common use during the T'ang dynasty was to pound the tea leaves, shape and press them into molds, and then dry them over heat, so that a tea brick was produced. A hole was punched in each, and the finished bricks were strung together, wrapped, and carried in baskets from poles all over the country. In remote areas, tea bricks were even used for money. (Although brick tea later fell from favor among the Chinese, it continued to be produced, especially for the Russian and Tibetan overland trade, and can still be bought today.)

The second volume contains Lu Yu's "Tea Code," and describes in detail the twenty-four articles of tea equipage necessary to the proper preparation of the infusion. Such was the fashion of the day that no family of social prominence could be without all the articles; social status was measured by their quality, so that it was common for households to buy tea articles made by skilled artists and keep them in especially built and designed cabinets. Lu Yu's specifications even included the color and type of teacups considered best to use (Yueh ware with a blue glaze to make the tea look greener) and the symbols that should appear on various larger implements. Only the lord of the house used this equipment; women and servants were not allowed to preside over any tea service.

Lu Yu gave poetic instructions for brewing tea, from finding proper water to boiling the water correctly:

*All quotations are from *The Classic of Tea* by Lu Yu, translated by Francis Ross Carpenter (Boston: Little, Brown and Company, 1974). This quotation, p. 74.

> When the water is boiling, it must look like fishes' eyes and give off but the hint of a sound. When at the edges it chatters like a bubbling spring and looks like pearls innumerable strung together, it has reached the second stage. When it leaps like breakers majestic and resounds like a swelling wave, it is at its peak. Any more and the water will be boiled out and should not be used [p. 107].

Since the quality of the tea infusion depends heavily on the quality of the water and whether it is boiled properly, Lu Yu's instructions probably did a great deal to improve the quality of tea then drunk.

It was common at the time to add salt to tea, although Lu Yu frowned on the addition of ginger, onion, orange, and peppermint previously in use. His instructions called for making tea directly in the teacup, pouring the boiling water on a ground-up chunk of the tea brick and waiting for the fragments to sink to the bottom. As one cup was drunk, boiling water was poured over the same ground leaves to make the second, third, and fourth cups. Although, of course, it is impossible to know what these teas tasted like, they were apparently pale in color and distinguished enough in flavor to charm the connoisseurs of the time.

The remaining sections of the book include quotes from Chinese texts mentioning tea, a list of the districts in China producing the best teas, suggestions for substitutions for some of the utensils (unless the family is an aristocratic one, in which case tea cannot be prepared without the twenty-four required implements), and instructions for tea merchants on how the *Ch'a Ching* should be copied and displayed for the edification of all.

The Sung Dynasty

Differences in the styles of eras had a considerable effect on tea and how it was drunk; during the Sung dynasty (960–1280), a romantic period of lyrical and elegant taste in all things, the hearty brick tea and sturdy teacups of the T'ang fell from favor. A more delicately flavored tea was created by Sung tea connoisseurs who ground tea leaves to a fine powder, poured boiling water over them in a cup, and beat the liquid to a froth with a bamboo whisk. No longer was tea flavored with salt and the other flavorings common previously; instead tea was drunk primarily for its own

aroma and flavor, although flowers such as jasmine, roses, and gardenias were sometimes dried and added to make scented teas. It was an era in which tea epicures sought new and rare varieties of tea, gave them poetic names such as "sparrow's tongues," "falcon's talons," and "gray eyebrows" (p. 25), and evaluated their merits in tea-tasting contests: in the cities, elegant public tea houses were built where drinking tea was a social art. The manufacture of porcelain, begun in the T'ang, produced more translucent, pure, and refined teacups to suit the age. An artistic and talented Sung emperor, Huei Tsung (1101–1125), became a patron of the art of tea and composed a treatise somewhat akin to Lu Yu's on the twenty kinds of tea and the rituals required with the new method of making it. According to Francis Ross Carpenter:

> Tea soon became so popular that Taoists claimed that it was an important ingredient in the elixir of immortality. The waste of fine tea through incompetent manipulation was considered one of the three most deplorable acts in the world (the other two being false education of youth and uninformed admirations of fine paintings) [p. 17].

Tea and this new method of drinking it were not confined to the educated classes in cities; Zen Buddhists included drinking tea in ceremonials before images of Bodhidharma in their temples, and since many in the lower classes at the time were Buddhists, this ensured the spread of drinking tea as a beverage rather than a medicine. Later, many of the rituals and customs of the Sung dynasty would be combined in the Japanese tea ceremony.

During this era, too, the cultivation of tea spread to areas like Anhwei and the Bohea Hills, later to become famous tea districts when tea was introduced to the West, and the export of tea to Mongolia and Tibet became common. With the Mongol conquest of China in 1280, however, court encouragement of tea-drinking and the code of tea ceased; the Mongol emperor apparently did not drink tea, nor did those in the Mongol tribes. Marco Polo, who visited the Mongol court in the late thirteenth century, does not mention tea in his journals. However, social tea-drinking among the populace certainly continued, though the elaborate tea cult of connoisseurs and scholars declined.

Ming Dynasty

It was after the overthrow of the Mongols in the Ming dynasty (1368–1644) that the three forms of tea we know now—black, oolong, and green—became prevalent. In fact, the process for manufacturing green tea was invented during the Ming dynasty. Many different kinds of tea were drunk, and Fukien tea, a sweet, light tea from the Bohea Hills, became the most celebrated tea in China; the Chinese claimed it would even purify the blood. In line with the atmosphere of the times, new methods of making tea were found. Steeping tea in cups or teapots became commonplace. Special cups with covers were used in order to drink the tea without catching leaves in the mouth. Small, individual teapots made into a wide variety of shapes, from egg-shaped to wheel-shaped to flower-shaped, graced the social tea ceremony in both homes and court entertainments. The round teapot shape we know today is based on one of the most favored teapot shapes of the Ming—that of the muskmelon. Tea-drinking was an important part of the social life of the Chinese, especially to polite society.

During the last decades of the Ming dynasty, foreign traders, ambassadors, and missionaries began to visit China and eventually sampled tea. A new era, that of the introduction of tea to the West, began.

Tea in Japan

Origins

Since tea was introduced to Japan by Buddhist priests in conjunction with the importation of Buddhism, it is not surprising that Japanese mythology links the origins of tea to Bodhidharma, or Daruma, as the Buddhist saint is called in Japan. According to the legend, when Daruma awoke with a start after falling asleep during meditation, he tore off his eyelids in anger at his weakness (which is why he is always depicted with a popeyed stare). Where his eyelids fell, tea plants sprang up. With their treasured property of warding off drowsiness, this relationship between tea and Buddhism continued to grow in Japan, culminating in the

evolution of the Japanese tea ceremony in the fifteenth century.

Knowledge of tea was brought to Japan from China in about A.D. 593, during the reign of Prince Shotoku, along with Buddhism, styles of Chinese art, and Chinese civilization in general. During the next century, many Japanese priests pursued their Buddhist studies in China, and some no doubt brought back both tea seeds and tea leaves, in addition to other artifacts of the T'ang era that have had a lasting impact on Japanese art and life. Authoritative historical records show that the Japanese emperor in 729 served powdered tea to Buddhist priests called to read Buddhist scriptures at his palace; the Chinese word for tea, *ch'a,* and the character for it were also imported and in use—the powdered tea served was called *hiki-cha.*

Apparently the first tea plantings were in Buddhist temple gardens; a Buddhist monk, Gyoki (648–749) planted the first tea bushes in the gardens of the forty-nine temples he built near the end of his life. At that time, tea was a rare and costly beverage, drunk only by the aristocracy and important Buddhist priests, and apparently was regarded primarily as a medicinal plant; when Emperor Kammu in 794 planted an enclosed tea garden near his new imperial palace, its administration was carried out by the bureau of medicine.

The early ninth century saw the spread of knowledge of tea and tea cultivation throughout Japan by various Buddhist priests, such as the saint Dengyo Daishi (also known by the name Saicho) and the monk Kobo Daishi, who brought tea seeds and information about cultivation and manufacturing from China and planted temple gardens with success. (Whether they gained this information from Lu Yu's *Ch'a Ching* is not known.) The twentieth-century tea garden in Ikegami is supposedly the site of the first plantings undertaken by Dengyo Daishi. Priests at Buddhist temples drank tea not only to help them maintain long meditation vigils, but also to help them consume less food. The spread of Buddhism to the general populace also spread the habit of drinking tea.

The tea brewed from the leaves of the tea plants in temple gardens must have been quite attractive, because during a visit to a distant temple by the emperor in 815, the tea he was served so impressed and pleased him that he ordered tea cultivated in provinces nearer the capital and imposed a tea tribute for his and the imperial court's use.

Although drinking tea was used as an excuse for conver-

sations about poetry and religion, it was still considered primarily a medicinal drink, albeit a delightful one. It was gaining in popularity in the capital as a purely social drink among the aristocracy when civil wars between Japanese nobles, or shoguns, each trying to gain control over the emperor, began a period of conflict that lasted two hundred years. There were few contacts with China during that time, and the constant battles between warring groups of samurai hired to fight for individual nobles interfered with the cultivation of tea gardens. However, it appears the Japanese still valued the medicinal properties of tea, as it was drunk as a remedy for the plague that swept Japan in 951.

At the close of the civil-war period, Japan revived contact with China, and this time imported the romanticism of the Sung era. As the Japanese had previously imported Buddhism, so now they imported Zen Buddhism, in vogue throughout southern China, and the Zen ritual of drinking tea from a single bowl before an image of Bodhidharma (Daruma) in their temples.

The reintroduction of tea to Japan after the civil wars owes much to the Japanese Buddhist abbot Eisai, who went to China to study the doctrines of Zen, bringing back with him in 1191 tea seeds that he planted in the grounds of various temples (one was in the Uji district, a region now known for the quality of its tea) and a commitment to propagate the doctrines and discipline of Zen.

Eisai also wrote the first Japanese book on tea, modeled somewhat after Lu Yu's *Ch'a Ching*, the *Kitcha-Yojoki* (Book of Tea Sanitation). It expressed his view of the sacred nature of tea and its medicinal benefits; he believed tea was "a divine remedy and a supreme gift of heaven for preserving human life." This view was reinforced for the general populace by the recovery of a great shogun, Minamoto Sanetomo, who, ill from overfeasting, was saved by tea and prayers offered by Eisai. The shogun, of course, began to drink tea regularly, and the tale of his miraculous recovery induced others to do so as well.

The introduction of Sung pottery techniques into Japan further enhanced and made fashionable the drinking of tea, as the skilled potter Toshiro produced tea sets utilizing imported glazes for the aristocracy. And the spread of tea-drinking was ensured when Eisai was invited to the capital, where he instructed samurai in the Zen discipline.

The Tea Ceremony

The Japanese tea ceremony, or *Cha-no-yu* (literally "hot-water tea"), developed in the fifteenth century from the Zen tea ritual, created an entire aesthetic cult of tea-drinking that ultimately influenced all aspects of Japanese culture. The cult, Teaism, is based on the "Zen conception of greatness in the smallest incident of life," on worshiping the beauty to be found even in the most mundane aspects of daily existence. Embodied in it, and in the tea ceremony, is a sense of simplicity, harmony, and austerity of almost a religious nature; indeed, tea became somewhat of a religion in Japan as well as an elevated art form that went way beyond the uses and appreciation of tea in the romantic Sung dynasty in China. In Japan, tea and the tea ceremony became symbols for refinement as well as a discipline that might lead to enlightenment.

The earliest set of rules for the tea ceremony was created by a priest, Shuko, who introduced tea-drinking to the ruling shogun Yoshimasa in the last part of the fifteenth century. The purity and simplicity of the ceremony appealed to the ruler, undoubtedly as a contrast to the decadent militaristic society of the times, with its atmosphere of political intrigue and treachery. The shogun built a special tea room, held frequent tea parties, and made Shuko the first priest of the tea ceremony. Thus began the tradition of the *cha-iins,* or tea masters, who presided over the tea service; so important was this ceremonial function that each of the powerful shoguns who ruled Japan felt it necessary to install one.

The rules of the tea ceremony as it is known today were codified in the latter part of the sixteenth century by a famous tea master, Sen-no Rikyu, who made the ceremony less elaborate and more aesthetic than it had been previously, and created the first independent tea house. The proportions and arrangement he established for it are those generally followed today: a nine-foot-square empty tea room designed to recall the simplicity and purity of a Zen monastery, a small room for washing and arranging the tea utensils, a portico in which the guests wait, and a path connecting the tea room and portico, intended to help the guests break connection with the outside world before they enter for the tea ceremony.

Since "the ceremony was an improvised drama whose plot

was woven about the tea, the flowers, and the paintings," as Kakuzo Okakura puts it, the guests and host had their roles to play. Traditionally, three to six guests are invited; after gathering in the portico, they follow the host down the path to the tea-room entrance—a low door designed to inculcate humility since all, no matter how noble or common, must bend to go through it. After washing and removing their sandals, the guests enter the tea room. While the host gathers materials for the fire, the guests examine the room decorations, usually a simple but beautifully chosen flower arrangement and a painting. As the host makes the fire and sprinkles incense on it, the guests watch; the guests return to the portico while the host assembles the tea utensils and the kettle is put on the fire to boil. The guests reenter when the host strikes a gong. He wipes all the tea utensils, then takes two and a half teascoops of powdered green tea from a tea jar, and puts them in a teabowl. Using a ladle, he pours hot water on the tea and stirs the tea briskly with the bamboo whisk until it froths. The teabowl is handed to the main guest, who sips it while drawing in breath, making a loud sucking noise, and asks politely about the tea's origin, then passes it to the next guest. The host drinks last and offers apologies for the poor quality of the tea, utensils, entertainment, and so on. After the guests admire the utensils, they bow and thank the host, leave, and the ceremony is ended.

Throughout the centuries, variations on the ceremony developed for each season and time of day; eventually a separate cult grew out of the flower arrangements so carefully created and displayed in the tea room. (While no longer as common as it once was, the practice of the five-hundred-year-old ceremony is by no means dead, nor is it confined to Japan.)

The Japanese were not always as subdued about tea as they were in the tea ceremony. In 1623 began an extravagant annual public tea ritual, the pageant of the "Tea Journey." Three huge tea jars were carried from the shogun's palace in Tokyo (then called Yeddo) to Uji, three hundred miles away, to bring back the season's new tea. A tea master and numerous attendants accompanied the jars first to Uji, then with the new tea to Kyoto, and finally to Tokyo. Along the way the group was treated royally and everyone was required to bow to the tea jars as the procession passed through their district. Eventually the expense of this imposing ritual proved too great, and in 1710, it was ended.

Tea-drinking not only was the basis of an aesthetic and meditative ceremony and the excuse for ostentatious pageantry, but also became a game of connoisseurship. The "Tea Drama," a game of tea-tasting, became fashionable as early as 1250 and persisted to the twentieth century, in spite of a shogun's attempt to forbid it in the fourteenth century. Tea connoisseurs would gather to taste teas "blind," trying to distinguish and identify as many as one hundred teas from different gardens.

Tea as art, religion, pageant, game: Japan developed the habit of tea-drinking into all of these long before the West had even sampled it. Centuries of tea-drinking and its attendant rituals have marked every aspect of Japanese life, from architecture to pottery to flower-arranging. According to Ukers, "The Japanese speak of a certain type of individual as having 'no tea in him,' when he is incapable of understanding the finer things of life."

Introduction of Tea to the West

Tea first came to the West by two travel routes: overland to Russia across Mongolia and the Siberian steppes, and by sea from Japan to Holland. But the first information Europeans had of tea came from the Arabs who controlled the land routes from Europe to the East, used before ships capable of sailing long distances had been built. The European view of tea as a medicine was certainly implanted in their minds from the very beginning. In 1559, a Venetian author gave this account of tea, which he had heard from a Persian merchant describing Chinese tea-drinking customs:

> They take of that herb, whether dry or fresh, and boil it well in water. One or two cups of this decoction taken on an empty stomach removes fever, headache, stomach ache, pain in the side or in the joints, and it should be taken as hot as you can bear it [quoted in Shelleck, p. 26].

In 1589, another Venetian author went so far as to attribute the long lives of Orientals to their habit of drinking tea.

But these were only hearsay accounts; the first Europeans to taste actual tea appear to have been missionaries. In

spite of the fact that Portuguese ships first reached China in 1516, the traders had little contact with the Chinese and were unacquainted with their customs. Although the Chinese wanted to trade, they were suspicious of Western intentions, fearing the traders wanted only to invade and conquer China, and therefore restricted the Portuguese to Macao, where a settlement, completely separate from the mainland, was built. Meanwhile, Portuguese priests traveling throughout China to bring Roman Catholicism to the populace partook of the tea-drinking custom; they wrote about and brought news to Europe of the great medicinal properties of tea and commented favorably on its taste. In fact, as early believers in temperance, they felt this nonalcoholic drink had much to offer Europeans, who might be persuaded to imbibe it rather than wine.

In spite of the Portuguese ships reaching China first and Portuguese missionaries writing favorably of tea, it was a Dutch writer, Jan Hugo van Linschooten, who inspired the Dutch to undertake voyages to the East and to import tea to Europe. By 1600, the Dutch had ten thousand ships at sea, and soon after formed the Dutch East India Company, one of the first of the European East India companies, all of which were empowered to act as governments—to make war and raise armies, regulate trade, and administer conquered nations. After conquering Java, the Dutch attempted to trade directly with the Chinese, only to meet with rebuffs. Part of the Chinese reluctance is attributed to the fact that many Dutchmen had red hair and a Chinese myth associated men with red hair with devils; in any case, the Dutch were known as "red devils" to the Chinese! Lacking direct trade contacts with the Chinese, the Dutch established trading settlements in Japan, helping the Japanese expel the aggressive Portuguese with cannons in order to win this concession. Thus it seems likely, though not certain, that it was Japanese green tea, not Chinese, that was brought to Holland about 1610. Introduced by the Dutch East India Company as an exotic medicinal beverage, it was so costly that only the aristocracy could afford both it and the tiny china cups and saucers, teapots, and tea jars that were thought the necessary accouterments for storing and serving it. Knowledge of how to serve it came from reports of how the Japanese and Chinese served it; the drink was so exotic and mysterious that it was felt necessary to follow the established customs precisely. Although how expensive tea was when it was first

imported to Holland is not known for certain, it is known that by 1666 the price had been lowered substantially to a mere eighty to one hundred dollars per pound! (A far cry from the five to fifteen dollars per pound the finest teas cost today.)

In Holland, tea became the rage; by 1635, it was the drink of the Dutch court; by 1637 it was being served by wealthier merchants' wives; by 1680, well-to-do housewives had special tea rooms added to their houses where they gave tea parties. During the latter half of the seventeenth century, the tea infatuation caused both medical controversy and social consternation. Women began giving elaborate tea parties every afternoon at which each guest drank ten to twenty cups of tea, ate cakes, talked scandal, and finished off the party by drinking brandy and smoking pipes. (Women in lower classes formed and joined tea clubs that met at beer halls.) Husbands complained the family was being destroyed because their wives gadded about, going to tea parties instead of supervising the servants. Reformers spoke and wrote of banning it to save the Dutch family.

Drinking twenty cups of tea in an afternoon might seem an enormous quantity of tea, but the cups imported from China were hardly big enough to hold two swallows. Tea was not yet drunk with milk, but sugar was sometimes added. It was drunk from the saucer—not from the cup—and slurped loudly as a compliment to one's hostess. Surprisingly, saffron was added to the water before the tea was brewed; the period is known as that of saffron tea.

Most aspects of life in Europe were changed by the popularity of drinking tea, and the growth of the pottery industry was no exception. Delftware, with its lovely blue and white colors, was an attempt to imitate the expensive porcelain Ming teacups imported from China. (Not until 1710 did the Europeans discover the process of making porcelain.)

In the health-conscious seventeenth century, tea was thought of as a medicine, albeit a fashionable one, and was first sold in apothecary shops. Today, it is difficult to imagine why tea caused such a medical controversy throughout Europe; some doctors claimed it could cure almost any illness, others claimed it would cause death. Although tea was not introduced to Germany until 1650, the tea-as-medicine controversy was started primarily by a German physician who published a medical treatise in 1635 warning against and condemning tea consumption: "It hastens the

death of those that drink it, especially if they have passed the age of forty years" (quoted in Ukers, p. 30). As the importers for the Continent, the Dutch had a financial stake in praising tea's medicinal properties. A famous Dutch doctor wrote in 1661:

> Nothing is comparable to this plant. Those who use it are for that reason, alone, exempt from all maladies and reach an extreme old age. Not only does it procure great vigor for their bodies, but it preserves them from gravel and gallstones, headaches, colds, ophthalmia, catarrh, asthma, sluggishness of the stomach and intestinal troubles [quoted in Ukers, p. 31].

In Germany, physicians and laymen alike took sides. One Jesuit propounded the theory that tea caused the "dried-up appearance" of the Chinese; another prescribed it for the maintenance of health; others thought it should be banned by public decree.

The German condemnation of tea as a medicine preceded its appearance in Paris, where the "poison or panacea" arguments reached their heights. One of the most famous French doctors, the conservative Dr. Guy Patin, declared himself heartily opposed to tea and records in his correspondence the medical response of condemnation and laughter to a paper given by a fellow doctor praising tea as a panacea: "Does Tea Increase Mentality?" Although most of the French doctors condemned and denounced tea both as a medicine and stimulant, aristocrats and the wealthy drank it anyway—no doubt fashion and hope for a more pleasant remedy than bloodletting prevailed over the denouncements. Among those who drank it was Cardinal Mazarin, the prime minister of France, who hoped it would cure his gout; one courageous doctor proceeded with experiments to establish the healthful effect of tea on gout. The medical faculty of the Collège de France reconsidered, pondered the effects of smoking tea leaves, and eventually a majority changed their minds about the adverse effects of the beverage. In spite of this, a small number of doctors who remained opposed to tea-drinking propounded their preference for making infusions from herbs such as sage. While all experiments to establish the medical benefits of herb teas failed, they began a history of the *infusion* in France, and herbs hitherto used as medicines began to be prepared as teas.

Even the royal physician involved himself in the disagreements, and it was linked to evangelistic movements. It was the drink that anyone with any pretense to fashion had to try. The literary circles of the day certainly drank it by the 1680s, and in fact the first reference to drinking tea with milk is found in one of Madame de Sévigné's letters. Her friend, Madame de La Sablière, the wife of a poet, put tea in her milk to warm it up. Racine, the famous dramatist, drank tea every morning. Eventually, of course, the medical controversy died down as drinking tea became more prevalent and few people seemed to die or recover as a result of imbibing it.

Unlike the introduction of tea to western Europe, tea was first brought into Russia by an overland route. It was not immediately a popular drink; in fact, the first men to bring reports of tea to Russia in 1557, two cossacks, brought no samples. And although a Chinese embassy to Russia presented the czar with a sample of tea in 1618, a gift of tea for the czar was rejected in 1638 by the Russian ambassador to the imperial court as "something for which the Czar would have no use."

While the medicinal and social benefits of tea traveled throughout the countries of Europe during the seventeenth century, it was not until the end of that century and the signing of a treaty between Russia and China that caravan trade across Mongolia and Siberia began, and not until 1735, when the empress established it, that it developed into a regulated trade. The journey, with three hundred camels in the caravan, each carrying six hundred pounds of tea, covered eleven thousand miles from Peking to Moscow, across the vast Gobi Desert and barren steppes of Siberia. It took sixteen months, and the great expense of undertaking such a long and arduous journey meant that tea remained an expensive item drunk only by the rich and the aristocracy. Obviously such a trek meant that the Russians would not import Chinese pottery as did the Europeans, and they developed their own tea-drinking customs, which persist to this day. A water-heating urn, called a samovar, held enough hot water for about forty cups of tea and a teapot filled with strong tea, rather like a tea concentrate, sat on top. A small amount of the concentrate was poured into glass cups in silver holders and hot water was added to fill up each. Slices of lemon were floated on top, and for those who desired it, a lump of sugar was held in the teeth while the

tea drinker sipped his tea through it, a difficult procedure for one not accustomed to it.

Tea in England

Today the habit of tea-drinking is linked with England in most people's minds, and it seems strange that the first mention of tea in English was in an English translation of a Dutch travel book and that the first tea seen in England was brought by the Dutch. If Linschooten's travel descriptions did not impel the English to sail to the Orient immediately for tea, it did inspire them with visions of wealth to be gained from Far Eastern trade of other items. As early as 1600 the English East India Company was chartered by Queen Elizabeth I, who gave it the vast privileges of a country—power to acquire territory and administrate it, make war and command troops, inflict punishment, coin money, and so on—so that it was later to form the basis of the British Empire. But up to the middle of the seventeenth century, the Dutch controlled the tea trade; although there are records of agents for the English East India Company drinking tea as early as 1615, apparently they never thought of importing tea leaves.

Tea was first brought to England from Holland by English aristocrats who had tried the beverage there, and a small amount was brought in on Dutch ships. After the Navigation Acts of 1651 forbade the importation of goods in other than English ships, tea was loaded on English ships in The Hague and brought to England by them.

The first public sale of tea was in 1657 at Garway's Coffee House in London; although the importation of coffee preceded tea by a few years, tea became an important drink, along with chocolate, at all the coffee houses (see Chapter Two for a detailed discussion of these). Known primarily as a health drink, tea soon appeared at other coffee houses and became popular. Garway's broadside advertising the new drink claimed vast curative powers for tea, following the tradition of the Continent:

> The Drink is declared to be most wholesome, preserving perfect health untill extreme Old Age. . . .
> It maketh the body active and lusty.

It helpeth the Headache, giddiness and heavyness thereof.

It removeth the obstructions of the Spleen.

It is very good against the Stone and Gravel, cleaning the Kidneys and Uriters, being drank with Virgins Honey instead of Sugar.

It taketh away the difficulty of breathing, opening Obstructions.

It is good against Lipitude Distillations and cleareth the Sight.

It removeth Lassitude and cleanseth and purifyeth adult Humors and hot Liver.

It is good against Crudities, strengthening the weakness of the Ventricle or Stomack, causing good Appetite and Digestion, and particularly for Men of a corpulent Body, and such as are great eaters of Flesh.

It vanquisheth heavy dreams, easeth the Brain, and strengtheneth the Memory.

It overcometh superfluous Sleep, and prevents Sleepiness in general, a draught of the Infusion being taken, so that without trouble whole nights may be spent in study without hurt to the Body, in that it moderately heateth and bindeth the mouth of the Stomack.

It prevents and cures agues, Surfets, and Feavers, by infusing a fit quantity of the Leaf, thereby provoking a most gentle Vomit and breathing of the Pores, and hath been given with wonderful success.

It (being prepared with Milk and Water) strengtheneth the inward parts, and prevents Consumptions, and powerfully assuageth the pains of the Bowels, or griping of the Guts and Looseness.

It is good for Colds, Dropsies, and Scurveys, if properly infused, purging the Blood by sweat and Urine, and expelleth infection.

It drives away all pains in the Collick proceeding from Wind, and purgeth safely the Gall.

And that the Vertues and excellencies of this Leaf and Drink are many and great is evident and manifest by the high esteem and use of it (especially of late years) among the Physitians and knowing men in France, Italy, Holland and other parts of Christendom [quoted from Ukers, p. 39].

The advertising campaign for tea as a cure-all had its effect; tea consumption continued to rise in spite of the

coffee houses' method of brewing it. A large amount of tea was infused at one time and the resulting mixture kept in kegs in the same manner as ale. Individual portions would be drawn off and warmed with water before being served. Certainly considerable sweetening must have been necessary to improve the flavor of the strong, bitter drink this must have been.

The drinking of tea was not confined solely to the coffee houses, which also sold loose leaves; the medical benefits encouraged the well-to-do to drink tea at home as well, in spite of stiff prices of thirty to fifty dollars per pound. Samuel Pepys, the indefatigable diarist, tried it in 1660, recording: "I did send for a cup of tea (a China drink) of which I have never drunk before." Tea-drinking as a male prerogative faded when Charles II married Catherine of Braganza, a Portuguese princess devoted to tea-drinking, in 1662. She lost no time in introducing tea as the fashionable drink of the Court, and ladies of the time began to serve tea at home, copying the serving methods in vogue on the Continent. Apothecary shops began to carry the new health drink; Pepys records in his diary in 1667: "Home and found my wife making of tea; a drink which Mr. Pelling, the 'poticary, tells her is good for her cold and defluxions."

The popularity of tea did not fail to arouse the pecuniary interest of the English East India Company. Judiciously, they brought from the Orient a gift of tea for the king and queen in 1664, and by 1669 had convinced the government to ban Dutch imports of tea, giving the English East India Company a monopoly on tea-importation.

By Queen Anne's reign, 1702–14, there were nearly five hundred coffee houses in London, and some were beginning to specialize in serving tea. Tom's Coffee House, established by Thomas Twining in 1706, was one of the first. Twining was also the first to recognize the commercial possibilities latent in the increasing numbers of women drinking tea; Tom's Coffee House became, in 1717, the first tea shop, The Golden Lyon, and, unlike the all-male coffee houses, it was open to both men and women. Fashionable women frequented it, paying a shilling for a cup of tea, at that time still served in the tiny China teacups that held barely more than a tablespoonful.

The vogue of gossiping while drinking tea provoked many works satirizing tea-drinking; Henry Fielding's comedy, *Love in Seven Masques,* asserted that "love and scandal are the best sweeteners of tea," a sentiment echoed by Pope,

Congreve, Addison, and other writers of the day. Yet the tea-drinking habit had not been established completely; when aristocratic ladies at the time began substituting it for ale at breakfast, they caused a considerable scandal.

By 1715, however, with the importation of the cheaper green tea (prior to this time, the tea imported was black tea, known as Bohea tea), tea-drinking became commonplace.

Meanwhile, tea had been introduced into Scotland by the Duchess of York about 1680; she brought it and the tea manners of the Dutch, including the habit of drinking tea from the saucer, back to Edinburgh after living in exile. And although Scots of all classes were drinking tea by 1724, it was in Scotland that denunciations of tea were the strongest, continuing the Continental tradition of the tea controversy.

In England and Scotland, however, the argument was not solely over tea's curative or medically detrimental properties; it was also a socioeconomic and moral argument. During the eighteenth century, arguments ranged from those of James Lacy, who wrote that "incessant tea-drinking results in a prodigious Depression of the spirits," to those of Jonas Hanway, who wrote that tea was "pernicious to health, obstructing industry, and impoverishing the nation." In order to prove his points, Lacy even experimented on dogs, injecting them with concentrated tea, and retained his belief in the evils of tea despite the lack of experimental evidence to bear them out. Hanway went so far as to calculate and publish the amount of lost labor time and therefore extra expense to the nation resulting from the time servants and workers spent drinking tea. An influential political economist of the period, Arthur Young, concurred that tea-drinking was an economic evil, and was convinced the effects of it on the national economy would be a disaster. Besides, he felt, it was too expensive an item for the lower classes to waste their money on, a sentiment echoed by *The Female Spectator*, which dubbed tea-drinking the "bane of housewifery," and by John Wesley, who exhorted his followers to "avoid the enfeebling effects" of tea-drinking that kept them from working as hard as they might and to donate the money saved to charity. Although a Scottish physician, Dr. Thomas Short, took a more balanced view of tea, advocating its benefits for "inflammatory Thicknesses of the Blood," "several Disorders of the Eyes," and preventing "Drowsiness and Dulness, Damps and Clouds

on the Brain," and warning of its uses by those with weak stomachs, an entire movement to ban the "tea menace" swept through the towns and counties of Scotland. It was thought that tea would make Scotsmen effeminate and weak, and many towns passed resolutions condemning the use of tea as "improper diet" except for those who could "afford to be weak, indolent, and useless." (In present times, most medical evidence indicates that tea is among the most innocuous of beverages.) In answer to all these denunciations of tea, Samuel Johnson, a great lover of the beverage, proclaimed in print that he was "a hardened and shameless tea drinker," and ridiculed the claims of those who denounced it. The controversy continued with claims that tea even corrupted the morals; the evidence cited for this were the attractive female servants hired as "tea-blenders" by noblemen, who supposedly served other functions for their masters. Emma Hamilton, mistress of Lord Nelson, claimed to have been a "tea-blender."

At least some of the tea drunk in the eighteenth century probably did cause adverse physical effects, because one of the ways of lowering its cost was to add other, cheaper substances to it. Sawdust and gunpowder were used to stretch tea, and licorice leaves among others were often dyed and sold as tea. Used tea leaves were even dried and resold. Consequently, a series of regulations forbidding the adulteration of tea were passed throughout the century, with higher and higher penalties advocated as the practice persisted. Since green tea was primarily the target of this practice, public confidence in it was eventually shaken.

Another source of poor-quality tea was the smuggling trade, prevalent in that century along the coasts of Cornwall, Kent, and Dorset, where caves and church crypts held tons of tea, connected to thoroughfares by tunnels. By 1780 it was estimated that half the tea sold in England had been smuggled into the country, largely because the duty on tea was so high. Selling tea inexpensively depended on smuggling it in, so as to avoid the taxes. Finally, with the passage of a bill reducing the tea duty in 1784, smuggling, as well as tea adulteration, abated. Public tea-drinking continued to grow, and in 1785 eleven million pounds of tea were brought into England.

In spite of tea adulteration, high prices, and medical, economic, and moral controversy, tea was the drink in vogue during the eighteenth century, inspiring the building of the London tea gardens. These areas grew out of the pleasure

gardens of the previous centuries, providing flowered walks, bowling greens, illuminated music pavilions, and dancing "for the relaxation and amusement of the best people." Both coffee and chocolate as well as tea were served at these tea gardens, but tea soon took precedence. Catering to both men and women, the gardens attracted the literary and aristocratic sets as well as ordinary people; opening fetes were always attended by the Prince of Wales, and Henry Fielding, Samuel Johnson, Horace Walpole, and Handel frequented them during the middle of the century. For only one shilling, they provided substantial entertainment, including fireworks and "the best music in England," and of course, advanced the habit of drinking tea.

In spite of British problems with tea and revolution in America at the end of the eighteenth century, and the Opium Wars in the nineteenth century (fought by the Chinese to end Britain's illegal exchange of Indian opium for Chinese tea), by the nineteenth century tea was a British beverage—a custom around which more customs could be created. One of these was the habit of afternoon tea, an invention of Anna, wife of the seventh Duke of Bedford. Custom at the time dictated only two planned meals a day: a huge breakfast in the morning and a large dinner at eight in the evening. During the middle of the day the servants were off duty, and consequently lunch was a simple snack affair. To ease the "sinking feeling" the duchess felt in the afternoon, she began ordering tea and cakes when the servants came back on duty at five o'clock, thus beginning a fashionable habit that persists to this day.

Since tea had been used for everything else, it was sure at some time to become an instrument for the church. In the mid-nineteenth century, temperance was the big issue, and although previous centuries had looked on the replacement of ale with tea as a scandal, this century looked on it as a blessing. Temperance societies all over Britain sponsored tea meetings to counteract the influence of drink. Before long the Church of England saw the potential for raising money in the tea meetings and sponsored their own temperance tea meetings, beginning an era of "chapel tea drinkers." In this atmosphere of Victorian England the British Empire was established, mostly built in the East through the planting and cultivation of tea in India and Ceylon.

Tea in America

Although the United States is now primarily a coffee-drinking nation, tea was the favored drink of American colonists until the tax on it became a focus for the Revolutionary War. That it captured the taste buds (or health consciousness) of Americans seems incredible, considering the odd ways it was prepared and served when it was introduced into some communities in the seventeenth century. In Salem, for example, tea leaves were boiled for some time to yield an extremely bitter drink that was drunk without milk or sugar, and then the tea leaves were eaten with butter as a vegetable! In other communities the tea liquid was thrown out altogether and just the boiled leaves were eaten.

Residents of New Amsterdam, however, had the benefit of being introduced to the drink by the Dutch, who sent several kinds of tea to America, along with Dutch tea customs, about 1650. The methods of using saffron water with tea, flavoring the infusion with peach leaves, and giving tea parties for ladies featuring tiny teacups imported from China reflected the Dutch influence prevalent at the time. The Massachusetts colony, influenced by the English, was drinking black tea as early as 1670, and in 1690 the first tea was sold there. Perhaps due to the cost of the China tea sets, ladies carried their own teacups, saucers, and teaspoons with them when they attended a tea party.

When the British took over New Amsterdam in 1664 and renamed it New York, tea customs there took on a British flavor. Although during the first part of the eighteenth century tea was still a very expensive item, it was not long before tea gardens imitating those of London flourished on the outskirts of New York, featuring fireworks, concerts, and coffee and tea. One of the gardens, Tea Water Pump Garden, became a fashionable resort, famous for the water from its spring. The poor quality of water in New York City and the excellent quality of the water from several springs located on the city's outskirts led to a thriving tea-water trade; pumps over the springs were constructed and peddlers hawked this spring water throughout the city as tea water for those who could afford the luxury. "Come and get

your tea water" was a familiar cry in the streets of mid-eighteenth-century New York.

By the time of the 1765 Stamp Act, passed by the English Parliament to raise money to pay for the recently ended Seven Years' War, tea was the most popular beverage in all the colonies of America. The Stamp Act, taxing tea and other items imported into the colonies, was only the first in a series of taxation measures that were to result in the Revolutionary War. Although the Stamp Act was repealed the following year, after protests on the part of the colonists and a number of Englishmen, the English government asserted the right of the English Parliament to tax the colonies without their representation, and passed the Townshend Acts in 1767. The colonists boycotted English goods rather than pay the taxes on tea, oil, lead, glass, and paint the act imposed. This boycott had an adverse effect on the English merchants concerned, and at their behest, this act was repealed too, except for the threepence-per-pound tax on tea; smuggling Dutch teas into the colonies was the colonists' response.

Naturally the English East India Company did not want to lose its former tea revenues to the Dutch; it persuaded Parliament to pass the Tea Act of 1773, which allowed direct importation of tea to America, enabling the cost of English middlemen and American importers to be bypassed. The act also provided that English duties on tea reshipped to the colonies would be reimbursed. What this meant was that even with the remaining threepence-per-pound duty to be collected from the colonists, English East India Company tea would be cheaper than the tea smuggled in by the Dutch.

But the colonists were not prepared to pay any tax at all to England, regardless of the low price of tea. They began to organize protests against the English tea taxes. Petitions were sent to Parliament, resolutions condemning the tax passed by communities, and demonstrations of protest held. Groups of women in Boston, Hartford, and other New England towns resolved to drink "Liberty tea"—stalks of the loosestrife plant—and other tea substitutes such as raspberry leaves, chamomile, and sage. In some communities it was impossible to buy tea without a medical reason. The Sons of Liberty, a secret patriotic organization active in most colonial cities, declared that since the tax was to be paid on the landing of the tea, no tea should be allowed to land. Along with other patriotic groups and merchants,

they embarked on a publicity campaign to prevent the English East India Company's American agents from unloading any tea that arrived and paying the duty on it. Resolutions were adopted in Philadelphia, New York, and Boston declaring that those who attempted to land tea would be enemies of the country, and in Boston, the Sons of Liberty, among whom were John Hancock, Samuel Adams, and Paul Revere, pledged to oppose any attempt with their "lives and fortunes" if necessary. A New York paper, *The Alarm*, warned on October 26, 1773:

> If you touch one grain of the accursed tea you are undone. America is threatened with worse than Egyptian slavery. . . . The language of the Revenue Act is, that you have no property you can call your own; that you are the vassels, the live stock, of Great Britain.

The consignees, or agents, of the English East India Company in Boston refused to promise not to accept, land, and unload any tea that arrived, and when they learned three ships with tea had sailed for Boston, they appealed to the governor of Massachusetts colony for protection of it and themselves when it arrived. But although the governor was willing, the town council of Boston and the council of Massachusetts advised the consignees to send the tea and ships back to London without unloading the tea, as defending the property of the English East India Company, they felt, was not their province.

When the ships sailed into the harbor, their captains were ordered by a town committee to unload all cargo but tea, and a watch was set up to make sure no tea was landed. The shipowners were willing to return to London with the tea still aboard, but according to the law, the ships couldn't leave the harbor until all their cargo was unloaded without a customs pass from the governor. He refused it, thinking the customs officials, backed by two naval ships, would seize the cargo at the end of twenty days, as was the law if the duty had not been paid.

But on the night of December 16, 1773, just before the twenty days were up, men dressed as Indians boarded all three ships and dumped the tea overboard, an event now known as the Boston Tea Party. While the British Parliament denounced the action and ordered the port of Boston closed, the other American colonies celebrated the event enthusiastically and resolved to follow with their own "tea

parties" when ships carrying tea arrived in their harbors. Only a week later, at the Greenwich, New Jersey, Tea Party chests of tea were burned in the Market Square by men disguised as Indians. In Charleston, South Carolina, the first few tea shipments were seized and allowed to rot in vaults, but when a great crowd threatened a group of seven ships arriving in 1774, the owners and consignees threw the tea overboard themselves, fearing the crowd might burn the ships. "Tea parties" followed in Philadelphia, New York, and Annapolis, and in Edenton, North Carolina, an actual tea party attended by fifty-one women resulted in a written and signed declaration of the ladies' intentions to boycott British goods and tea, which they sent to a London paper for publication. British attempts to repress this spirit of protest eventually resulted in the Revolutionary War.

During and immediately after the American War of Independence, no American patriot drank tea, but when independence was won, two facts eventually led to a direct tea trade with China. First, now that drinking tea was not a form of selling out to the British, Americans acknowledged that they had acquired a taste for tea; and second, other than tea, there was no Chinese cargo to be had in sufficient quantities to fill up each ship. At the end of the eighteenth century and the beginning of the nineteenth, a tea trade with China developed that was peculiarly American; ships from Atlantic ports sailed around Cape Horn to the Pacific Northwest, where they loaded furs, and then transported the furs across the Pacific to Canton and Foochow (Minhow), where they were exchanged for tea, silks, and spices. Great fortunes were made in tea during this century; among those who profited greatly were John Jacob Astor, Stephen Girard, and Thomas Perkins, all of whom recognized the vast profits to be made in trading furs for tea.

The Clipper Ship

As the American tea trade grew in importance, merchants clamored for the new teas of each season to reach them more quickly. One of the most romantic eras in American maritime history resulted when the clipper ships were built to answer the demand for speed. The inspiration for them was the *Ann McKim*, a three-masted schooner based on the design of the fast privateers (called Baltimore clippers)

built for the War of 1812. The *Ann McKim,* built by a merchant for the China trade, proved to be fast, but had a small cargo capacity. While this design seemed unprofitable to other merchants, J. W. Griffiths, a ship designer, improved upon her design, conceiving the first true clipper ship, the *Rainbow*. Arguments about his design prompted bets on whether the *Rainbow* would float or sink, but by her second China voyage the superiority of the clipper design was proved. The *Rainbow* was so fast that she brought back the news of her arrival in Canton herself; she made the trip to Canton in ninety-two days, and back to New York in eighty-eight.

By 1849, the monopoly of the English East India Company to bring tea into England had ended, and the English Navigation Acts, allowing only English ships to land goods in England, had been repealed. American merchants built a fleet of clipper ships to capture the English tea trade. Donald McKay, known as the designer that made the clipper ship famous, was responsible for many of those ships. The English were forced to build their own version of the clipper ship in order to compete, and the race was on. The annual race to London from China with the season's new teas was an important event; the winning ship received a ten-shilling-per-ton premium for her tea, since the first tea sold for sixpence a pound more than that of the slower ships. Frequently, the crew would receive a five-hundred-pound prize from a pleased owner, who made a tidy fortune himself. Faster and faster clipper ships were designed and built, and the day a ship was launched in Aberdeen (where most of the English ships were built) or in New England was declared a holiday. Schools were closed, brass bands played, and townspeople gathered at the docks to wish the ship Godspeed.

American clippers sponsored their own San Francisco to Canton races, and as more American clippers transported men and supplies to California during the Gold Rush years, English shipping companies built and launched rival ships for the London–Foochow route. During the tea season, discussion of the race was the all-consuming topic, and when the telegraph was invented, men posted at points on the route would telegraph the hour at which the tea clippers swept past them. Probably the most exciting of these races was the Great Tea Race of 1866, talked about for a generation. The run was sixteen thousand miles from the Pagoda anchorage at Foochow to the London docks, and the winner traditionally was the first ship to throw the sample boxes

of tea on the dock. The *Ariel* and the *Taeping* left Foochow on the same day in 1866, and both were racing up the Channel ninety-nine days later. But although the *Ariel* arrived at Dungeness and put up signals for a pilot boat to bring her into the dock an hour before the *Taeping*, the *Taeping* had a faster pilot and drew less water, thus docking a scant twenty minutes before the *Ariel*. (The race was considered a tie.) Sadly enough, the excitement of these races came to an end with the building of the Suez Canal in 1869; the golden age of the clipper had lasted only twenty-five years.

Tea in India

Although some early legends linking the discovery of tea with Buddhism cite India as the source of the first tea drinking and cultivation, the West did not discover that the tea plant is indigenous to northeast India until the nineteenth century. The peoples of that area had probably already been drinking tea for hundreds of years at that time; British reports indicated that tea was eaten in some areas as a vegetable, a sort of pickled tea, while in others an infusion of the leaf, mixed with churned butter and salt, was drunk, as was the prevailing custom in Tibet. Other hill tribes, whose chiefs subsequently turned out to own natural tea plantations, cut the leaves into small pieces, boiled them, and squeezed them into balls to be dried in the sun. But in spite of the late introduction of its tea to the West, India and Sri Lanka (formerly Ceylon) now dominate the world tea market.

It was the English East India Company that eventually established the first tea plantations in India, but confusion over the differences between the indigenous Indian tea plant and the Chinese tea plant and the assumption that only the Chinese tea plant was worthy of cultivation were responsible for the slow growth and experimentation of the Indian tea industry.

As early as 1774, employees of the East India Company were discussing the possibilities of growing tea in areas other than China, and a few tea seeds were sent to the British emissary in Bhutan for him to plant there. By 1778, a famous British naturalist, Sir Joseph Banks, had been hired by the East India Company to suggest crops that might be

grown by the company for profit. He advocated the growing of tea, suggesting importing Chinese growers and tea makers to India to help start the industry. In spite of his enthusiasm, however, little was done for nearly fifty years. Although it is usually claimed that the East India Company had no incentive to start a tea industry until its monopoly on Chinese tea ended, there were actually other reasons for the delay: those areas in India suggested for cultivation were still under native control, Bhutan seemed a likelier bet for cultivation than India, and last, but in some ways most important, the indigenous tea plant of the Assam district had not yet been identified as tea.

From 1815 to 1831, three major reports of indigenous tea plants (and samples) were sent to the East India Company's botanist at the Agricultural and Horticultural Society of Calcutta, two from Assam, stating that natives drank an infusion made from the leaves of the plant; but Wallich, the botanist, insisted the plants were not tea, but camellias. As a result of the confusion, the first experiments in growing tea in India involved importing Chinese tea seeds and plants in Assam.

The governor-general of India, William Bentinck, received a proposal that the East India Company begin plantings of tea where the camellia grew, since the China trade was beginning to be more uncertain and there was some doubt that the Chinese would renew their treaty in 1833, when it expired. He in turn appointed a tea committee, including the botanist Wallich, to develop a plan for introducing tea culture into India. They dispatched a representative to China to seek seeds, plants, information on cultivation, and workers. At the same time, the committee sent out descriptions of the conditions of soil, weather, and so on, known to be needed for the successful cultivation of tea, to local British representatives, searching for likely cultivation areas. Again, Wallich (and the committee) received reports of indigenous tea plants growing in Assam; indeed, one report was from a man who had reported it previously. Sample leaves processed by members of one of the hill tribes, along with leaves, fruit, and blossoms were sent for identification; this time Wallich was finally convinced it was indeed a tea plant. The English, who thought black and green tea were two different plants, dubbed this indigenous plant the Bohea or black tea plant.

A scientific commission was charged with investigating the experimental cultivation possibilities of this indigenous bush. The commission was divided: one group favored im-

porting China seeds on the basis that the native plants would yield an inferior, "jungly" tea; the other group favored cultivating the Assam tea plant. China seeds were chosen as the basis for the experimental plots, but then disagreement arose about where they should be planted. At great cost, more than fifty thousand Chinese plants were imported and planted in various areas; some died on the way, others were mistakenly planted in poor soil; a few survived. At one point, in order to ensure that the East India Company received the very best Chinese seeds, a British traveler was paid to disguise himself as a Chinese and penetrate the interior of China.

The English, assuming that all Chinese were knowledgeable about tea, imported Chinese workers willy-nilly, some of them shoemakers and carpenters who knew nothing about tea plants, but in spite of these problems, the first Indian tea manufactured from the imported Chinese plants was shipped to England in 1838, where it was well received. Subsequently, both the imported Chinese plants and the indigenous plants were cultivated; at the end of the century, tea growers were to lament that the Chinese plants had ever been imported, as they brought about the growth of a hybrid plant in India deemed less satisfactory at low elevations.

Nonetheless, the experiment was a success, and private individuals came to India to start tea plantations and make fortunes. Gradually, the Assam plant took over; the Chinese plants produced an inferior yield in most districts. Despite the many hardships that lay ahead for the Indian tea industry, within three generations 788,842 acres were producing 432,997,916 pounds of tea annually, and the industry employed one and a quarter million people.

Tea in Sri Lanka (Ceylon)

Although the first tea plants in Sri Lanka (Ceylon), Assam plants imported from India and plants imported from China, were cultivated on an experimental basis in the 1840s and 1850s, tea cultivation was not widespread until 1875, when the coffee blight was destroying the island's coffee industry. Coffee had then been grown in Ceylon for nearly two hundred years, mostly in small gardens owned by villagers. When the British took the island from the Dutch, they began

investing money in coffee estates; the first European estate was established in 1824, and more Europeans arrived each year to clear huge tracts of jungle, plant coffee trees, and make their fortunes. When the blight struck in the 1870s, more than 275,000 acres were being cultivated, yielding an export of over a hundred million pounds of coffee annually. The European planters and the local village coffee industry were ruined. Despairing but determined, some planters tried planting Cinchona seeds in the rows between the rotting coffee trees—these would eventually yield quinine—but the successful tea-cultivation experiments begun before coffee's decline inspired others to uproot the coffee trees and plant tea. In a scant twenty years, Ceylon's single-crop coffee economy became a single-crop tea economy, with 305,000 acres planted to tea; even today, 80 percent of Ceylon's export trade is tea.

Iced Tea and the Tea Bag

Both the tea bag and iced tea are accidental twentieth-century American inventions. The first iced tea was served at the St. Louis World's Fair during a heat wave in 1904. Since Americans of the time drank primarily green tea, an Englishman, Richard Blechynden, had been sent to the fair to introduce Midwesterners to black tea from India and Ceylon. But the sweltering fairgoers weren't interested in anything hot to drink. To induce the public to try his tea, Blechynden finally poured it into glasses, added ice, and sold it as iced tea. The word spread, and iced tea became the most popular summer thirst-quencher of the fair, and later of Americans.

An attempt to economize prompted the invention of the tea bag. In 1908, a New York City tea importer, Thomas Sullivan, began sending tea samples to his retailers in small silk bags, rather than in the sample tins holding larger amounts. Impressed with the convenience of the self-straining, premeasured bags for brewing tea, the retailers ordered tea in the bags from Sullivan, assuming he had intended them to steep the tea in hot water right in the bag. And so the tea bag was born.

CHAPTER NINE

How Tea Is Grown and Processed

The Botany and Cultivation of the Tea Plant

The tea plant is a tropical and subtropical evergreen that belongs to the Camellia family. The Camellia plant most familiar to the West is the shiny, green-leaved *Camellia japonica* with its red, white, or pink flowers, but by far the most important Camellia is *Camellia sinensis,* whose young leaves and unopened leaf buds are processed in various ways into the dried tea leaves familiar all over the world. *Camellia sinensis* has been grown in China for thousands of years. Yet, interestingly enough, the wild plant from which cultivated tea must have been developed was not thought native to any part of China until recently.

In the 1830s, when the first attempts were made to introduce the tea plant known then—the Chinese variety—to northeast India, a plant of the same genus was found growing wild in Upper Assam. At first it was thought the wild plant was distinct from the Chinese plant. The differences seemed obvious: if unpruned, the China variety grew only to a height of twelve to fifteen feet, and it had smaller, rounder leaves. It was more cold-hardy, and the processed leaf yielded a light, flavory cup of tea. The Assam variety was far more vigorous and prolific, grew to thirty or forty feet, had larger leaves, and yielded a darker, stronger beverage. It was found to be more cold-sensitive than the China variety. Later, the tea plant was found to be native to the area where India, Burma, Tibet, and China share their borders, but some botanists still believe that tea was introduced to China from Assam. Whatever the origin of the Chinese plant, it is now thought the variety simply developed from the wild tea plant during hundreds of years of cultivation; it and the Assam plant are now considered the two varieties of *Camellia sinensis.*

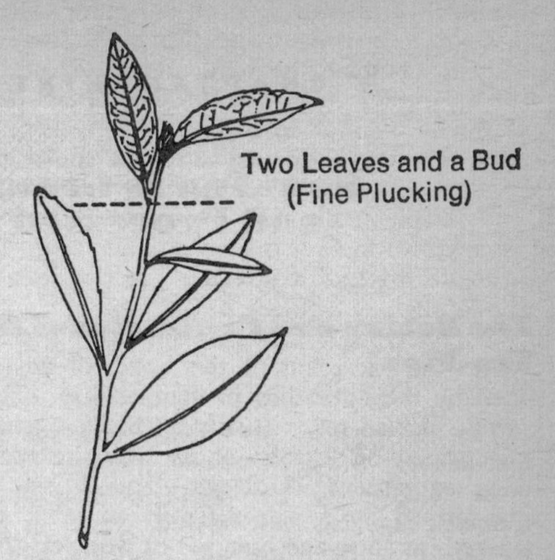

PLUCKABLE SHOOT

TEA BUSH

Many hybrids (or *jats,* as they are called in India) of the China and Assam varieties exist, some developed purposely to combine the hardy character of the China plant with the prolific character of the Assam plant. In India it was found that at low elevations, a hybrid close to the Assam variety did best, whereas in cooler climates in high elevations (as in Darjeeling) a hybrid with predominantly China character did best. As might be expected, the China type is grown in China, Taiwan, and Japan. Elsewhere in the world—in Sri Lanka (Ceylon), Africa, South America, Indonesia, and, of course, Assam and other parts of India—the Assam type or China-Assam hybrids predominate.

With the exception of the leaves of wild tea plants collected by the hill tribes of southeastern Asia for making a kind of pickled tea, virtually all the tea grown in the world is cultivated on estates, or as they are called in northern India, tea gardens. These may range in size from a quarter-acre farmed by a single family to giant plantations with hundreds of acres and hundred of workers.

When cultivated for the production of tea leaves, the bushes are never allowed to grow to the height they might attain in the wild state. Instead, they are pruned to produce a flat-topped bush about three feet high, so that each growth of new leaves may be picked with relative ease. Pruning also prevents the bush from going to seed and keeps it in a vegetative state where it simply produces new leaf suitable for picking, year after year. A tea plant may remain productive for over a century. After the plant is pruned back—at first this is done every year, and later at longer intervals—it is given a rest period to put out the amount of foliage required to sustain the plant. After that, consistent picking of the new growth resumes. Only about half the leaves produced during the life of the bush are actually picked and processed for market.

The tea plant grows only in tropical or subtropical climates, flourishing particularly in warm areas with a great deal of rain. Tea, especially the China variety and very close hybrids, tolerates a cool, dry season, but there must be at least one warm, rainy season per year. The plant will grow easily and luxuriantly all year round in certain constantly warm climates. The plant is equally tolerant of a wide range of soils, although it prefers light, sandy loam. Like the wine vine, it will grow in soils too poor for any other crop. Since tea is a monoculture—a crop grown year after year in the same location—it is universally fertilized,

and in some areas heavy fertilization has increased yields per acre enormously.

There are two methods used to propagate the tea plant. One involves taking seeds from tea bushes, known as "bearers," that are allowed to grow to their full, unpruned height (this may be as much as eighteen or twenty feet), and planting the seeds in a nursery, where at first they are kept damp and hot. After several months the seedlings are transplanted to the hillsides of the estate and normally attain productive status in three or four years, though they do not reach full production until eight or nine years old.

Tea is what is known as a self-sterile plant and must be pollinated from flowers of other bearers; unfortunately, it is impossible to ensure that fertilization occurs only from selected bushes. In addition, even if fertilization could be perfectly controlled, such seeds might naturally give rise to plants that do not have the character of the parent plants. According to Harler, it is possible for an expert tea taster to recognize marked differences between teas made from leaf plucked from different bushes on the same estate. This fact is not so much a dramatic demonstration of an expert's tasting ability as it is a demonstration that tea bushes grown from seeds of bearers may differ widely in character and quality. Because of this, the second principal method of propagation, that of using cuttings or graftings from selected plants to develop new bushes, is now used more frequently, as it ensures that the progeny will be genetically identical with the parent bush, or "clone." This method of propagation has been used with success since the late nineteenth century in Japan. In Taiwan, new bushes are simply developed from older bushes by layering—a branch of a selected bush is stripped and bent into the ground to form roots and ultimately a new tree.

Recent research in tea has helped to isolate some of the significant factors in cultivation and processing that have a bearing on the quality that ultimately appears in the teacup. Most important is the inherent quality of the general variety of tea plant grown, and the inherent quality of the individual bushes used. Climate, soil, and weather play a large role in determining how much of the inherent quality of the bush will be brought out from year to year and from picking to picking. In many tea-growing districts, the finest teas come from higher elevations, where the bushes are subject to considerable differences in climate and weather from those at lower elevations. The cooler climate at higher

elevations results in slower growth of new leaves and the entire yield is quite small. The substances present in the tea leaf responsible for the aroma and flavor of the beverage appear to be present in greater concentration in tea grown at such high elevations. Some of the best teas of Sri Lanka (Ceylon) and East Africa are grown at altitudes of six thousand feet or over; the much-esteemed Darjeeling teas of India are grown at similar altitudes in the foothills of the Himalayas. Not all the finest teas of the world are high-grown, however; superior Formosa oolongs, the best Assams, and the rare Lung Ching green tea of China, to take but three examples, are all grown at low elevations, in some cases merely a few hundred feet above sea level.

Naturally, the harvesting and processing of the leaf must be done so as to ensure that all the quality and character present in the unpicked leaf is retained. The chemistry of the substances present in (and, for that matter, on) the tea leaf that give rise to desirable fragrance and taste in the beverage made from the leaf is only partially understood, and not all the qualities in a cup apparent to the tea taster have been correlated with chemical analyses. But although laboratory research has not settled all questions, a good deal of practical information has been established through trial and error about which field methods and factory processes best retain and enhance the quality of the tea.

The crop taken from the tea bushes consists of young leaf shoots and the unopened leaf bud, because these are rich in caffeine and the organic compounds that are responsible for the smell and taste of tea. Picking—which is really plucking and is often called that—is either "fine" or "coarse," which simply refers to the size of the shoot that is plucked. "Two leaves and a bud" is fine plucking, whereas three or more leaves and a bud is considered coarse plucking. High-quality teas are almost always harvested with fine plucking, as this ensures that only the youngest, most flavorful topmost shoots are gathered. Unlike many crops, tea is plucked or harvested at least three times a year and sometimes dozens. In certain climates tea can be picked all year round, while in climates where a cool dormant season occurs, picking takes place in specific seasons—the spring, before the monsoon, in the autumn, and so on. The frequency of picking depends largely on the number of "flushes" (as new growths of pluckable shoots are called) that occur during the year, and the quality of leaf sought. A balance

has to be struck between frequency and fineness of plucking, fertilizing, and pruning, in order to stimulate the bush to produce its maximum growth of high-quality leaf.

Although tea cultivation is still a village industry in many parts of the world, with farmers cultivating small plots of tea according to traditional methods, often alongside other crops, to a great extent the world's tea production is in the hands of large estates, where modern methods are used in every aspect of the cultivation and processing. Since tea is an important export for many countries—vitally important to a country like Sri Lanka, 60 percent of whose export earnings come from tea—most of them sponsor research into all aspects of tea, and more or less oversee the development of the industry as a whole, right down to the distribution of fertilizers to improve yields and pesticides to cope with the scores of insects that find the leaves of the tea bush particularly succulent.

The Processing of Tea

The processing of tea begins with harvesting. The methods of turning the fresh green leaves into the various forms of dried tea leaves in loose teas vary from simple (green-tea production) to more complex (black-tea production). What follows is an outline of what is called the orthodox method of black-tea preparation on a large estate, from harvesting to packing the chests, with brief discussions of the manufacture of green and oolong teas and some recent innovations.

Harvesting

A typical tea estate in most of the principal tea countries has three thousand to five thousand tea bushes per acre, and the estate may be five hundred to a thousand acres in size. Although certain experimental plots of heavily fertilized, especially selected bushes have yielded eight thousand pounds of fresh leaf per acre, one to two thousand pounds per acre is considered a high yield. The bushes are set in rows about four feet apart, and depending on the contour of the land, fields may be terraced. Plots of tea are almost always set out with a number of shade trees that act as windbreaks and provide mulch as well as some protection from the hot sun for tender leaves. Each tea bush puts out up to a thou-

sand shoots a year, depending on district and climate, and must be plucked in regular rotation every six days to two weeks during the growing season.

Tea requires an enormous amount of hand labor. A typical large estate will employ several hundred workers. It has been estimated that it takes one worker one year to produce eight hundred pounds of tea. It takes two to three thousand shoots—each one of which must be plucked by hand—to produce one pound of tea, or about four pounds of plucked, fresh leaves to produce one pound of black tea. In many tea countries, women do the harvesting, moving through the waist-high, often fragrant tea fields each day to pluck as much as forty to sixty pounds of leaf, shoot by shoot. They choose the young growth, snap them off between thumb and forefinger, and toss them into the tall baskets or sacks tied to their backs. (Plucking by shears is common in Japan, but it has not proved useful elsewhere.) At midday and early evening the baskets are collected and taken to the estate "factory" to be weighed. Large estates commonly have their own processing centers, or factories. Probably because the term "factory" is used, it is common to speak of tea manufacture, although nothing is added or taken away from the leaf; preparation by manipulation and heating merely gives it a dry, stable form so that it can be used to make a beverage by infusion.

The Three Basic Types of Tea Manufacture

The main biochemical constituents of the tea leaf are substances known as polyphenols, often (and imprecisely) called "tannins." These soluble substances are transformed in processing and are responsible, ultimately, for the taste, strength, body, and color of black tea. The tea leaf also contains caffeine, pectin, aromatics, and small amounts of enzymes.

Once the leaf has been plucked, processing the finished leaf must begin as soon as practicable. Biochemical changes start to take place immediately after plucking, and the processing of the tea leaf is designed to take advantage of these transformations in the leaf, first by augmenting the change and then by arresting it. Provided the processing can take place within certain time limits (and in certain districts within certain temperature limits), the quality of the tea can be brought out and preserved.

Any of the world's teas falls into one of three categories: black, oolong, or green. These divisions are based solely on differences in the methods of processing the tea leaf. Black teas (the ones most familiar to the West) are black in appearance and produce red-brown liquor in the cup; green teas are green in appearance and yield yellow-green liquors; oolong teas are greenish-brown in appearance and make an amber-colored beverage. It is possible to make green, black, and oolong teas from the leaves of a single tea bush, and all over the world it is commonplace for greens, oolongs, and black teas to be made from the same varieties of the plant. As a practical matter, however, certain districts, areas, and estates generally specialize in the production of one of these categories of tea, not only because of tradition and expertise but also because of market demands. Countries may specialize as well: virtually all Japanese tea is green; almost all Indian tea is black; China produces all three types.

Green tea undergoes the least elaborate process and thus is the simplest to explain. Basically, the fresh, plucked leaves are steamed or heated in a perforated cylinder or boiler for several minutes to halt the natural enzymatic activity that begins in the leaf juices when the leaf is torn from the bush. The steaming prevents the juices from oxidizing and thus halts the process, which, if left uninterrupted, would result in black tea. The leaf is also softened by the steaming, making it easy to roll. Then it is dried, by machine or by hand, in a pan over heat. Drying reduces the moisture content of the leaf, thereby preventing any further chemical changes. There are any number of various ways (or styles) into which the leaf may be rolled: balled, flat, curly, thin, twisted, and so on (a description of some of these green-tea-leaf styles is given under the entries for Japan and China in Chapter Eleven). The heating and rolling process may be repeated or not, depending on the leaf style. In making tea with these leaves, contact with boiling water releases the natural vegetative fragrance and flavor that were stabilized—captured, as it were—in the steaming and drying process.

Black-tea manufacture is more complicated, though basically the leaf merely undergoes more elaborate manipulations than with green tea, manipulations that encourage the natural enzymatic activity of the plucked leaf in order to turn the tea black. In brief, fresh green leaves are withered after picking—spread on racks to dry out—and then rolled—crushed and broken by rollers to release the

leaf's juices, which then oxidize (or "ferment," as it is called) and turn the leaves brown. The leaves are then fired —dried by hot air to arrest further oxidation. The aromatic quality of the juices that have been dried on the crushed leaves is released by contact with boiling water when tea is made, and the dried oxidized leaves' juices impart their flavor, scent, and color to the beverage.

Oolong teas are prepared similarly to black teas, but are given a very short withering period and are only partially oxidized. The green leaves are allowed to turn only partially brown before drying, so that oolongs share some of the taste characteristics of both green and black teas.

But in order to understand more fully how black teas develop their special character, a more detailed look at the steps of black-tea manufacture is necessary.

Withering

On arrival at the estate factory, the fresh green leaves are thinly spread out on tiers of racks, often constructed of Hessian cloth held taut on wires. These racks may take up several stories (called withering lofts) in a large factory building; in some estates, tea leaves are withered in wire-mesh troughs. Where the climate is suitable, the leaves wither (lose their water content) naturally. In wet weather or humid climates, warm dry air is passed over the leaves or up under the trough-withered leaves by huge fans. In eight to twenty-four hours, the leaves have become soft, pliable, and flaccid, having lost much of their moisture. The fresh, acrid smell of the leaves when plucked develops into a marked, fruity odor. Sufficient withering has occurred when a handful of the leaves has lost its springiness; by then the leaves weigh only half of what they did when picked. This is known as full wither and prepares the leaves for the rolling operation that follows.

Rolling

After withering, the leaves are taken immediately to large rolling machines, each holding several hundred pounds, that twist and roll the leaves, breaking down the leaves' cellular structure and liberating the juices. The substances contained in the leaves are brought into full contact with one another and exposed to air, and enzymatic action begins. (The enzymes do not come into contact with the other leaf

substances until the leaves are torn or crushed.) At this point the leaves begin to darken in color and exude a crushed-apple smell. The twisted lumps that emerge from the rollers are broken up by coarse sieves, or roll breakers; the coarsest leaves are returned for further rolling. After the rolling process, which takes about one and one-half hours, the tea leaves are taken to the fermenting rooms.

Oxidation, or Fermentation

This step is responsible for the characteristic dark color of black teas. In large rooms with a cool, humid atmosphere, the leaves are spread in a layer about one inch thick on cement or tile floors (sometimes concrete or glass tables). The juice that has been squeezed out onto the surface of the leaf by rolling changes color, from yellow to red to dark brown, due to enzymes mixing with polyphenols and pectins and combining with oxygen. Hence the step is really oxidation, although the traditional term is "fermentation," in spite of the fact that the chemical changes have nothing to do with true fermentation. The absorption of oxygen gives the leaves a bright, coppery color, and the juices, which are astringent and bitter when colorless, become mellowed, developing the characteristic flavor of black tea. This step takes anywhere from twenty minutes to over three hours, depending on temperature; fermentation is completed when the leaves have developed full fragrance—sometimes described as nutty, spicy, or floral. (If fermentation were allowed to continue, most of the aroma and flavor would be lost and the beverage itself would be practically black.) For green tea this step is omitted, and this is the key distinction between green teas and black teas—which is why green teas are called unfermented and black teas fermented. Oolong teas, as mentioned before, are only partially fermented; oxidation is stopped when the outer edges of the leaf have changed color. Oolongs thus have a characteristic greenish-brown color to the dry leaves, rather than the full, dark-brown or black appearance of black tea.

Drying, or Firing

In order to arrest the process of fermentation at the point where maximum aroma and flavor are preserved for the tea, the fermented leaf is dried by hot air (fired) to destroy the enzymes and to reduce its moisture content to

about 3 percent. The oxidized, flavorful juices that have been dried on the surface of the crushed leaf are soluble and remain relatively stable until they are brought into contact with boiling water when the infusion is prepared by the consumer, at which point the characteristic aroma and flavor of the tea brew is released.

Drying takes about half an hour. Highly automated oven-like machines move the coppery-colored leaves on perforated trays at a speed regulated to avoid scorching, exposing them to a continuous blast of hot air at several hundred degrees. Depending on the factory setup, the tea may be fired twice, but the juices are fixed at this step, and the tea takes on its characteristic black appearance.

Orthodox and Unorthodox Manufacture

The preceding describes what is known as orthodox manufacture, developed in the late nineteenth and the early twentieth centuries in India and Ceylon. Used widely today all over the world, it requires much less labor than the original Chinese method, in use since the beginnings of tea manufacture, which required hand labor for each step in the process. Leaves were withered for a few hours in the sun, cooled, then rolled in the hands to bruise the leaves gently and laid out to cool. The entire sequence was repeated a number of times, until fermentation was judged, by aroma, to be complete. Firing was accomplished by rolling and manipulating the leaves in a hot pan and then cooling them, again a process repeated several times. The enormous variations possible in the details of this procedure allowed for enormous variations in the teas produced, but of course the teas had to be produced handful by handful. Shortly after the introduction of tea to India, planters found ways to simplify the entire procedure. The procedure developed became known as "orthodox." Today, orthodox manufacture is considered to produce the finest teas.

Unorthodox procedures, as they are called, are those that eliminate or significantly reduce some of the laborious steps that remain in orthodox procedure. Attempts to reduce withering time or eliminate it altogether were not successful at first because unwithered leaves simply mash in the roller. A number of teas today are first shredded in the Legg Cutter (originally designed for cutting tobacco), then rolled, given a short fermentation, and fired. Legg-cut-system teas have a great deal of strength and color, but often

have a brassy or raw taste, so the method is not used for top-quality teas. Since nonwithered teas tend to lose juice because of their excess moisture, a number of machines have been developed to mangle and mince the leaf before, after, or in conjunction with rolling. Some of these machines have rather descriptive names, such as the Dreadnought Equalizer, a sort of giant screw that smashes the leaf to the desired size. There are continuous-process machines, too, the best known of which is the Rotorvane. Probably the most popular of these systems, however, is the C.T.C. (for crushing, tearing, and curling), invented in the early 1930s. It results in very full oxidation and is said to improve teas with little natural quality. Due to the method and the fact that the leaves are reduced to small, fine, broken sizes, they make a strong, colory cup quickly, an advantage for teas in tea bags. Because of this, the better C.T.C. teas command better prices than poor orthodox teas. However, according to some authorities, unorthodox teas do not keep as well as orthodox teas; they are said to go stale quicker on the shelf. Most (but not all) of the less-expensive teas produced in India are manufactured by unorthodox methods, as is true in a number of other tea-producing countries.

The Grading of Teas

Typical tea drinkers may know little about tea production, but chances are that they have heard of "Orange Pekoe," and if so, are almost certainly misinformed about its meaning. "Orange Pekoe" (pronounced peck-o) is not a *kind* of tea, but merely a term used to describe a certain size of black-tea leaf. To say that a tea is an Orange Pekoe tells you nothing whatsoever about the quality or flavor of the tea.

Leaf sizes of teas are important to the trade for a number of reasons. The tea as it comes from the drier could be used to make a beverage, but because of the manufacturing process, the dried tea leaf is composed of large and small whole leaves and broken leaves of various sizes, from large pieces to small particles. In making the beverage, the smaller broken pieces would brew faster than the large pieces or leaves, releasing their color and flavor more quickly, and thus tea composed of various leaf sizes would not infuse in a uniform fashion. Varied leaf sizes would also present difficul-

ties in packing because the smaller particles would sift down to the bottom of the package. Therefore before it is packed for shipment, the tea is sorted by size.

The dried leaves are sifted by machinery—a great improvement over sifting by hand—through meshes and sieves of various standard sizes, each of which will permit a leaf or broken leaf of a certain size to pass through. Depending on the practice of the particular estate, the leaf may also be sorted in the green-leaf and fermentation stages in order to facilitate handling of given leaf sizes. The sizes into which the black-tea leaf is sorted are known as "grades," the two principal divisions of which are leaf grades and broken grades. Leaf grades consist of larger leaves left after the broken grades have been sifted out. Broken grades—and there may be some smaller leaves in these as well—make up 80 percent of the total crop. Leaf grades and broken grades are further subdivided and each individual leaf size or grade has a specific name.

The usual divisions and subdivisions used for black-tea gradings, from the largest to the smallest, are as follows:

LEAF GRADES

Souchong: Bold, round leaves yielding somewhat pale liquors.

Pekoe (Pek.): Leaves are shorter and less wiry than Orange Pekoe, but the liquors often have more color.

Orange Pekoe (O.P.): Thin, wiry leaves, sometimes with yellow "tip" (bud leaf). The liquors are somewhat pale.

BROKEN GRADES

Broken Pekoe Souchong (B.P.S.): Larger than Broken Pekoe and paler in the cup. Often used as a filler in blends.

Broken Pekoe (B.P.): More color in liquor than B.P.S.; often used as a filler in blends.

Broken Orange Pekoe (B.O.P.): Quite obviously smaller than leaf grades, it often contains tip, and yields liquors with good color and strength; consequently is much in demand for blends.

Fannings (FNGS): In some grading systems, also known as Broken Orange Pekoe Fannings. Much smaller

than B.O.P. Gives quick brews with good color; consequently is also sought for blends.

Dust (D): The smallest grade produced, used for strong, quick-brewing blends.

There are further subdivisions in use (B.O.P. No. 1, Orange Fannings, and so on), but these are not of great significance. The term "Flowery" is sometimes used as a preface to the main grades given above. "Flowery Broken Orange Pekoe" simply means B.O.P. that shows a lot of tip. These yellow-gold particles seen in black tea are sometimes confusingly thought to be flowers by tea enthusiasts, but the tea plant flowers only when it goes to seed; a producing tea plant is never allowed to flower. These tips are not flowers but small, tender, just-opening leaf buds. They are considered to add much to the appearance of the dry leaf, but cannot be taken as an indication of the cup quality of the tea. Uninteresting teas may be "tippy" in appearance, while many superb teas show no tip at all.

Many of these terms, such as Pekoe and Souchong, derive from the names used by the Chinese in grading their teas, but today they often do not correspond to their original meanings. Pekoe was used originally to describe young leaf buds of a particular appearance. To some extent, this terminology is still used to describe the leaves on the bush: the bud leaf is the Flowery Orange Pekoe, the next lower leaf, Orange Pekoe, and the next larger leaf, Pekoe. If teas were made from a single bush, it would make sense to say that the Flowery Orange Pekoe would yield the highest quality because the smallest leaf of a given bush is the best leaf. But since the largest, coarsest leaves on one bush may be far better than the smallest leaves on another bush, the quality of all the leaves plucked is evenly distributed throughout all the grades that are manufactured. Thus, for all practical purposes, the consumer, whether he be an unfussy tea drinker or the most demanding connoisseur, can ignore grading designations, since they are irrelevant to cup quality. (Doubtless part of the confusion in this respect is that, to the layman, the word "grading" carries a connotation of quality judgment as well as of sorting.)

Green tea has a completely different nomenclature for leaf sizes, and it is concerned not only with size, but also with the style or configuration (twisted, flat, pellet, and so on) that the leaf has been given in drying or firing. Unfortunately the nomenclature is not as well standardized as the

one for black tea; different ones are in use in different countries. The principal divisions of China green teas are: Chunmee, Gunpowder, Hyson, Young Hyson, and Sowmee. The principal grades of Japanese greens are Pan-fired, Basket-fired, Guri, and Natural Leaf. For a more detailed description of these grades, which again have no direct bearing on the quality of the tea, see the entries for *China* and *Japan* under the Guide to the World's Teas in Chapter Eleven.

The Packing of Tea

Each individual estate continues plucking and manufacturing tea throughout the season, but does not send off each day's production. Instead, teas of each grade are collected until there is a sufficient quantity to make up a "chop," or an invoice. Throughout the entire season each estate will make up a number of chops. "Chop" comes from the Hindi *chapna,* "to stamp," and thus a chop of tea means a number of tea chests all bearing the same brand or estate or garden mark. Since the quality of each day's pluckings differs, each grade is bulked (mixed) individually to make sure that a sample from any chest of any grade of the invoice is representative of the grade in appearance and the cup quality of the entire chop. This is important, since the trade depends on the reliability of samples as indicative of the quality of particular chops or estate marks at particular seasons.

Tea is packed by machine in aluminum-lined, plywood chests (sometimes paper-lined as well) to protect the flavor and resist moisture. The chests, which measure about 19 x 19 x 24 inches, hold about 90 to 120 pounds of leaf and larger broken grades. Fannings and Dust are often shipped in half-chests (14 x 14 x 16) of 80 to 100 pounds. A shipment from a typical estate might consist of:

30 chests Broken Orange Pekoe
15 chests Broken Pekoe
10 chests Orange Pekoe
15 chests Pekoe
5 chests Souchong
10 chests Broken Pekoe Souchong
12 chests Fannings
3 chests Dust

These hundred or so chests comprise a chop, the quality of which depends principally on the type of tea grown, the climate, elevation, soil, weather, and a number of other

factors that determine the range of quality of teas that are normally produced in a given tea district.

Some individual estates or gardens naturally have a much greater reputation for quality than others. These are, as might be expected, well-run estates with fine tea varieties grown in particularly favored conditions, which can be depended upon to produce some of the finest teas from their districts in any given year. Since there are at least a few harvests each year, sometimes a dozen, each may vary significantly from the last. In Darjeeling, for example, the tea plant hibernates during the cold, dry winter, producing leaf only from April to November. In the spring, fine tea can be produced from the first flush (new growth of small soft shoots), but the finest teas of the year available from Darjeeling are from the second flush, after the lull in growth following the first flush. The bulk of the Darjeeling crop is grown during the monsoon season that starts about mid-June and lasts until autumn, and does not show the prized character associated with fine Darjeeling. After the rains end, a small crop of autumnal leaf is gathered before the end of the season. This is superior to the "weathery" summer teas but has thin liquors. Even the finest estates from the finest tea-producing districts will ship chops of widely varying character and quality during the year, and these differences are reflected in the prices individual shipments command in the international tea market.

The Marketing of Tea

The tea market is international in scope, and necessarily so. Although many tea-producing countries, such as India, consume a substantial amount of the tea they produce, most tea-producing lands export the great majority of their tea, and in some instances—this is true of Sri Lanka—depend heavily on tea as a major source of export earnings. On the other hand, the countries that are the biggest consumers of tea, both in sheer amount and in per-capita consumption, are mostly all non-tea-producing lands, entirely dependent on imports (see page 190). The tea trade has become a highly organized and interdependent market, in which exporting countries normally send their teas to all tea-drinking parts of the globe and importers in tea-drinking

lands maintain constant contact with the more than three dozen countries where tea is grown.

Forty years ago, Ukers estimated that the number of servings of tea consumed each year in the world would fill a teacup so large that an ocean liner floating in it would look like a rubber duck in a bathtub. Today, one would have to find an even more mind-boggling comparison, but the message is clear: tea is big business. The actual structure of the trade is of more interest to the student of international finance than to the tea enthusiast, but the principal means by which the price (and value) of tea is fixed is fascinating. While some tea is sold directly from the estates to foreign and domestic buyers, most of the world's teas are sold at auction in a number of key cities. In the producing countries, some of the main centers are Calcutta for north India; Cochin for south India; Colombo for Sri Lanka; and others include Chittagong and Nairobi. In addition there are important auctions held in the principal tea-trading cities, notably London, Amsterdam, Antwerp, and Hamburg. Buyers in importing countries bid on teas at these auctions in competition with buyers from all over the world, either directly or through agents in the principal centers.

Prior to the auctions, teas are shipped and warehoused so that they can be examined and sampled. Holes are bored in a chest from each chop or invoice; a sample of the tea is taken out, sampled by expert tea brokers, and forwarded to leading tea buyers in various parts of the world. The actual method of tea-tasting is discussed in detail in the next chapter; at this point, it is important only to note that tea-tasting reaches such a high level of precision that there is never any difference of opinion about the character and quality of any individual tea. Differences in prices offered for different teas are based solely on the demand caused by the needs of buyers for teas of varying characters and qualities, not by differences of opinion over the quality of specific teas.

Buyers are not merely interested in the finest teas; the variability in the quality and quantity of the product inevitably means that tea packers and suppliers all over the world must blend teas from a number of sources in order to be able to supply their customers with a constant supply of tea with a consistent character and quality at a given price. Some of the complex factors blenders and buyers take into consideration in making blends are mentioned in the next chapter, but here are some of the more general demands:

British buyers want strong, colory teas for blends that will make a satisfying beverage when served with milk, and consequently are interested in quick-brewing broken grades of the full, pungent teas from Assam; Continental Europeans are interested in the appearance of the dry leaf and want tippy leaf grades, as well as the more delicately flavored teas; Americans pay no attention to appearance and are especially interested in the smaller, broken, quick-infusing grades for use in tea bags; and so forth. All alike want fine flavorful teas to add character to their popular medium-quality blends and want fair quality but inexpensive teas to use as blenders to keep the cost down. During various seasons when certain teas are in short supply, other teas will be in great demand, and prices will vary considerably. The finest teas always command a stiff price, particularly if there is little available. The best Darjeelings may sell for ten times the price of standard-quality Darjeelings.

Virtually all teas sold at retail are blends. The major blends, familiar to everyone as the brand names on every grocery shelf, may be composed of dozens of teas from various parts of the world. Far more expensive gourmet teas, offered in much smaller quantities, may consist of a blend from two or three estates of a particular district. Single-estate teas may be available to customers from time to time, but these are not necessarily better teas than the finest district blends.

This wide range of needs creates a lively market: as many as fifty thousand chests (five million pounds) of tea may trade hands in a single day at one of the major auctions. Having made the highest bid, the buyer either ships his newly purchased tea to fill an order for a customer or, if he has purchased it on his own account, will send samples to potential buyers in various tea-importing countries. In a trade as complex as tea, there are any number of variations in the way tea may be sold or purchased. Particularly important to the trade are brokers, who operate either in the producing and exporting countries or in the importing countries. They buy (and sell) tea for customers who do not have an expert tea-buying staff. There are also importers who do their own buying and purchase teas to sell in turn to large tea firms, wholesalers, and retailers. A few of the largest tea firms (for example, Thomas J. Lipton, Inc., Standard Brands, Inc., Salada Foods, Inc., Tetley, Inc., Brooke Bond Foods, Inc., and The Great Atlantic and Pacific Tea Co.) may simply buy their tea directly from their

own agents in the producing countries, then do their own blending, packing, and retail distribution.

There are three basic forms in which tea can be purchased by the retail customer: loose, in tea bags, or in instant form. A merchant who purchases tea in chests from importers will simply scoop out a half-pound of tea into a paper bag for you on the spot. Loose tea in bulk (as it's called) is not as common as it once was, although it is reappearing in the United States, usually in specialty food shops or bean coffee shops, for customers who enjoy picking out their teas this way. Loose tea, however, is most commonly seen in packages or tins, and these range in character and quality from the everyday supermarket blends to some of the finest teas in the world. A well-stocked shop may offer teas packed locally; teas packed in England or the Continent and shipped to the United States; teas packed in the producing country by small firms, importers, or large firms; and even teas packed under the store's name. A few of the better loose teas in tins are available by mail order (see Appendix).

Teas packed in tea bags are widely available, but for the reasons given in Chapter Twelve, fine teas are rarely available in this form.

Soluble tea (called instant tea), developed in the 1930s, is really more a tealike drink than an alternative form of the beverage; a would-be tea enthusiast would not find in it the fragrance and flavor of this ancient brew.

CHAPTER TEN

How to Taste Tea

A tea drinker can have a quite uncritical palate and yet derive enormous enjoyment from tea; knowing how to tea-taste in any formal sense is not a prerequisite to appreciating it. But having some discrimination about what you sip from your teacup heightens appreciation and thus makes tea-drinking more rewarding and interesting. Tea-tasting is a way of exploring the world of fine tea to become aware of the characters different teas have and to learn to distinguish the difference in quality among ordinary, fine, and superlative teas. The kind of amateur tea-tasting I advocate falls far short of the experience, practice, and skill necessary for professional tea-tasting, but it will without doubt enhance your enjoyment of tea and can be as interesting and entertaining as wine-tasting, coffee-sampling, or cheese-nibbling. Professional tea tasters are more concerned with evaluating tea quality than appreciating it, but these two aspects of tea-tasting are closely allied. A description of why and how the experts taste helps tea lovers understand what they can learn from even very simple comparative tastings.

How Tea Experts Taste Tea

There are several points along the route that tea takes from bush to grocer's shelf where some assessment of its quality is called for. In spite of the rapid growth of technological improvements in the production of tea, no scientific analysis yet devised can replace the judgment of an expert tea taster after cup-sampling. In the districts of origin, cup-sampling is primarily a means of quality control over the processing, and when the tea is purchased, either directly or at auctions, it is a way of establishing the tea's character, quality, and relative value. Brokers and agents cup-sample on the spot at major markets; samples are also flown air-

mail to buyers and brokers all over the world. Governments in importing countries where legislation provides for control over the quality of tea that is imported—as in the United States—cup-sample all imports. In brief, at any point in the tea market where there is some need to describe the tea and put a value upon it, cup-sampling is the method of evaluation.

There are two basic methods of tasting in common use: the British and the American. Actually there is little difference between the two except in the equipment used, so I'll simply describe the American method. American tea buyers and tasters use equipment quite similar to that used for coffee cup-sampling, except that there is no need, of course, for sample roasters. The necessary equipment consists of a long, waist-high countertop or a round wood or marble table four feet in diameter with a revolving top (the outside edge is slightly lower than the rest of the top, creating a sort of shelf); thin, white handleless cups ranged around this shelf; a shallow pan or tray to hold the sample tea behind each cup; bright light from a window (ideally north light); a scale to weigh out samples; a source of filtered water; two or three kettles and a stove to boil the water; and a spittoon (or "gaboon," as it is called in the trade), a stool, and a spoon. Most tea tasters find tap water piped through a charcoal filter satisfactory.

A tea taster examines the tea before and after preparation in order to determine, as much as possible, its character, quality, and value; in each state—dry leaf, infused leaf, and liquor—the tea reveals a good deal to the expert eye, hand, and palate. As previously explained, the dry leaf is simply the processed tea in the state in which the consumer purchases it. The "infused leaf" is the wet mass of leaves left after the preparation of the beverage. (Confusingly, tea leaves in this state are called the "infusion" by tasters, whereas tea drinkers commonly call the brew or beverage itself the infusion. In the interest of clarity, I will use the phrase "infused leaf" whenever possible, and save the term "infusion" for the entire process or method of brewing.) The "liquor" is the liquid part of the brew that results from pouring boiling water over tea leaves and allowing the mixture to steep for a number of minutes.

A tasting session begins with selecting the tea to be sampled. It is possible to evaluate several hundred samples a day, but since the nose and palate tire quickly, only two or three dozen will be tasted at a given time. A portion of

each tea selected is dumped into a sample tray and appropriately tagged. First the dry leaf is examined simply by appearance. Black tea's fully withered leaves look black, obviously, green-tea leaves look green, whereas oolong leaves look partially withered. The "varnish" of dried tea juices that cover the leaf in black teas is called the bloom or complexion; its evenness is a sign of good quality. Shortcomings in the manufacture of the tea can be detected by the practiced eye: brown leaf in orthodox teas may indicate underwithering; blistered leaves and grayness are caused by overrapid firing; well-twisted leaves indicate full withering, and so on. The presence or absence of fiber, dust, and stalk is noted, as well as the care that has been taken in sorting and grading; whether the leaf is choppy, flaky, uneven, or bold (big for the grade size) will affect the quality of the tea. Nonexperts tend to be unduly impressed with "stylish" teas, or teas with an impressive appearance, particularly those containing a high proportion of white or golden "tips" (buds). Whether or not a tea has "tip" has nothing to do with cup quality. The presence of tip usually—but not invariably—indicates careful handling of the leaf during manufacture. It is primarily a cosmetic attraction. Some of the best Darjeelings—the ones with the highest cup quality—are entirely black in appearance.

A rough test of the freshness of the tea is made by gently pressing some in the hand; new teas are somewhat more springy than old teas and less likely to crumble easily. Finally, the dry leaves may be smelled, usually by warming some in the hand, exhaling into them to moisten them, and then inhaling. By appearance alone, Ceylons, Javas, Africans, Indians, and in fact most black teas are difficult, if not impossible, to distinguish, but the aroma detected from them in the hand is sufficiently distinct to permit the expert to tell them apart—and even to give a reasonably accurate assessment of their probable quality.

This entire dry-leaf analysis, it should be understood, in practice takes only a few seconds while the taster mentally compares his impression of the leaf with his knowledge and experience with that type of tea and that particular garden.

Next, a small amount of each tea (usually thirty-five grains, one-tenth to one-quarter ounce, or two to three grams—about the weight of a well-worn dime) is carefully weighed out and put in a cup. (Thirty-five grains is considered the standard measure for a cup, and also a tea bag; on this

basis one pound of tea yields a standard two hundred cups.) The sample tray with the corresponding tea is placed behind it to allow comparison of the dry leaf with its infusion. The cups hold five to six ounces when filled to just below the brim. When all the samples are in the cups, water is brought to a rolling boil and the cups are filled in order. The taster pulls up a stool, positions a tall spittoon between his legs, and hovers over each cup in turn with his tasting spoon.

The analysis of the infused leaf begins shortly after all the cups are filled, since the open cups permit the taster to watch "the agony of the leaves"—as the unfolding of the tea leaves in boiling water is called. Open, flat leaves infuse quickly; well-twisted leaves take longer to yield their full flavor. (Generally speaking, smaller leaves will yield more body in the brew than the larger leaves from the same plant.) In practice, the taster may wait a few minutes for the cups to cool and the teas to release their color and aroma. Then he scoops up a large portion of the infused leaf from the bottom of the cup for a close look and a sniff. The aroma released by the infused leaf is as powerful and revealing, if not more so, than that released by the liquor. Along with the all-revealing sniff, the taster looks at the infused leaf for color, evenness, and brightness. Quality black teas (congous are an exception) have a bright, penny-coppery-colored infused leaf; a dull-brown color warns of poor liquor; mixed, uneven, and green color in the infused leaf of black teas indicates that the liquor is apt to be raw or thin in taste.

Now the taster looks at the appearance of the liquor itself, although, of course, he has been noticing it all along. He is primarily concerned with its brightness and color, and again compares it mentally with his experience of previous teas of this type. The possible shades of tea colors are many and varied; in order to facilitate comparisons, the light must be both bright and consistent, and anything that might influence judgment is eliminated from the tasting. This is why the cups are white and of uniform size (and are handleless, because the slight shadow a handle might throw on the inside of the cup hampers objective judgment).

Strength of color does not necessarily indicate strength of flavor. A light, bright greenish-yellow liquor is a sign of quality in a green tea, and the liquor will have body, strength, and pungency; a dull, dark, or brownish-yellow color, on the other hand, often indicates old or poor leaf. Young green teas yield very light liquors. The finest oolongs

have a much paler amber color than those of poorer quality, and some of the finest Darjeelings yield a light-colored liquor compared to the dark cups of many black blends. The amateur is often subconsciously tricked into thinking a dark, rich-looking cup of tea is more flavorful than in fact it is. (Since it takes a minimum of three minutes for all the flavor and aroma characteristics to be infused from the leaf, the quality of the finished brew must be judged according to the length of infusion, not by color.)

The taster is now ready to confirm or supplement his impressions so far by tasting the liquid. All the previous steps take very little time in actual practice, and so does the tasting. The taste is the final test and the final determiner of quality. All the other tests have been signs or portents of cup quality; the taste confirms or denies these signs. While the tea can be sampled directly from the cup, it is far faster and more efficient to use a spoon. The ideal temperature for tasting the liquor is said to be 106° to 110°F. Much above that temperature and the palate may be scalded and the taste buds desensitized. Many tasters examine the dry samples and infused leaves while waiting for the liquor to cool to around that temperature.

The taster sucks the liquid—about a tablespoonful—off the spoon with considerable force, enough, anyway, to make a loud sucking noise. The noise just accompanies the proper technique, which is to create enough suction with the mouth and lips to spray the liquor over the entire palate and carry its aroma into the nasal passages. A swish around the mouth, and the liquid is spat into the gaboon. Often a taster will take at least two slurps from each cup, the purpose of the first slurp being to clear the palate of the impression of the previous cup tasted. The mechanics of the slurping method allow all the senses of the mouth and nose to experience the tea liquor. By sucking the liquor into the back of the mouth, the olfactory nerves in the nasal passages are strongly stimulated and the entire tongue is bathed in the liquid. Of the four dimensions of taste (salt, sour, sweet, and bitter), sweetness and saltiness are tasted on the tip of the tongue, bitterness at the back, and sourness at the back edges. Astringency or pungency of tea is not a taste per se, but a sensation felt on the gums and cheeks. The body, or thickness, of the tea is the impression of weight or viscosity experienced when the liquor is swirled around in the mouth. A good deal of the sensation of taste is actually experienced by the nose, not the mouth,

as anyone with a head cold can attest; for this reason, most of the tea taster's efforts are aimed at accentuating the olfactory sensations.

Perhaps not surprisingly, there are considerable similarities among the descriptive terms tea tasters, wine tasters, and coffee tasters employ. Each has its own particular and sometimes peculiar terminology, however, and although the vocabulary used by tea tasters is close to that of coffee tasters, it is not identical. Certain key terms, such as "flavor," have meanings that only partially overlap. The following list covers most of the tea-tasting terms in common use; it covers only terms used to describe the general characteristics of tea, the liquor, and some common tea terms. It does not include terms that apply only to the appearance of the dry leaf and the infused leaf. In compiling the list, I have been guided by contemporary usage in the U.S. tea trade and by the lists given by Harler and, to some extent, Ukers. Some of the descriptions are not the technical ones used in the trade, but are my own attempt to explain terms in a nontechnical fashion.

Note: Italicized terms appear elsewhere in this list.

A Tea Taster's Glossary

Aroma The odor of the tea liquor (and the infused leaf); also called nose or fragrance. It may be lacking, faint, medium, full, expansive, *flowery*. A complex aroma is often described as a bouquet. The character and quality of flavory teas is partly aroma. See *flavor*.

Astringency See *pungent*.

Baky An undesirable flavor characteristic of black teas from which too much moisture has been driven off during firing. Not as strong as *burnt*.

Biscuity A descriptive term sometimes applied to the aroma of well-fired Assam tea.

Bite See *pungent*.

Bitter An unpleasant acrid taste arising from several causes. See *green*.

Black currant The aroma and flavor of some fine Darjeelings are sometimes described as reminiscent of black currants. See *muscat*.

Body The tactile sensation of weight and substance of the liquor experienced in the mouth. The impression of vis-

cosity is not due solely to the amount of soluble solids, but is accentuated by flavor and pungency. Body may be described as thin, medium, full, and so on. In black teas, full body denotes a strong, thick, concentrated infusion.

Brassy Undesirable flavor tang in black teas caused by underwithering.

Bright Characteristic of all fine teas. Bright teas have liquors with a lively, limpid, or sparkling appearance. Usually an indication of good quality, as opposed to dull-looking liquors. Also a taste description. See *dull*.

Brisk The opposite of *flat*. Related to but not merely a pungency quality, it is described as a "live" character found in the taste of good black teas. It is not related to age.

Burnt A smell and taste of burnt organic matter due to excessive firing temperature.

Character Loosely, the general quality of a tea. More specifically, the quality of aroma and flavor that can be associated with country, region, district, or even garden of origin.

Chocolaty A term used to describe the flavor of certain fine Darjeelings, a slightly *toasty* flavor similar to that of some Keemuns.

Clean Usually used to describe dry leaf free of dust, fiber, and stalk, but also often applied to thin, plain tea liquor of no other distinction than that of being free of undesirable taste characteristics.

Coarse A liquor lacking aroma and often with undesirable taste qualities as well, due to irregular firings or poor leaf.

Color Color varies with tea type and origin, but should be bright, limpid, or deep, as opposed to stewy and *dull*. A black tea with a concentrated red liquor is sometimes described as colory.

Complex Characteristic of very fine teas whose nose and taste give the impression of a subtle mélange of flavors.

Common Untainted but nonetheless poor-quality teas yielding plain, dull liquors.

Cream A milky film that forms as certain black teas (particularly Assam) cool. Usually indicates some briskness and strength though not necessarily *flavor*.

Delicate Subtle as opposed to assertive, intense, or penetrating aromas and flavors. A delicate tea may possess considerable complexity, however.

Dull Opposite of *bright*. Muddy, brownish color and appearance in the liquor arising from poor manufacture or poor leaf. Not an encouraging sign.

Earthy A dank flavor taint due to damp storage conditions.

Fine Term of praise; usually synonymous with flavory. See *aroma* and *flavor*.

Flashy Often a very recently picked *self-drinking* tea that is exceptionally alive in the cup. See *new*. This character is ephemeral and sometimes develops into a rounder, more mellow quality with age.

Flat A soft, rather tasteless tea lacking *brisk*ness, *strength,* and *pungency*.

Flavor (a) Used to describe fine quality indicated by the presence of a sweetish or honeylike aroma-taste complex —a bouquet that can be tasted as well as sniffed. Such a tea is described as flavory. (b) Specifically, certain flavor nuances found in the taste of the liquor—almonds, toffee, and so forth.

Flowery Characteristic of the fragrant *aroma* of many fine teas; often used in describing high-grown Ceylons and South Indians. (Not to be confused with the perfume of scented teas—see Chapter Eleven.)

Fresh Sometimes confused with *green*. Usually refers to recently manufactured teas and those teas that have not been on the shelf so long they have become *stale*.

Fruity A flavor taint due to bacterial infection; however, a piquant fruity quality is characteristic of oolong.

Full Used to describe liquors of black tea with strength but with little briskness. Full teas are not bitter, but ripe, round, and smooth.

Gone off Tainted or moldy tea that has been spoiled by improper storage or packing. Also applied to out-of-condition teas that are merely too old, but this state is more precisely termed *stale*.

Green As applied to black teas, a raw, bitter taste due to underfermentation. It is not related to actual age. Sometimes confused with *fresh*.

Hard Used to describe a black-tea liquor with great pungency and bitterness; a raw, rasping, or harsh quality related to greenness.

Hay A flavor characteristic found in certain teas at certain seasons; a woody, grassy, or stalky flavor. Undesirable in black teas, not always desirable in oolongs and greens.

Heavy Thick, strong, colory black-tea liquors with little briskness.

High-grown Most, but not all fine teas are from high elevations, but in districts where quality is related to altitude,

the *aroma* is more expansive and the *flavor* is more *intense*.

Intense Usually applied to *flavor* and taste to indicate a concentrated, penetrating quality.

Light Not to be confused with *delicate*. A light tea lacks *body* and *aroma;* related to *thin*.

Lively See *brisk, flashy*.

Malty A character associated with, and a desirable quality of, Assam teas.

Mature Used to describe fully fermented black teas; see *full*. Not related to actual age; should not be confused with *mellow*.

Mellow The desirable qualities a black tea may take on with a certain amount of age. Few teas develop with age. See *winy*.

Metallic An undesirable coppery tang found in some black teas.

Muscat Common description of the *aroma* and *flavor* of some fine Darjeelings.

New Term used to describe recently picked and processed tea.

Plain Characteristic of the liquor of *light* or *thin* tea.

Point A tea has point if it has some desirable quality, such as liveliness, *brisk*ness, or fine fragrance.

Pungent An astringent puckery sensation given to the gums; it is a quality of the liquor and not a *flavor*. Also called bite. Pungency gives tea its refreshing quality; excessive pungency gives tea a *bitter*, harsh, rough character.

Raw See *green, hard*.

Rich Sometimes said of a *full, mature* tea, but it suggests an opulence of *flavor* as well. See *winy*.

Round See *full*.

Sappy Full, juicy liquor; *brisk*.

Self-drinking Said of a tea that possesses all the requisites of quality and thus does not need blending. Self-drinking teas can come from a variety of origins.

Smoky A desirable characteristic fragrance and *flavor* of some China teas, especially Lapsang Souchong, which varies from faint to strong. Also found in other teas due to faulty manufacture.

Smooth See *full*.

Stale A tea that has lost most of its quality through excessive age. Stale teas have faded aromas and a characteristic dead, papery taste.

Strength Thick, concentrated liquors with pungency. In black teas, also colory and creamy.
Sweet A light, pleasant tea of no great character or quality.
Tainted A tea with strange foreign aromas and flavors, usually because of molds or storage with odiforous substances. See *gone off*.
Tarry Pronounced, heavy *smoky aroma* and taste, as in Lapsang Souchong.
Thickness See *body, strength*.
Thin A weak, dilute tea, usually because of poor leaf.
Toasty A term sometimes used to describe the *aroma* of fine Keemun, occasional Darjeelings, and sometimes other highly fired teas.
Vegetative Green teas often have distinct vegetative aromas and flavors, from new-mown hay to seaweedy to delicately herbaceous.
Winy A fine Darjeeling or Keemun properly kept six months to a year or more may take on a *mellow*, winy character.

On Tea-tasting Expertise

A tea taster's skill is focused primarily on the description and evaluation of teas. Even though tea tasters may enjoy the superb quality of an occasionally superlative tea, however, by and large their days are devoted to the analysis of far more commonly available teas, seldom with rare teas. After years of assessing teas, experts become so familiar with many teas that they can recognize them "blind." Expert tea tasters can, in fact, identify hundreds of teas blind—including those from specific gardens. But such an ability is not the point of tasting tea. Identification per se has little to do with tasting expertise. It is analysis and evaluation that are important in tasting, and this is true whether the object of scrutiny is wine, tea, coffee, cheese, or any other beverage or foodstuff requiring careful description and evaluation.

Like the expert wine taster, the tea taster has a well-stocked mental library of previously tasted examples. The amateur tea lover can hardly remember the difference between one tea and another unless they are tasted side by side; the expert's memory is quite clear and precise because it is built on daily acquaintance with the world's teas. It is this sensory background that enables an expert to register

with precision whether a present perception of a tea is typical, out of character, blemished, tainted, or unusually outstanding. There is little, whether a virtue or a fault, that would be missed by such a palate.

Practically anyone has the latent ability to distinguish among many teas, provided they are tasted next to each other. It is surprising how easy it is to notice even slight differences among teas when tasted this way, even though it takes much more practice to be able to express these differences with any precision.

A tea taster's job consists of much more than finding the bright, high-grown flavorful teas among given samples. In most cases, tea tasters are also concerned with tea-blending, and their buying is connected with that in mind. As was mentioned earlier, the demands of the marketplace and the vagaries of an agricultural product like tea conspire to make virtually all teas that appear on the marketplace blends. In most cases this is an advantage, since only a minute fraction of the world's teas (at least in terms of production) are self-drinking teas—or teas which can be drunk on their own with full enjoyment and which can't be improved with judicious blending. The variations of the weather in the various tea districts of the world, the weather variations experienced by individual gardens, the perceptible changes in character and quality of the teas from individual estates from picking to picking, and even the variations from one week to the next from the same bush make it extremely difficult to obtain a consistently high-quality product throughout the season from a given garden. That, coupled with the fact that few teas can be marketed successfully except in fairly large quantities, makes it difficult for even a supplier of gourmet teas to offer teas from single estates or tea gardens.

The well-known supermarket blends of the famous tea empires—Lipton's, for example—must use a great many teas from a great many sources in order to supply a consistent blend throughout the year. To keep a given blend a consistent quality and character, tea buyers and blenders have to create their teas from an ever-changing flavor palate of the world's teas. If they have been using a particular Java tea over the past few months to supply a certain nuance customers look for in the blend, a change in the weather may necessitate a change to East African teas to supply the needed note. To create a blend strictly by recipe—30-percent Ceylon, 40-percent Assam, and 30-percent Java (or whatever the ideal formula might look like)

—is really a recipe for disaster, since the characters of these teas will change considerably throughout the year, and thus, so will the blend. Buyers of major blends may not be the most discriminating customers of tea, but they do insist on consistency of taste.

The ability to put together a blend from two to twenty or more different sources is not something that *automatically* comes with tasting expertise. It is an additional skill learned only after considerable experience at the tasting table. Although with experience tasters develop the ability to gauge which teas will merge and blend and which teas are incompatible, only actually mixing proportions of the liquors of various teas tells the blender if a particular combination will harmonize and create the quality and character sought.

Of course, there are other considerations that enter into the blender's picture besides the necessity for consistency. The particular character, flavor, and quality must be achieved at a reasonable price, and preferably as economically as possible. The buyer thus looks for reasonably priced teas with distinctive characters that will contribute substantially to the quality of the blend and will do so even if used in small quantities. Some teas will force their character upon other teas and dominate the blend. Such a tea may lack other qualities, but it may provide one of the things the blend needs. Other useful teas are those of middling, ordinary flavor that can be used as cost reducers in relation to the average blend costs. These teas ideally fade into the flavor background and are substantially improved by the more flavorful teas. Only expertise and artful work at the tea table will tell blenders if they will achieve a higher overall quality for the cost ratio if they use half as much of a tea twice as good as the base tea but twice as expensive, and so forth.

There are still other considerations. Is the blend to be used for iced tea? In that case it should not cloud when cooled. In what area of the country will the blend be sold? Water conditions vary widely, and blenders often have samples of regional waters they use in determining a blend that will go well with the water supply of a particular area.

Blenders may try milk with the blend; if it has good color with milk (this, of course, means black teas), it indicates that the blend is fairly balanced between color, strength, and briskness. Skim milk is sometimes added to check the color of a tea since this can enhance color differences.

The techniques employed by professional tea tasters are easily adapted by amateurs to increase their appreciation of tea. You need only a set of uniform cups, a teaspoon (or balance scale if you're fussy about exactitude), a spoon, a kettle, tea, and preferably a counter area next to the kitchen sink. Reasonably good comparisons of teas can be made by preparing samples that are spoon-measured, using the standard measure of one level teaspoon per cup. Because a teaspoon of tea does not always weigh the same, however, there's some imprecision; a teaspoon of broken-grade leaves weighs more than one of open, flat, or spidery leaves, so a cup made from the former may be thought stronger than it actually is. If you require exactitude, use a scale to weigh out the same amount of tea into each cup. (The kind of balance scales used in college science courses are perfect, offering sensitivity to a hundredth of a gram; they cost about twenty dollars.)

A typical tasting procedure, using spoon-measuring, would go something like this: on an uncluttered counter top next to the kitchen sink, arrange a half-dozen cups (tasting more than six teas tends to be confusing). I use plain white handleless china bowls of a six-ounce capacity purchased at on Oriental import store. (I think they were intended as small soup or dessert bowls.) Double-check to make sure no soap remains from a previous washing; if in doubt, rinse vigorously with hot water and shake out.

Arrange each tin or bag of tea to be tasted behind a cup to prevent mixups, and with a measuring spoon, scoop out a level teaspoon of leaf from each tin. Dump it in the cup in front of it. Put a quart of cold water in a kettle. Draw cold water from the tap, making sure the water runs for a few moments so you don't use the water that has been lying in the pipes. (Such water is often flat.)

While waiting for the water to boil, make a list of the teas to be tasted. When the water boils, promptly fill to the brim each cup, in order. The leaves will begin to unfold immediately, but wait until the cups have cooled slightly before spooning up the leaves from the bottom for a look and a sniff. Record your impressions on a note pad, trying to be as concrete as possible ("grassy," "flowery," and so on, rather than "heavenly," or "weird"). The spoon can be rinsed between cups, but professional tasters normally

just shake it. When the teas cool and can be tasted comfortably, try slurping exaggeratedly from the spoon to get the best effect. The sink provides a convenient and hard-to-miss spittoon. Use after spraying the liquor over the tongue and swishing it around the mouth.

When sniffing or slurping, try to concentrate on the impression gathered in one or two tries. Excessive sniffing quickly tires the nose, and overtasting dulls the palate. Record your impressions on each in turn before resampling any teas.

For the beginner, it's instructive to start with an overview of the world's teas, although it isn't really a comparison because it isn't meaningful to compare greens, oolongs, and blacks together. Later you'll want to compare teas that are roughly similar so that their individual differences stand out. Try all black teas, or China blacks vs. Indian blacks, or Indian blacks vs. Ceylon blacks, or as you get more adept, teas from the same region, such as a series of Darjeelings. Close comparison tastings allow each tea's particular virtues and shortcomings to come to the fore.

Direct comparison tastings are obviously the best way to discover the best teas for the price. For complete objectivity, they should be tasted blind—that is, with the identifying bags and tins out of sight. This ensures that your judgment is not unduly influenced by the name on the label. To taste blind, simply number the bottoms of the cups with a China marker in order from left to right and make a list of the teas by number. After weighing out the samples but before pouring in the water, put the tins and the first list away. Shuffle the cups around and make a new left-to-right list—A, B, C, and so on. After tasting the teas and noting your impressions next to the letters, lift the cups to find out which number—and hence which tea—was A, B, C, and so on. Of course, you can cheat at this by paying attention to the appearance of the dry leaf in the cups, something that may not be easy to avoid if they are quite different, but for the amateur this method is sufficiently blind.

As your expertise increases, you might try tests that two people give each other: the delta test (two cups hold the same tea, the third is different, pick out the different one); picking out the tea that matches a given cup from a series of three or more; and so on.

After you've explored the world of teas, you might want to try blending your own. Although many prefer the classic

tea types unblended, you might try adding one-sixth of a fine Earl Grey to a fine China black or one-fifth Formosa Oolong to a Darjeeling to serve guests something a little different. A pinch of Lapsang Souchong adds an effective note to many fine black teas; a combination of one-fourth green tea and three-fourths oolong is lovely. Try sampling the blend while cup-tasting, spooning out the liquor from the separate teas to combine and sample in another cup. That way the proposed proportions can be sampled for compatibility and effect. Many combinations that sound good in theory may be quite disappointing in fact. There is no law of chemistry such that any two or more teas thrown together will make up one another's lacks or accent one another's virtues. In order not to waste tea on a poor blend, try the combined liquors before mixing several half-pounds of tea together.

CHAPTER ELEVEN

A Guide to the World's Teas

The following far from exhaustive list does not include teas grown primarily for local consumption (as in Fiji and the Azores) or tea districts in the experimental stage or too small to be of commercial importance (as in Australia, Guatemala, Bolivia, and so forth). A number of tea-producing countries are mentioned whose teas do not at this point appear on retail shelves under country or district-of-origin names. They are mentioned not merely for the sake of completeness but because many of these tea lands produce quality teas that could be marketed as district blends. At the least, their silent role in the familiar tea blends of major tea packers ought to be acknowledged. For the convenience of the tea novice, I've included common tea terms as well.

It is probably true that every tea district having good conditions for tea-growing produces, or could produce, a small quantity of fine to outstanding tea. Nonetheless, there are only a few areas that consistently produce fine tea in quantities sufficient to be of commercial importance in the world market. Because the teas of some countries are described here as "useful blenders," the reader should not imagine that the quality of that country's tea never rises above this level. In certain seasons and depending on market conditions, tea buyers and blenders may draw upon any of the world's teas for good-quality blends. Of course, this isn't to say there aren't distinct peaks of quality produced among teas. The very finest teas are produced in very small quantities and consequently occupy a fractional percentage of the international tea trade. In this respect they are no different than fine wines, and like fine wines, they have reputations that add luster to the less-exalted growths produced in their countries of origin.

Note: Italicized names and terms appear elsewhere in this list.

Africa Although these teas are of considerable and growing commercial importance in the world market, they do not, so far as I know, appear on the retail level under

PRINCIPAL TEA EXPORTING AND TEA IMPORTING COUNTRIES

PRINCIPAL TEA EXPORTING COUNTRIES (MILLIONS OF POUNDS ANNUALLY)

(ALL FIGURES APPROXIMATE)

Country	Millions of pounds
SRI LANKA (CEYLON)	444
INDIA	440
KENYA	104
CHINA	95
INDONESIA	93
TAIWAN	47
BANGLADESH	40
UGANDA	33
ARGENTINA	30
TURKEY	25
JAPAN	4

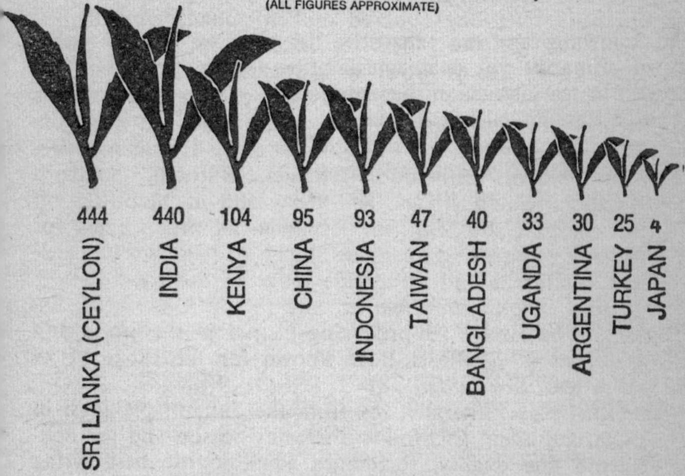

PRINCIPAL TEA IMPORTING COUNTRIES (MILLIONS OF POUNDS ANNUALLY)

(ALL FIGURES APPROXIMATE)

Country	Millions of pounds
UNITED KINGDOM	460
UNITED STATES	170
EGYPT	66
AUSTRALIA	59
CANADA	47
U.S.S.R.	43
IRAQ	42
SOUTH AFRICA	42
IRELAND	27

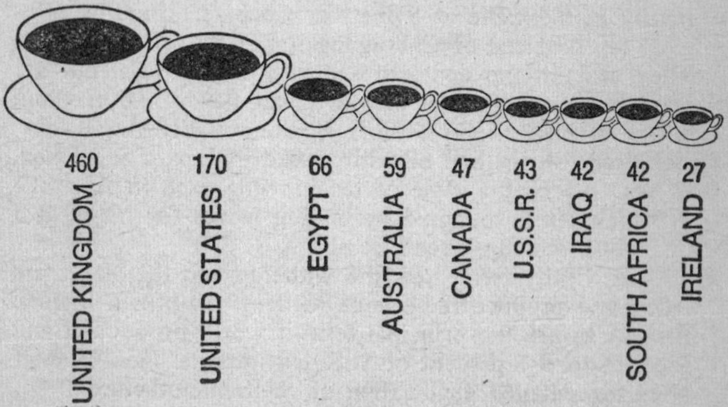

the names of their countries of origin, even though the better teas from some African countries are of excellent quality. The high-grown teas of Kenya resemble good Ceylons and are often used, along with other African teas, in major blends. The tea industry in Africa is relatively new, quite modern, and is certain to be of greater importance in the future. Almost all African production is black tea. Kenya, where tea is grown at altitudes of 6,000 feet, has the highest production of any African country, currently over one hundred million pounds annually.

Malawi has the oldest tea industry in Africa, dating from 1887. Tea is grown at altitudes to 4,000 feet, and some forty-five million pounds are exported. Uganda is second only to Japan in the yields obtained from its plantings—almost 1,350 pounds per acre. Tanzania, Zaire, Mozambique, Cameroon, Rwanda, Burundi, Southern Rhodesia, South Africa, and the island of Mauritius off the coast of the Malagasy Republic, all produce tea for export in increasing quantities, much of it grown in excellent conditions and of a wide range of quality.

Argentina See *South America.*

Assam The largest tea-producing district in the world and a district in northeast India known for the range of its black teas. See *India.*

Autumnal teas Literally, tea from the autumn pickings; in India, autumnal teas follow the rainy season and are considered fine quality, sometimes equal to the best spring teas, although often on the light side.

Bancha A coarse-leaf Japanese tea. See *Japan.*

Bangladesh Bangladesh has some 100,000 acres of tea under cultivation. Almost all production is black, known primarily in the trade as Sylhets or Cachars (after the principal tea districts) or Chittagongs (after its principal port). They are not the equal of the best Indian teas, but are good blenders, have a smooth clean flavor and medium body. At best, they resemble medium-quality Assams.

Basket-fired A method of curing used in Japan. See *Japan.*

Billy tea A frontier style of tea brewing used in Australia in which tea is prepared by boiling leaves for hours in a tin vessel, or billy, over a campfire.

Black tea Fully fermented and withered tea; the leaves are black and produce red-orange to deep red-brown liquors. Black teas are the principal teas of world production and account for 97 percent of U.S. tea imports. (See Chapter Nine for detailed explanation of their manufacture.)

Ceylon Formerly the name of Sri Lanka. The teas of the country are still known in the trade as Ceylons. See *Sri Lanka*.

China (Note: Many types of tea produced in the People's Republic of China are produced on Taiwan (Formosa) as well. Thus, there are mainland and Formosa examples of various traditional teas, such as Keemun, Gunpowder, oolong, jasmine, Lapsang, and so forth. See *Taiwan*. Tea from China was not available in the United States from 1951 to 1971, when the embargo on trade with the People's Republic was lifted.)

According to legend, tea-drinking originated in China some 4,700 years ago (see Chapter Eight). China dominated the tea market long after the beverage was first introduced to the West in the late sixteenth century. By the 1930s, China's share of the world tea market had dwindled in the face of competition from the vast modern tea-producing districts of India, Sri Lanka, and elsewhere in Asia and was drastically reduced when World War II cut off trade. China today is beginning to regain a share of her former importance as an exporter of tea, and some famous China names are reappearing on retail shelves. China has never ceased to be an important producer of tea, since her domestic consumption is enormous. Up to 1939 China was the largest producer of tea, and today it is grown in half the provinces of the country, presumably by farm communes in the mountainous regions. The provinces of Yunnan, Szechuan, and Kweichow formerly produced tea primarily for local consumption, but have gained in considerable importance in recent years. The People's Republic currently exports about ninety million pounds a year.

China is to tea what France is to wine. The range, quality, and variety of Chinese teas are so vast they have never been properly codified. Traditional divisions and subdivisions listed thousands of teas. Today, however, the traditional terminology is undergoing considerable change as some names are dropped and new ones are added to the list of teas currently produced. In general, the traditional classifications have been simplified, although the number of Chinese teas still runs to hundreds of varieties that are exported in bulk as well as in packages under various proprietary names—Goldfish, Temple of Heaven, and so forth. In brief, there are four main categories of China tea: black, green, oolong, and scented.

China black teas Of all China black teas, the ones most familiar to the West are commonly known as congou teas. Congou means "time and labor," and interestingly enough, has the same two characters as "kung fu." Lest anyone get the impression that a swallow of Chinese congou will take your head off, let me hasten to assure you that congous rank high among the fine teas of the world. The two principal divisions are north China congous and south China congous. The north China congous—those from the provinces of Kiangsu, Anhwei, Hunan, and Hupei—were the traditional English breakfast teas. Of the major varieties of north China congou—Keemuns, Ningchows, Pingsuey blacks, Ichangs, and so on—the Keemun is the most famous. It is often said to be the best black tea produced in China, and has been called the Burgundy of teas because of its superb bouquet. It is, at its best, one of the finest teas in the world. Its aroma is highly distinctive but difficult to describe. Aromatic and penetrating, it is rich and perfumelike without being lush or floral. It is quite complex and subtle, which is perhaps why it is so evocative; one is tempted to speak of the subtle scents of long-unopened jewelry boxes, hints of incense or distant pine smoke—except that the mention of smoke is liable to suggest the direct tarry-smoky quality of a Lapsang Souchong, something no fine Keemun should have (although Ukers does describe other north China congous as having a slightly smoky flavor). The Chinese say that the bouquet of fine Keemun is like the perfume of an orchid (that is, the subtle scent of a Chinese orchid); the less poetic-minded will probably find it reminds them of toast hot from the oven. It is sometimes suggested that the reason Keemun is the classic English breakfast tea is that its fragrance is brought out by the addition of milk. In any event, the thick red liquor from the fine, tightly rolled leaves of this superb tea has a deep, rich, concentrated flavor, and to my taste suggests something of the austerity of Bordeaux rather than the softer qualities of Burgundy. Keemun is the best-keeping of the black teas; fine specimens will keep for years if well-stored, and take on a mellow, winy character. Naturally, all the foregoing applies only to really fine Keemun; middling examples have a scent rather like pigskin and a strong, simple taste. One sometimes sees Gray Keemuns—these are simply given extra han-

dling in manufacture and thus show a more polished leaf, and hence a slightly gray appearance.

The south China congous—especially those from Fukien province—are somewhat lighter in character than north China congous (Ukers calls them the clarets of China teas). In this category fall the Pan Yongs, Paklums, and Chingwos, which vary from full, colory blenders to brisk, fragrant, very fine teas with bright red liquors. Souchong is a name given to large-leaf south China congous (elsewhere Souchong is also a term for a specific leaf size in several tea-grading systems). The most famous of them is Lapsang Souchong. This Fukien-province tea is a rich, thick, red brew with a very distinct tarry scent and flavor imparted to it by purposely smoking the leaf while drying it. Its quality varies, and its potent aroma and tarry, "kippery" flavor can be either light (in which case it is quite intriguing) or heavy (in which case it can be overpowering). To some palates it is an acquired taste.

The list of black teas currently exported include those from Kweichow, Szechuan, Kwangtung, and Yunnan. The quality range here again is considerable. Yunnan black tea is perhaps the most individual in character and most commonly seen of this group. Grown mainly at high altitudes, it has strength, briskness, and character, and a full, attractive aroma. Do not confuse Yunnan black with the Pu-Erh teas of Yunnan, which have a powerful, unpleasant musty smell. These teas are prepared by a type of pickling process and are held in great esteem (at least in the East) as digestive remedies.

China green teas Chinese green teas come primarily from the provinces of Fukien, Chekiang, Kwangtung, Kwangsi, Yunnan, and Anhwei. China greens are known by their leaf styles as well as by district names. These styles are similar to the grading system of leaf sizes used in black-tea manufacture in that they describe the shape and size of the dry leaf after processing. By themselves, such descriptions are not a guide to cup quality. The principal ones today are Young Hyson, Hyson, Chunmee, Sowmee, and Gunpowder. Young Hyson greens are prepared from young leaves and made into a long, thin, twisted style. Hyson was originally associated with a kind of tea, but now indicates older leaves and a coarse style of preparation. Sowmee is associated with a small, twisted type similar to Young Hyson, but appears to be used for certain broken grades as well, while Chunmee is a "hard," twisted style. Gun-

powder indicates that the leaves have been rolled into tight little pellets. Known as "pearl tea" to the Chinese, Gunpowder is made from small- to medium-sized leaves that are rolled into various sizes, from pinhead (very small) to pea leaf (large). Gunpowder is one leaf-style description that has an indirect bearing on quality. Most green teas do not keep as well as black teas, and stale quickly. But small-sized Gunpowder, due to the tight roll of the pellets, keeps the best of all teas, black or green.

Chinese greens at their best are among the finest greens produced. Clear and rich, they often have substantial body and pungency that belie their clear pale liquors. The aroma can be sweet and floral, or like spring meadows or cool forests—after all, green teas are only steamed before drying, and it is not surprising that the best China greens possess an ethereal but appetizing vegetative fragrance. Poor greens can be smoky, pungent to the point of bitterness, raw, and even a trace metallic in flavor. Probably the most famous China green tea is Lung Ching ("Dragon Well"), a Hangchow tea from the province of Chekiang. At its best, its coarse, flat leaf yields an exceptionally light, clear liquor with a complex, expansive aroma that rises off the cup, at once both distantly sweet and faintly herbaceous, and a delicate, yet lingering, haunting flavor. It is tea at its most refined, an ethereal brew for contemplation, and one of the world's great teas. Unfortunately, it is rare and expensive, and it is not easy to find a fresh specimen. Other superb Chinese greens include Pi Lo Chun ("Green Couch Spring") and Maojian from Kweichow.

China oolong tea Oolong is taken from the Chinese *wu-lung*—"black dragon." As a partially fermented tea, it partakes of some of the qualities of both black and green teas. Due to its method of manufacture, a weaker but drinkable second pot can sometimes be made from the infused leaves left from the first pot. Most China oolongs come from Fukien province, and vary widely in character and quality. The lower-quality oolongs have stalky, grassy scents and flavors and thin liquor. At their best, they are beautiful teas, with full, fruity-sweet aromas and flavors to match. The best-known China oolong is Ti Kwan Yin (also spelled Teh Kuan Yin; "Iron Goddess of Mercy"), a Fukien "cliff tea." Unfortunately, the name is used loosely today by tea merchants. A genuine example has a full, exquisite aroma and a long, rich taste. Ming Xiang is another fine oolong type sometimes seen.

China scented teas "Only common teas require scenting" is a Chinese adage, but the popularity of teas that have the added fragrance of flower blossoms is long established in the history of tea. Given good-quality tea and scenting material, the result can be quite attractive. See *Scented tea* for a more detailed description of the method and types.

Other China teas In her long history, China has produced other categories of tea: compressed tea (pressed into bricks or tablets from dust grades for the overland trade), faggot tea (tea wrapped in two-inch bundles), white tea (a flavorless tea produced from tips only), and other oddities. Few are commonly seen, and none are of great interest for the tea lover.

Congou Originally a Chinese term for all hand-fired, i.e., traditional method Chinese black teas. Now a very broad, inprecise term. See *China.*

Darjeeling Tea district in northeast India; source of one of the finest Indian teas. See *India.*

Dimbula Tea district in Sri Lanka. See *Sri Lanka.*

Earl Grey See *flavored teas.*

English breakfast teas These are traditionally Keemuns (see China black teas under *China*). The term was broadened in the United States to include China congou blends; today many teas labeled "English Breakfast" are often India-Ceylon blends of varying quality, as are "Irish Breakfast" blends.

Estate A tea plantation. In northeast India tea estates are called tea gardens.

Flavored teas Since the beginnings of tea in China, various flavorings and fragrances have been added to teas to enhance their scent and flavor. Cinnamon, orange rind, cardamom, oil of bergamot (an oil from the rind of the fruit of *Citrus bergamia*), and dozens of other ingredients and spices have been used to add interest to tea, often to teas that would be of little interest if nothing were added to them. Nonetheless, certain flavorings are widely popular, so that flavored teas are produced in a number of countries. In particular Earl Grey tea, which uses oil of bergamot, is a black-tea blend put out by a number of tea packers. It is not drunk by the Chinese, in spite of the fact it is said to derive from a recipe given to an envoy of Earl Grey, the British prime minister at the time, by a Chinese mandarin in 1830. Depending on the quality of the tea blend and the scent used, the character varies from something that smells like cheap perfumed soap to a heady,

attractive sachet scent. While the exotic quality of flavored teas is welcome on occasion, many find them too cloying for everyday use. The same can be said of scented teas, which are a special type of Chinese tea. See *Scented teas.*

Formosa See *Taiwan.*

Formosa oolong See *Oolong* and *Taiwan.*

Grades Tea grades are leaf sizes or styles of preparation of the dry leaf and have no direct bearing on cup quality. (See Chapter Nine for a detailed discussion.) See *orange pekoe.*

Green tea Tea that has been neither fermented nor withered. Instead, the leaves are simply sterilized in steam, hot air, or hot pans to prevent fermentation. The leaves are green in color and produce light, pale, greenish-yellow liquors, often with considerable aroma, body, and flavor. Green teas are produced in *China, Taiwan,* and *Japan,* and to a lesser extent elsewhere.

Gunpowder A style of green tea in which each leaf has been rolled into a pellet. See China green teas under *China.*

Gyokuro In Japanese, "pearl dew"; a very fine green tea made from shaded bushes in the Uji district. See *Japan.*

Hyson See *young hyson.*

India More tea is produced in India than in any other country in the world: almost a billion pounds a year, almost all of it black tea, from over 880,000 acres. India exports slightly less tea than *Sri Lanka*—about 440 million pounds currently—because her total domestic consumption has surpassed that of the United Kingdom.

Assam district Although the tea plant grows wild in the Assam district of northeast India, it was not until the British initiated large-scale plantings of tea in the nineteenth century that Indian production of tea began in earnest. Today it is one of the world's most modern tea industries. Tea is grown in the northeast, northwest, and south of India, of which the northeast districts are the most important, particularly that of Assam and its subdivisions. This is not only the largest single tea-producing area in the world, but is known for the range and quality of its teas. The finest Assams are superb drinking, proof that not every fine tea must be grown at high elevations. Assams are known as rich, heavy, malty, very pungent teas, ranging from orange-red to deep red in color, and form the backbone of many of the world's major blends. The best have a full, savory nose and flavor, along with

strength and thickness, and make a very sturdy, satisfying cup, almost bouillonlike in depth of character. Less outstanding Assams are merely hearty or pungent to the point of hardness. The manufactured leaf varies from black to brownish, and is sometimes tippy.

Darjeeling district North and west from Assam is the Darjeeling district, source of one of the finest teas in the world. Grown in the foothills of the Himalayas at elevations from 1,000 to 6,000 feet, the finest black tea from this area is unique in character, with an exquisite bouquet and flavor that make it the most prized of Indian teas. Red-gold in the cup, fine Darjeelings have an aroma that is best described as a complex fragrance that reaches right out of the cup. It has been described as nutty; others find it reminds them of black currants; most often it has been described as similar to the fragrance of muscat grapes. Superb examples have in addition an almost winelike character to the taste, because of their deep, subtle, lingering flavor. Full-bodied, but delicate; clear, brisk, and penetrating; clean yet rich and memorable, a first-rate Darjeeling is an incomparable tea. It should be stressed that not every Darjeeling meets this description. Only the best pluckings—usually June and October but most particularly the second flush of spring—from the best gardens possess true Darjeeling character. Lesser Darjeelings are of considerably less interest, though they can make a satisfying cup. The best command high prices, keep well if properly stored, and, it should be noted, are not necessarily tippy in appearance.

South India teas South India teas are produced all year round from hill-slope estates in Madras, Kerala, and Mysore. Tea-growing conditions are much closer to those of *Sri Lanka*, so that in cup quality South India teas resemble Ceylons. The tea from the Nilgiris, in particular, is noted for fine, high-grown flavor.

Other tea-producing districts in India include the Terai and Dooars in the northeast, producing colory teas for blending, and the districts of Kangra and Mandi in the northwest, which produce mostly green tea of fair quality.

Indian teas are graded according to leaf size into Broken Orange Pekoe, Broken Pekoe, Orange Pekoe, Pekoe Souchong, Souchong, Fannings, and Dust (see Chapter Nine for an explanation of these). As with other leaf-grading systems, such categories are not a guide to cup quality.

Indonesia, Malaysia, and Southeast Asia Indonesia exports

about ninety-five million pounds of black tea per year from some 165,000 acres planted to tea. Tea has a long history in Indonesia, having been first planted in Java in 1684. By the nineteenth century the industry was well established, and today the region has regained much of its pre-World War II importance as an exporter of tea. Grown in a variety of conditions, the tea ranges widely in quality; the best high-grown Javas resemble better Ceylons. Most Javas and the similar teas from Sumatra are described as "useful blenders."

Malaysia does not export as much tea as it once did, due to increased domestic consumption. Its climate is best suited for large yields rather than quality.

Southeast Asia produces both green and black teas in the north and south of Vietnam. The recent protracted war has cut production and exports drastically. Production follows traditional Chinese methods, and quality is said to be useful for blending. Some Chinese-style teas are made, including *Jasmine.*

Iran Iran produces over forty million pounds of tea annually, but consumes most of it domestically. Some is exported, principally to the United Kingdom. Tea was introduced to Iran in 1898, and today the country has considerable acreage planted in the north near the Caspian Sea, where rainfall is sufficient for tea cultivation. Iranian tea is often described as similar in quality to U.S.S.R. tea: thin and often lacking in cup qualities, but well-made.

Japan Tea cultivation was first introduced to Japan from China about A.D. 800 (see Chapter Eight). Japan's tea industry today is composed of a great number of small farmers, but its efficiency is extremely high, with yields sometimes reaching 1,500 pounds per acre. There are some 133,000 acres planted to tea, from which over 200 million pounds are harvested annually. Japan exports only four million pounds, however, of which about 80 percent goes to the United States. (Japan, in fact, is a large importer of tea.) Virtually all Japanese tea produced is green tea; less than one percent of the crop is black.

Japan produces some of the finest green teas in the world. Ukers calls Japan greens "the white wines of teas," an apt description, since they vary, as white wines do, from very light and delicate to rich and mouth-filling. The Japanese divide their own teas into a number of categories according to their origin, use, manufacture, and leaf style. Only the most common are covered here. Bancha

is the lowest category of tea, made from the last of the three or four harvests traditional during the season. It is a coarse, plain tea and is primarily for domestic consumption. Sencha is the tea of commerce, the principal type exported. Made from the first and second pickings, it comprises about three-quarters of the total annual harvest. Its quality varies over a wide range. The best are pale, limpid green in the cup, have an exquisitely refined fragrance and a delicate, refreshing flavor. Gyokuro is an especially fine tea made from specially shaded bushes. Comparatively little is made and little is exported. Matcha (or Hikicha) is the ceremonial tea, and almost none, apparently, is exported.

Over half the yearly production comes from the prefecture of Shizuoka, and the city of that name is the center of the Japanese tea industry. The principal subdivisions of Shizuoka teas are Enshu teas and Suruga teas, each of which has further subdivisions. Enshu teas are thought, on the whole, superior to Suruga teas, and are light in color, but rich and full in the cup. Of the other tea districts in the country, the second most important is that surrounding Kyoto, from which the finest teas in Japan come, the Gyokuro teas of *Uji*. Three weeks before plucking, the bushes are covered with straw shades. This practice is said to be responsible for the particular intensity of the Gyokuro (or "pearl dew") teas and slightly increases the caffeine content while lowering the tannin. Uji Gyokuro produces a gold-green liquor in the cup, a full, attractively vegetative complex scent, and a rich, mouth-filling taste with a depth of flavor that will surprise those who imagine that a pale tea must be weak and flavorless. The Matcha, or ceremonial tea, is always powdered after drying and is prepared by whipping the powder into hot water with a whisk (see Chapter Eight). The resulting frothy beverage is unique but no improvement over Gyokuro, which is prepared in a rolled-leaf form, although Matcha is also made from shaded bushes.

Japanese teas are also categorized by leaf size and methods of preparation. Both hand and machine processes are used to steam the leaf, after which it is cooled and rolled. Pan-fired teas are rolled and rubbed in hot iron pans, and consequently the light-green medium-sized leaf has something of a polished appearance. Basket-fired teas are made from long young leaves, well-twisted, so that the appearance suggests pine needles or "spider's legs." Natural-leaf

teas are prepared in a similar way to pan-fired or basket-fired teas but are not rubbed. (Virtually all Sencha is natural-leaf tea. Guri teas are curly leafed, and there are further gradings as well. These differing methods of preparation affect the appearance only, not the taste.

Jasmine Tea scented with jasmine blossoms. See *Scented tea.*

Java See *Indonesia.*

Keemun One of the finest and best-known China black teas. See *China.*

Lapsang Souchong A China black tea with a distinct smoky-tarry scent and flavor. See *China.*

Lung Ching One of the finest China green teas. See *China.*

Malaysia See *Indonesia, Malaysia,* and *Southeast Asia.*

Nuwara Eliya Tea-producing district of *Sri Lanka.*

Oolong Partially fermented and partially withered tea. The leaves are greenish-brown and produce an amber-colored brew. Oolongs are produced in *China* and *Taiwan.*

Orange pekoe (pronounced peck-o) A grade or size of leaf used in black-tea manufacture. It is not a kind of tea nor is it any indication of quality (see Chapter Nine).

Pan-fired A method of curing used principally in *Japan.*

Pouchong Pouchong teas are the type used as the base of scented teas (see *Scented teas*). Only slightly fermented in processing, they are closer to greens than oolongs; unscented pouchongs can be extraordinarily fine in quality. See *Taiwan.*

Proprietary These are tea blends that carry trade names given to them by the firms that developed the blends. In that sense, all the major brands are proprietary blends. In addition, many tea firms have special blends that they market under various names. Examples are Dowager (Fortnum & Mason), Lady Londonderry (Jackson's of Piccadilly), Constant Comment (Bigelow), Prince of Wales (Twinings), and so forth. Of course, character and quality vary considerably.

Russian caravan tea These are blends of China and Indian teas (often Darjeelings) associated with the Russian market in days past. They are sometimes sold as Russian-style teas by various firms, and quality varies considerably. These should not be confused with Russian tea that is grown in the U.S.S.R.

Scented tea Scented teas are certain China teas given a particular fragrance by the addition of traditional "scenting material" such as flower blossoms: rose, laurel, lotus, ly-

chee, and so on. Jasmine blossoms, however, are considered to have the fragrance that harmonizes best with tea and are often added to pouchong teas (see *Pouchong*) to give them an ethereal floral scent. Traditionally, layers of the blossoms were strewn between layers of tea in a chest so that the delicate scent soon permeated the whole. These days, hot air is passed through the petals to scent the tea so that the petals can be used more than once. Exhausted blossoms are used to decorate the teas. Produced in both China and Taiwan, jasmines at their best yield a cup with all the concentrated, heady bouquet of a garden in bloom. Inferior jasmines may not be scented with jasmine, but with roughly similar *chu-lan* blossoms. See *China* and *Flavored tea.*

Sencha The ordinary export teas of *Japan.* These cover a wide range of quality.

Seychelles A small amount of full, rich, flavorsome black tea from this Indian Ocean island off Africa is packed in London.

South America South America is identified so strongly in the public mind with the production of coffee that it comes as a surprise to learn that a considerable amount of tea is produced as well, not only for domestic consumption but export. Again, to my knowledge, none appears on retail shelves under the name of the country of origin. Argentina has the largest acreage of tea under cultivation, well over 100,000 acres. Much of it is grown at the southern limit of tea-growing conditions, and its best teas are considered good quality. They are used widely in blends, especially during seasons when comparable quality teas from northern-hemisphere lands are in short supply. Peru also exports high-quality tea and has considerable plantings in excellent locations, some at 5,000 feet altitude. Brazil has most of its plantings in the Santos district and exports a good deal of the tea it produces. Ecuador is growing in importance as an exporter, and there are small plantings in Chile, Colombia, and Bolivia. As expected, most of South American tea is black, though Ecuador and Brazil produce green tea as well.

Southeast Asia See *Indonesia, Malaysia,* and *Southeast Asia.*

Sri Lanka Sri Lanka, formerly Ceylon, is the largest exporter of tea in the world, shipping some 444 million pounds annually from her acreage of nearly 600,000 acres of tea. Her principal customers are the United Kingdom and the United States. Until 1869, coffee was the chief

crop of the island, but after a blight destroyed the coffee industry, planting was begun again with tea, which now accounts for 60 percent of the country's export earnings. The tea districts of the island are located in the central mountains and the foothills of the west and southwest. Some 120,000 acres of tea are grown above 4,000 feet, and the tea from such altitudes is considered superior to low-grown tea.

There are several thousand large estates and many thousands of small holdings, virtually all devoted to the production of black tea. Much of Sri Lanka's tea is sold at auction, where it commands good prices. The tea industry is modern, well-organized, and the better teas are well-made: black, often tippy, and graded by leaf size into Broken Orange Pekoe, Broken Pekoe, Orange Pekoe, Fannings, and Dust. These are sometimes qualified by the term "flowery," indicating a higher percentage of tip. Such gradings have nothing to do with quality, which is in fact closely related to the altitude at which the tea is grown. Low-grown tea (below 2,000 feet) is strong, but undistinguished. Medium-grown tea (that from 2,000 to 4,000 feet) shows more character, but is still rather plain. High-grown tea (above 4,000 feet) has the character one associates with good to fine Ceylons (as the teas are still known in the trade): strong and full but delicately flavored. Tea is grown as high as 7,000 feet, and the best examples are among the finest teas in the world, with a full, flowery, even sweetish aroma sometimes reminiscent of honeysuckle, and a brisk, refreshing, direct flavor.

Ceylons are used widely in major blends and fine Ceylons often appear as Ceylon blends. On occasion, one sees district names: Uva, Dimbula, Nuwara Eliya, and so forth. Dimbula is said to be perhaps the best district, Nuwara Eliya is noted for its flavory teas, and so on, but relatively little emphasis is put on district names in the trade, since elevations can vary as much as 3,000 feet within a given district. Much more emphasis is placed on estates known for the high quality of their teas, and the best Ceylons are typically made up of teas from several fine estates, the choice depending on the season and harvest. While tea is produced throughout the year, the finest Ceylons are produced in January and February and again in July, August, and September. The best estate teas of the early season are not usually the best teas of the later production, due to the

monsoon rains falling on different sides of the mountain ranges at different times of the year.

In sum, the best teas of Sri Lanka are high-grown but not necessarily single-district teas. One should remember too that gradings such as Flowery Orange Pekoe are descriptions of the appearance of the leaf and have nothing to do with cup quality.

Taiwan The tea industry on the island of Taiwan (or Formosa, as it is also known) was developed comparatively late in Chinese history—in the early part of the nineteenth century. By the end of that century tea propagation and manufacture—particularly that of oolong—had begun on a commercial scale, developed primarily by Fukien tea merchants. Under the Japanese occupation of the island from 1895 to the end of World War II, the tea industry was considerably expanded. Some fifty million pounds of tea are currently exported from plantings of about 85,000 acres, all clustered in the northern end of the island. Black, oolong, and green teas are made and exported, and since the end of World War II many traditional types of Chinese teas—though not all—have been successfully imitated and produced in quantity on the island. The result is that Chinese nomenclature is also used for Taiwan teas.

The consensus in the tea trade seems to be that many mainland teas are not necessarily better than the teas that have been developed on Taiwan in direct imitation. The green teas vary widely, from rather poor examples that smell somewhat seaweedy and occasionally smoky due to careless preparation and have a rather harsh, metallic tang to the taste, to very fine, flavorsome, pungent teas. Formosa greens are seen in Gunpowder, Chunmee, Sowmee, and other traditional green-leaf styles (see China green teas under *China* for a detailed description). Taiwan produces Keemuns, Lapsang Souchongs, and other black teas as well as scented types such as jasmine, and again the range is wide. Some examples are superb; some undistinguished.

The one tea of Taiwan that is often cited as superior to its mainland original is oolong. As with the mainland oolongs, quality varies considerably. But at their best, Formosa oolongs (as they are usually known) reach an unmatched peak of quality. Their full fruity-sweet aroma and piquant flavor is often described as peachlike, balanced by a refreshing, faintly herbaceous fragrance and taste. In poor oolongs this nuance is liable to be a distinct stalky-

weedy character, and the fruity quality may be nowhere in evidence. At once both light yet rich, lush yet refreshing, charming yet elegant, it is no surprise that first-rate Formosa oolongs are called the champagnes of teas. Their quality is another proof that not every fine tea must be grown at high elevations, since most of them are grown several hundred feet above sea level. The best are considered to come from a single picking in June or July (depending on weather). The greenish-brown leaf produces an amber liquor, often very pale in especially fine examples. It is also possible to make a drinkable but lighter second pot from the same leaves with the better oolongs, and the more delicate liquors of the second or third pots are often preferred by the Chinese.

Another superb tea from Taiwan is pouchong (see description under *Pouchong*). The best examples produce an exceptionally pale green liquor and an expansive bloom of an aroma, as complex and attractive as an herb garden after a summer shower, and a delicious, clear, exquisite taste to match.

Turkey The Turkish tea industry did not begin until after 1939, but the country now has some 100,000 acres of tea under cultivation and produces some ninety million pounds of tea a year. Turkish tea is similar to Russian and Iranian tea: rather light and thin in the cup and lacking real quality, but it can be quite satisfying when enlivened with a slice of lemon. Turkey also exports green tea.

Uji One of the finest tea districts of Japan. See *Japan*.

U.S.S.R. Tea has always been a popular beverage among the Russian people since its introduction in the eighteenth century, but attempts to cultivate it were not made until 1892, when plants were set out near the Black Sea in the Caucasus. In spite of the extreme northern latitude at which the tea is grown—snow is not uncommon—the climate is not completely inhospitable to the tea plant, and today a vast acreage is planted to tea, mostly in the Republic of Georgia. Most of the 136 million pounds of tea produced each year from about 185,000 acres goes to supplement the considerable imports that are required to meet the domestic demand for tea, but some Soviet tea is exported, principally to eastern Europe. The liquor is typically light-colored, the body is on the thin side, and the flavor lacks depth, strength, and character. It is best drunk Russian style—that is, plain with a slice of lemon, which adds a welcome sharpness to the taste.

Uva Tea district in *Sri Lanka.*

Young hyson A leaf size used in grading China green teas. See *China.*

Yunnan Newly developed tea-producing district of *China.*

CHAPTER TWELVE

How to Buy Tea

Tea can be bought knowledgeably or blindly; as in buying anything, you're always better off knowing something about the intended purchase so that getting your money's worth isn't merely a hit-or-miss proposition. Tea is no exception to the general rule, "You get what you pay for," but the catch is that the rule is only general. There are plenty of specific instances in which you won't get better tea by paying more, and may get tea of poorer quality. The guidelines in this chapter are to help you ensure that if you're paying for quality, you'll get quality.

It's nice to know, however, that in the United States there are certain minimum standards all imported tea must meet. Before going into the subject of price versus value and how to shop for it, let's take a look at the role played in this country by the quality standards for tea set by the U.S. Board of Tea Experts and enforced by the U.S. Tea Examiner.

The Tea Act and Tea Labeling

In the earliest days of the tea trade, stretching tea with used leaves, tree bark, or other vegetation was common. Unscrupulous adulteration of tea continued to plague the trade at all levels until the late nineteenth century, when tea-importing countries passed legislation to curb the practice. The Food and Drugs Act of 1875 in Britain made importation of impure tea a criminal offense and subjected such teas to seizure. In the United States, the Tea Importation Act of 1897 extended the provisions of an 1883 law allowing an importer to refuse to accept shipments of worthless tea. The new act introduced the notion of setting minimum quality standards for each type of tea imported each year. While the law was designed to benefit importers, it had the happy result of

protecting the consumer and in that sense was an example of one of the earliest American consumer-protection efforts.

Today, bolstered by further legislation, the Food and Drug Administration of the U.S. government essentially passes on the purity and the quality of all the tea brought into the country. Standards are set in the spring each year by the Board of Tea Experts, composed of six members appointed from among tea importers, packers, and brokers by the commissioner of Food and Drugs and the FDA supervisory tea examiner. From various tea samples submitted by the trade, the board selects one tea to represent each major type imported into the country. The character and qualities of these teas will come to represent the minimum standards any tea brought into this country must meet. In years past, up to eighteen different standard teas were needed to cover the wide range of types imported, but the emphasis on a few major types has today reduced the standards to seven: Formosa oolong, black tea (except China, Formosa, and Japanese black); China, Formosa, and Japanese black; Canton type (traditional scented types like jasmine); green tea (all types); scented black (such as Earl Grey); and spiced (flavored teas).

Duplicate samples are packed and supplied to the board members and are available to the trade as guides to the quality of teas that may be brought in. These standards are used by the U.S. Supervisory Tea Examiner in New York and the two additional tea examiners in the port cities of San Francisco and Boston as the standards for purity and quality that every imported tea must meet, including teas blended and packed in Europe. The provisions of the Tea Importation Act require that imported tea be warehoused under bond against illegal disposition until passed by the FDA examiner for that port. (The sole exceptions to this rule are the tea samples sent from abroad to importers or teas brought into this country in small amounts by those returning from abroad, or those ordered by mail from abroad by individuals for personal use.)

In passing on teas, the examiner usually takes a sample from each invoice, or chop (lot), for cup-sampling purposes, and gives the dry and infused leaf and the liquor as close a look as any tea buyer. He or she watches particularly for excessive amounts of woody stems, decayed leaves, deceptive imitation of other teas, scenting ingredients other than those permitted (as in the traditional types such as jasmine), the presence of paste, gum, paraffin, artificial coloring, and ma-

terials that may be dusted on the leaves to improve appearance, such as talc, gypsum, barium sulfate, kaolin, and clay. The examiner is concerned with seeing not only that the tea is free of illegal additives, contaminants, or adulterants, but that it equals or surpasses the appropriate standard tea in purity, quality, and fitness for consumption.

The U.S. examiners reject, on the average, about 0.5 percent of the over 170 million pounds of tea currently imported each year. The figure is low in part because of the general knowledge in the international tea trade that tea brought into the United States is carefully examined and because it is costly to have tea rejected: such teas must be destroyed or reexported. An importer may appeal the FDA examiner's rejection to the U.S. Board of Tea Appeals, again composed of government officials and industry members, which will compare the tea in question with the standard a second time. The examiner's findings are rarely overturned, so that rejections are not automatically contested.

In 1971 the Nixon administration announced that as an economy measure the government would no longer engage in tea-tasting. The tea industry was quick to explain to the public that the tea-tasting was no frivolous waste of the taxpayers' money but a valuable consumer-protection activity, and quite inexpensive as far as government expenditure usually goes, about $150,000 a year. The tea industry itself is levied an import tax (about 3.5 cents per hundred pounds) as an inspection fee, which goes to pay for most of the government's expense in passing on teas.

The Tea Importation Act does not ensure that every tea for sale in the United States is a high-quality tea—only that the inspection process makes it unlikely that any adulterated, defective, or completely worthless tea escapes detection. A tea lover interested in seeking out quality tea needs to look more critically at the tea he or she buys, and one of the first things to look at is the label.

These days consumers are rightfully interested in the authenticity of labeling; they should pay attention to the wording on tea tins and shop bins. Tea packed in tins—the sort put out by large packers as lines of teas—should, according to broad provisions of the Food, Drug, and Cosmetic Act, which governs such matters, carry a name of origin only if the majority (51 percent) of the tea contained in it is in fact from the district or country named. More precisely, a tea simply labeled "Darjeeling" should be 100-percent Darjeeling; tea labeled "Darjeeling blend" or "Darjeeling type"

ought to be at least 51-percent Darjeeling; and, in any event, a tea labeled with a name of origin should exhibit something like the character and quality a customer reasonably associates with the name. (I say "should" and "ought" because some producers, at least, seem to think labeling practices are not as closely observed as they should be.) So far, I have not encountered or heard of tea being mislabeled widely on the retail level (as is all too common with exotic coffee beans). At worst, some teas are misrepresented as being fancier quality than they are. The high order of expertise possible in tea-tasting allows considerable precision in identifying teas blind, and this alone will continue to keep creative relabeling of bulk teas on the retail level to a minimum. Of course, there is nothing to keep an unscrupulous merchant from stretching his teas with cheaper teas, except knowledgeable customers who insist on getting their money's worth. Until fine tea achieves something like the popularity of fine coffee, however, there is little worry that customers will be getting inauthentic teas on the retail level. Now, a tea lover's biggest problem is finding fine tea and making sure it isn't stale.

Price Versus Quality

There are three notions that the American buyer of fine tea should jettison before attempting to shop for tea. The first notion is a belief that English tea is necessarily better than tea packed in the United States. Despite the continuing importance of the British market to the international tea trade, London is no longer the center of world tea that it once was. This country is second only to Britain in total consumption among tea-importing nations. American importers, therefore, operate directly in the world auctions and tea-producing centers, just as the British do, and there is no lack of tea-tasting expertise on this side of the ocean. There are firms in the United States just as there are in Britain that specialize in importing fine teas, both in bulk for specialty shops and outlets and for packing, in many cases, under their own names. (The appendix mentions a few under Shopping for Fine Tea and Coffee by Mail).

Teas packed in England (and other foreign-packed teas) cannot effectively compete with U.S. teas in terms of the quality for the price—all things being equal. Although there

is no duty imposed on tea itself (whether it is brought in directly from a producing country or from a country like Britain, which reexports a good deal of the tea it imports), there is a 10-percent duty imposed on the individual containers in which tea is packed. And since the tea is shipped twice—once to the foreign packer and then to the United States—freight costs are higher than for the American importer bringing in tea directly in bulk and packing it in the United States. Don't be impressed with tins of tea that say "imported from England." Remember that *all* tea brought into the United States is imported tea, because none is grown here, just as all tea brought into the United Kingdom is also imported.

Undoubtedly for many Americans there is a certain cachet attached to drinking English tea, in the same way wine lovers are attracted to French wine. English tea seems to some the obvious choice for fine tea. Certainly some of the tea packed by British firms is indeed of very high quality, but much is certainly not worth the price asked for it—at least by the time it gets to these shores.

The second notion a prospective buyer should abandon is the idea that finding many varieties of fine tea in tea bags is easy, or that purchasing any tea in that form is economical. Yes, one can find some fine teas packed in bags, but because tea tends to pick up the smell of the packaging and can quickly go stale in bags, very few are packed this way, certainly nothing like the variety of teas available in loose form. There are really no advantages in convenience to tea bags that are not outweighed by their disadvantages (see Chapter Thirteen for fuller discussion). Add to this the fact that such packaging is far more expensive than packing the tea loose (not to mention a 17.5-percent duty on foreign tea bags!) and there is little reason to look for tea packed in bags.

Third, many people attracted to tea as well as longtime tea lovers cannot seem to rid themselves of the idea that drinking "expensive" tea is an enormous luxury. As I pointed out in the introduction to this book, fine coffee and tea are the most inexpensive gourmet items available. At their cheapest, both coffee and tea—but particularly tea—costs but a few cents a cup. The very finest coffees and teas cost twice this tiny figure, or about a nickel a cup. It is one thing to suggest to a wine lover that he or she could get much better wine for twice the price, and quite a different matter to suggest to the tea lover that he would get a lot more out of his teacup

if he doubled his tea budget. Good wine is at least several dollars a bottle and finer wine quite expensive. Even if a wine lover is well aware of the finer taste experiences to be found in more expensive wine, he or she may well not be able to afford such expenditures. It is difficult to believe that tea drinkers who can consider drinking better tea in the first place would really find their budgets crippled by spending twice as much on tea. Tea is probably the lowest cost-per-serving item on anyone's menu, yet a good many people who think nothing of spending dollars on a few bites of cheese or steak or a few gulps of wine, consider ten or fifteen dollars a pound for tea an extravagant expenditure, something on the order of consuming caviar by the scoop.

There seem to be two reasons for this. Consumers are used to regarding tea, like coffee, as extraordinarily cheap items on the grocery bill. The idea that they might be paying two to five times the price of supermarket tea seems somehow like conspicuous consumption. Second, even tea lovers, who ought to know better, seem mezmerized by the price per pound, when they ought to be thinking of the price per serving. One pound of tea yields *two hundred* cups of tea. A bottle of wine, by contrast, yields six glasses. That means a six-dollar bottle of wine is one dollar a serving. But even a tea priced at twelve dollars a pound would only be *six cents* a serving! What's more, a dollar a glassful is not much to pay these days for fine wine, and many of the world's superb wines cost two to three times that—or more. But for five or six cents a serving, one can expect the world's finest teas, excepting a few rareties that might cost as much as a *dime* a cup.

Whereas on the one hand I think readers shouldn't fall prey to false notions of economy when it comes to fine tea, I certainly do not advocate rushing out to buy the most expensive tea available. There are plenty of overpriced teas for the quality, from cheap to expensive. Although one shouldn't be misled into thinking that ten dollars a pound for two hundred servings is a lot to pay for really fine tea, one should never pay more per pound for tea than what it's worth. In this regard tea lovers who compare teas directly and don't allow themselves to be swayed by image, advertising, and what everyone else drinks are at a great advantage. They can focus their preferences in an objective fashion, discover which teas are more reputation than cup quality, and which are sleepers and offer a great deal of quality for little money.

Buying and Storing Tea

On Advice

The renewed interest of Americans in fine teas has encouraged many retail outlets to devote shelf space to one or two lines of tinned teas, and sometimes to add jars or bins of loose teas. Specialty stores usually carry several lines of teas put out by large tea blenders and packers in addition to their chests of bulk tea. This may look like a bewildering variety of teas to the neophyte, who, despite the enticing smells, may have little idea what to choose.

Unfortunately, very few of the merchants selling tea are knowledgeable about the subject, and the vast majority know as little as the average customer. They are, therefore, in no position to give sound advice or even guide prospective tea lovers to teas they might enjoy. In a specialty shop stocking a variety of gourmet foods, detailed knowledge of tea is too much to ask; unfortunately, even many merchants who specialize in coffee and tea are not particularly knowledgeable about them. In many cases tea has been added as an afterthought to the coffee. There are exceptions, but it is important for the would-be tea enthusiast to recognize that these days retailers are more enthused about the growing interest in fine tea than they are knowledgeable about the commodities they sell. Besides, helpful as it would be to find a source of sound advice, if you don't know anything about tea it is impossible to judge how sound it is. In short, there is no substitute for knowing something about tea yourself.

On Selection

In most outlets the buyer of tea will be making his selection from lines of tinned teas rather than from loose tea in bulk. It is far less trouble for a retailer to carry a line of teas than to obtain chests of teas in bulk from importers. Even those merchants who want to carry fine teas in bulk find it difficult to obtain small but consistent shipments of better teas.

Because of the complex nature of the tea trade, direct importing is out of the question for a retail shop. Instead, fine tea must be obtained from direct importers or from them through buyers in the world's tea centers who are willing to add a few chests of the desired tea to the volume ship-

ments that make up the vast majority of the trade. The majority of retail merchants who sell loose tea in bins rarely cup-sample their wares or are competent to do so; instead, they rely on the judgment of the importer to supply tea of the desired quality at a desired price. The quality and consistency of the tea in a given outlet often depends as much on the retailer's supplier as it does on the retailer.

On Storage, Staleness, and Spoilage

Curiously enough, loose tea in bulk does not dry out and become stale as quickly as tea in tins, because in a chest of tea the surface area of the leaves exposed to the air is small compared with the volume of tea—and it is the exposure to air that causes staleness. In tins, particularly small tins, the opposite is true, and many teas are past their peak of flavor after a year on the shelf. The fact that most of the teas so packed are already a year or two old by the time they reach the retail level simply aggravates the problem. A six month's difference in age is noticeable in many, though not all, teas.

Even though a stale tea is by no means undrinkable, it will have faded substantially in both flavor and aroma, and if old enough, have a flat, dull taste. Anyone who doubts this should try the following experiment: set out an ounce of good tea on a saucer, keep the rest tightly capped in its tin. Several weeks later make a cup each from the exposed and the unexposed tea and compare them. The faded quality of the former should be apparent even to the neophyte.

Much, of course, depends on the type of packed tea. Fine Keemuns and Darjeelings are particularly noted for their keeping qualities. Certain Keemuns may keep their character for years. Green teas (with the exception of Gunpowder greens) lose their quality relatively rapidly and are best appreciated within a year after harvest, a state of freshness in which few fine greens reach retailer's shelves. Small-sized Gunpowder greens, however, due to the pelletlike configuration of their tight rolling, are the longest-lived of teas, green or black. Oolongs do not stale as quickly as most greens, but they do not keep as well as blacks. Then, too, top-quality teas fall off in quality the quickest; they have more to lose.

Under ideal conditions teas last at least a year if tinned and up to two years in unopened tins. It is unwise to purchase more tea than you can use within six months or a year, because there is no practical way to extend this life-

span in storage. If you buy bulk loose tea, you'll get it in a paper bag, in which case you'll need an airtight container to put it in at home to retard staling. Some merchants will tin a half-pound of tea for a small extra charge, a worthwhile investment if you don't have suitable tins at home. Tins, by the way, are superior to jars for keeping tea because prolonged exposure to light seems to have a deteriorating effect on quality.

Tea has considerable hydroscopic qualities and quickly picks up moisture and taints. As moisture is second only to air in its staling effect on tea, keep tea in a cool, dry place; don't refrigerate it because moisture condensation may result from temperature changes when you take the tea in and out of the refrigerator. Always keep your teas tightly tinned and away from the spice rack, the onion bin, the kitchen stove, cooking odors, and mothballs. Teas can even pick up the odor of other teas. Lapsang Souchong will eventually lend its smoky smell to other teas packed with it if the teas are wrapped only in paper and packed together.

On Purchasing, Sampling, and Tasting

Wherever you shop, you should keep in mind the following points: (1) always buy in small quantities first, and (2) always cup-sample these before buying large quantities. No tea is worth the money if you discover you don't like it. By taking home a small sample and trying a cup or two before buying a half-pound or more, you can decide if the tea lives up to expectations or is a disappointment. It may be stale—in which case it will show a dead flavor, little aroma, and a papery nuance to its taste—or it may be simply wonderful. But by trying a small amount first, you avoid overcommitting yourself. Some shops with bulk teas will sell a one-ounce sample packet, an admirable idea, since it allows wide sampling for very little outlay. Unfortunately, if packed ahead of time, they quickly go stale on the shelf and give customers a poor impression of the tea. Many merchants can't be bothered with such small purchases and require a quarter-pound minimum purchase of any tea. In any event, it won't cost you much to try a number of different teas or the same tea type from a variety of outlets.

In trying teas, there is no better method than cup-sampling them at the kitchen sink in the manner described in Chapter Ten; only by direct comparison tastings can one really distinguish tea characters and qualities, form some idea as to

whether a tea is worth the price, and discover one's preferences. In comparative shopping for teas one soon discovers that fine Darjeelings fetch a stiff price compared with other Indian and Ceylon teas, and that many teas from mainland China are quite expensive for the quality. Darjeelings are expensive because they are among the most prized of the world's teas and in great demand. China teas are high-priced in part because of their comparative scarcity on the world market. With practically any given tea type it is possible to find a tea twice as good as another but costing only half as much.

To keep analysis of the qualities of teas being tasted in perspective, always include one good standard supermarket brand of tea. It is surprising to many how some of the better-known gourmet teas fail to equal the quality of the best of the major blends. If one is unduly influenced by reputation and fancy packaging, it is a good idea to taste the teas blind so that one doesn't imagine virtues or faults to exist where there are none (see Chapter Ten for details of blind tastings).

Tea-tastings with like-minded friends share the cost, add to the fun, and help dispose of the tea. Even so, you may have a few pounds of middling-quality tea left over that you don't want to drink or serve. Providing the teas aren't actually so poor as to be worthless or defective in some way, save them for iced teas or blending experiments.

Many shops offer custom blending of teas. For the reasons given in Chapter Ten, blending is a hit-and-miss affair at best if done simply by recipe. That isn't to say that it isn't possible for an amateur to create his or her own personal blend. Some guidelines that can be followed, along with some suggestions for blends, are given in Chapter Ten.

Those tea enthusiasts who do not live near any outlet that can supply them with good- to fine-quality teas need not despair. The appendix on Shopping for Fine Coffees and Teas by Mail lists several direct importers of tea that offer their own mail-order lines of fine teas, in addition to several shops that sell their teas by mail.

CHAPTER THIRTEEN

How to Make Good Tea

It makes little sense to go to the trouble of finding and the expense of purchasing fine tea and then fail to bring out all its inherent cup quality by brewing it improperly. Fine coffee may be ruined if made improperly; although it is almost impossible to ruin tea, it is easy to make a very poor cup. Most tea drinkers, like most coffee drinkers, think they know how to make their favorite beverage. Actually, although most tea drinkers are aware of the basic methods of making tea, they are fuzzy on the details of careful preparation and often omit critical steps because they don't understand the reasons for their importance. The rules for making tea properly are short, simple, and so often repeated on the sides of tea tins that most tea enthusiasts think that's all there is to say about the subject. On the contrary, there is quite a bit more to say: in this chapter I plan to do more than merely repeat the "golden rules"; I'll try to explain why they are considered essential to good tea preparation. By understanding this, the tea lover can know when and how to bend the rules to fit circumstances and which shortcuts will not shortchange quality.

Modern tea-drinking follows the Chinese practice of combining tea leaves and boiling water to produce an infusion that brings out the character of the tea. Other methods of tea preparation are much in the minority: the practice of powdering tea leaves and adding them to hot water is confined to the tea ceremony of Japan; the practice of making a kind of stew of tea by boiling the leaves for ten or fifteen minutes (as in parts of North Africa) or for as much as a day (as in the billy tea of the Australian bushman) is confined primarily to areas where the stimulant properties of tea are paramount. Even with the basic modern method, however, there are style differences: in cold climates like Britain, where a hot, comforting beverage is appreciated, tea preparation aims at producing a hearty cup; in the East, where tea may be drunk constantly, the brew prepared would seem weak

and unsatisfying to the British palate. But notwithstanding variations in the intended use of the beverage, it is oversimple to say that the right way to drink tea is the way you like it best. It is oversimple because, first, a great many tea drinkers, particularly in the United States, do not realize how much more satisfying a beverage their favorite tea could be if only a little more care were taken in its preparation, and, second, it is frankly a waste of time to attempt to appreciate the subtleties of fine tea unless the tea has been prepared in such a way as to bring out its distinctive character and flavor.

Of course, there's no real dispute possible with personal preferences; after all, there are those people who like fine red Bordeaux ice-cold. If you like tea laced with clover honey, then by all means enjoy your tea that way. Personally, I'm fond of a spoonful of honey in a hot mug of tea and lemon, particularly when laid low by winter weather, and I find spiced, iced tea a refreshing summer drink. But if you want to be able to notice the subtleties inherent in a truly fine tea, experience has shown that adding a gob of honey or cooling the tea and adding spices are not aids to analysis; there is really only one way to prepare the tea so that all its character is revealed. Just as the full appreciation of fine wine demands attention to the details of proper uncorking, decanting, and pouring, so too fine tea demands attention to proper methods of preparation that might be unnecessarily fussy with ordinary tea.

The Essentials of Proper Tea Preparation

For some reason, too many Americans who think nothing of squeezing their own oranges or shelling chestnuts regard making a proper pot of tea a mystery only the British can fathom. This is nonsense. The cardinal rules for tea-making are all common sense, and what is more, are foolproof *if* followed exactly. Unlike making a successful soufflé, successful tea-making requires not one whit of previous experience. All that is required is good tea, freshly boiling water, and the patience to wait five minutes. In fact, all the rules invented for the proper method of preparing tea derive simply from the need for the manufactured tea leaf to come into contact with fresh, boiling water and infuse for a sufficient length of time to yield all the fragrance, flavor, and charac-

ter the leaf possesses. Lists of rules differ in their wording, but the following one is typical:

1. Use a teapot.
2. Put in one teaspoonful of tea per cup.
3. Bring water to a boil and pour on leaves.
4. Brew for five minutes.
5. Serve at once.

Behind these rules, however, are a number of assumptions that are rarely discussed, and for which many tea enthusiasts need an explanation. Let's take these rules in order.

Teapots

The value of using a teapot for making tea is not merely that it is more convenient to make several cups in one batch; the use of a pot is an aid to proper infusion and permits easy removal of the brew from the leaf. Tea can, however, be made right in the cup, as is done by tea tasters in cup-sampling, and in fact, the Chinese frequently make their tea that way, placing a lid on top of the cup to keep it hot and sliding the lid slightly off one edge to sip the tea off the leaves.

Teapots have been used throughout most of the history of tea; they originated in China, where they evolved from early wine vessels. Since that time the number of different teapot variants developed and employed at one time or another has been enormous. Many of the pots in museum collections are fascinating examples of the sheer inventiveness, not to mention artistry, that has been lavished on the simple pot. Devices for boiling eggs and for dispensing sugar, cream, and/or hot water into the teapot by tipping or twisting the pot, or by pulling plungers or turning dials are among the more unusual variations to be found. By far the most common addition to the simple pot with handle, spout, and lid is an inset infuser. The advantage gained by having an inset infuser is more than offset by the added difficulty of cleaning a more complicated pot. (Of course, such infusers have another use, that of removing the leaves at the proper time, something I'll explain shortly.) Leaves can simply be shaken out of a pot, the few stragglers rinsed out, and the whole kept spotless with little effort.

In short, I think the simplest teapot designs are the best. Of the simplest designs, the fat, round earthenware pots have the added advantage of ease of cleaning (no odd interior corners) and good retention of heat during brewing.

Porcelain is also excellent. Sterling-silver pots are satisfactory, though they tend to draw off heat from the brew. Metal pots are difficult to keep scrupulously clean inside, and rubbing the inside walls with anything abrasive is not recommended, on the grounds of taste as well as possible health hazards. Perfect cleanliness is as essential in a teapot as it is in the teacups used. A teapot, unlike a cast-iron frying pan, does not need seasoning with a layer of old brown tannin from previous brews. That would merely add a bitter flavor to the tea. Some argue that teapots and teacups should never be washed in soap, merely rinsed in scalding water, claiming that an invisible layer of soap is deposited. Since hot tea will reveal to the taste any failure to rinse the pot and cups completely, extracareful rinsing is advised. Many dishwashers do an excellent job of washing and rinsing tea utensils, depending on the washer and the design of the pot and cups.

Preheating the pot is one of those admonitions to the tea maker that Americans puzzle over, and with good reason, since it is not always a necessary step in making good tea. It is often recommended because in cold climates a pot sitting on the shelf may be quite cold and will consequently rob the brew of heat while the leaves are infusing. Rinsing out the pot with scalding water never hurts and is a good idea if the room temperature is cold. It's not necessary to splash some near-boiling water from the kettle into the pot; just fill the pot with hot water from the tap and let it stand for a few minutes. There seems to be no consensus on whether or not to dry the pot before adding the tea leaves. I usually content myself with giving the pot a vigorous shake upsidedown.

Measuring Tea

American tea drinkers often botch this step. "One teaspoonful per cup" means exactly that, not a haphazard spoonful. Silverware spoons vary greatly in size, so use a measuring spoon; a teaspoonful of tea means a level or very slightly rounded teaspoonful. Unfortunately, teas vary considerably in volume, depending on the type of manufacture or leaf style used. A teaspoonful of small, wiry broken grades of black tea will weigh more than a teaspoonful of a rough, bulky-style oolong. To compensate, use a slightly more rounded measure of the bulkier teas. The ideal is to weigh one's tea out (one-tenth ounce or three grams per

cup), though admittedly this is asking for too much precision in one's afternoon tea. I do not subscribe to the "plus one spoonful for the pot" advice. This does not take into consideration the number of cups being made and is liable to make too strong a pot except for those who normally dose all their tea with liberal amounts of milk and sugar.

Americans err most in not realizing that one teaspoonful for each cup is relative to the amount of water put in the pot. It is surprising how many tea drinkers wanting three cups of tea put three teaspoonfuls of tea in a pot and then proceed to fill the pot to the brim with water, forgetting that the pot holds six or eight cups. Naturally, the resulting brew is insipidly weak. One cup of tea is six ounces of liquid; the typical pot holds one quart when filled—thirty-six ounces or six cups. (For those who have a small scale, the ideal amount of leaf for one quart of tea would be eighteen grams, or about two-thirds of an ounce.) Measure your pot to find out its capacity so that you'll know how many spoonfuls are required for a full pot. Error results in overly strong or overly weak tea. In making less than a full pot of tea, you'll have to measure the amount of water you want to boil, since the vast majority of pots lack any internal markings or guides. Unfortunately, this is a time-consuming chore with most narrow-necked kettles (which is why I use a wide-mouthed kettle with a lid).

Water for Tea

The third step is to bring the water to a boil and pour it on the leaves. Simple as this sounds, probably more errors are made with this step than with any other. First of all, the water must be fresh-drawn, aerated water. This means that it must be drawn from the cold-water tap, not, despite the practice of a disconcertingly large number of people, drawn from the hot-water tap. Hot water is stale water, de-aerated by virtue of standing in water heaters or boilers for hours at a time. Tea made from such water is dead-tasting and dull, because only aerated water brings out the full character of tea. For the same reason, water from the tap should be allowed to run for a minute or two before filling the kettle, to ensure that the water to be boiled has not been standing in the pipes for hours.

Next, the water needs to be brought to a boil. This means over high heat, and a boil means a vigorous, rolling, rollicking, furious, bubbling boil. It does not mean a fizzling

simmer or something short of a true boil. (If you use a whistling kettle, check to see that it alerts you at the exact moment of first boiling, not before or sometime after the boil begins.) Before the water boils, it is not hot enough to release the fragrance and flavor of the leaf. If it continues to boil, it becomes de-aerated and flat. Then immediately dash the water into the pot onto the dry tea leaves and put the lid on the pot.

"Bring the pot to the kettle, not the kettle to the pot" is actually sound advice. If there is an excessively lengthy pause —say, the time it takes to stroll across the kitchen—between the time the water reaches the boil and it is poured on the leaves, the water will sink rapidly in temperature and its effectiveness with the leaves will be diminished. While bitter failure will not result if the tea enthusiast doesn't instantly dash the boiling water onto the tea leaves, he or she ensures success by having the waiting pot next to the heating kettle, so that when the water reaches full boil, the kettle can simply be picked off the heat and the water splashed on the leaves in one easy motion. In the time it takes to do this, the temperature of the water subsides a few degrees to the optimum temperature—about 200° to 205°F.

Anyone who doubts that promptness with the kettle improves the eventual cup quality should try the "five-minute infusion test" devised by Gervas Huxley:

> Put a rounded teaspoon of tea into each of three eight-ounce glass tumblers. Into the first pour water that hasn't reached the boil (say, about 190°F.); into the second overboiled water (say, water that has been boiling for 10 minutes); and into the last water that has just come vigorously to the boil. In the first glass (underboiled) the leaves rise to the surface and stay there, and the water fails to extract all the ingredients from the leaves. In the second (overboiled) glass, the leaves remain a soggy mass at the bottom, and full extraction fails to occur. In the glass in which freshly boiling water was used, most of the leaves circulate up and down due to the presence of air particles, and full extraction occurs.

After saying all this, I would like to add a proviso. With very fine, delicate green teas one derives slightly better flavor by removing the boiled water from the heat and letting it "set" for about ten seconds before pouring it on the leaf, so

that harsh flavors will not be extracted. The Japanese wait a number of minutes in some cases, even letting the boiled water cool to 160°F if the very best green tea is being prepared. (They also use stronger proportions of leaves to water and steep the brew for only a minute or two.)

The quality of the water used to make tea can be just as important as how it's boiled. Major tea brands package regional blends so the tea will be compatible with the type of water found in the area: small grades of thick, full-bodied teas do best in soft-water localities; brisk, full, flavory teas are preferred for hard-water areas. In general, although Keemuns, Darjeelings, high-grown Ceylons, and many greens tolerate hard water well, soft water is generally considered superior to hard water for tea-making, as it extracts flavor better and quicker.

If you don't enjoy the taste of what comes out of your home tap, you might not want to add that particular tang to your choicest teas. In that case, investigate bottled water. Some spring waters give excellent results; other have excessive mineral content and are too hard. Distilled water gives superb extraction, but it is quite flat (this can be alleviated somewhat by pouring the water back and forth between containers before boiling).

Brewing Times

Once boiling water has been poured directly on the leaves and the lid put on the pot, there is little to do but wait for the tea leaves to infuse properly and see that the infusion is kept warm. In cold climates, a tea cozy, a sort of quilted hood or cover, may be slipped over the teapot to keep it hot. Some people go so far as to put metal teapots over low flames, but this often results in making a kind of stew out of the steeping tea.

How long the tea should brew depends on the type of tea and the strength desired—from a minimum of three minutes to a maximum of six, and in almost all cases five minutes. It has been determined by chemical analysis that after three minutes the maximum amount of soluble matter (flavor and aroma) and caffeine (stimulant) with a minimum of tannin has been extracted. (This is based on the proportion of one teaspoonful per six-ounce serving; a stronger proportion, naturally, would yield the same strength of flavor in less brewing time.) The liquor at this point may strike the tea drinker as lacking in body and pungency and will seem

weak if milk is added. Past the three-minute point further tannin is extracted from the leaf, increasing the strength of the brew, but little further flavor is contributed. Thus, three to four minutes is often recommended for teas to be drunk without milk, and four to five minutes for teas to be drunk with milk. In practice, however, I find a five-minute brew is ideal for the majority of teas, yielding a brew full enough not to seem weak if milk is added, but not so strong that it requires milk. Some well-twisted leaf teas may need six minutes to achieve complete extraction. Only by experimentation with particular teas can you determine the most suitable length of brewing time. In any event, don't attempt to guess the time elapsed; always use a clock or, even better, a timer. Color is no guide to whether the tea is ready, as it will differ from tea to tea and season to season, and is affected by the type of water used. Some teas simply brew darker than others. Darkness is no indication of strength; some of the most pungent teas available are green teas, which look quite colorless in the cup.

While the tea is infusing, it is not a bad idea to lift the lid and give the mixture a quick stir with a spoon. This ensures that the flavor and strength is evenly distributed throughout the pot. At least, do this just before pouring, to make sure that the first cup poured won't be weaker than the others.

Serving

When the tea has infused for the proper length of time, pour it off the leaves promptly. It does not take much in the way of dawdling for the brew to reach seven minutes or more, a length of time guaranteed to produce a rough cup. If you don't want to pour the tea into cups immediately, pour it into a preheated suitable serving pot. Use a strainer to keep stray leaves from escaping through the spout (get a stainless-steel one; the cheapest kinds eventually corrode and rust).

This covers the basic rules in about as much detail as the average tea drinker, or even tea enthusiast, cares to know about the subject. To sum up, I'll restate the rules in a slightly expanded, more complete form:

1. Use a clean, warmed teapot.
2. Put in one teaspoon of tea leaves for each six-ounce cup of tea to be served.

3. Bring the required measure of fresh, cold water to a rolling boil and immediately pour on the tea leaves.
4. Cover and let the tea brew for three to five minutes, depending on the tea.
5. Stir once and promptly pour the liquid off the leaves. Serve.

Second-potting, the Samovar, and Tea Bags

This, however, is not the end of the matter to tea drinkers in many parts of the world, who refuse to believe there is nothing more to be done with leaves. Connoisseurs maintain that, since the maximum of fragrance and flavor is achieved from the initial brew, the same leaves should never be used again for a second brew. The Chinese, however, commonly indulge in "second-potting" and sometimes "third-potting," making additional albeit progressively weaker tea from the same leaves. The British often "water" the leaves, adding additional hot or boiling water to the leaves of a partially empty pot. The advantages of second-potting and watering are not merely that of making the tea stretch further, but of allowing an increased consumption without excessive intake of stimulant. Because caffeine is highly soluble, most of it is extracted in the first brew. It has been found that the caffeine level of a pot of tea made from once-used leaves is less than half that of a brew made with fresh tea leaves. The disadvantage is that the fragrance and flavor of the tea are reduced, along with its stimulating qualities; one eventually ends up with a cup that has little but tannin to say for itself. For the caffeine-sensitive, however, second-potting might provide an alternative happier than abstinence. Black teas fare poorly when second-potted, but green teas can sometimes tolerate second-potting well. Some connoisseurs are willing to argue that oolong shows best in the second pot; I would not go so far as to claim that but I will admit that its fruity, piquant delicacy often lasts into the second brew.

"Watering" tea should not be confused with making very strong tea and then cutting the liquor with water. Such a method is actually akin to making a tea concentrate, something the Russians do as a matter of course. Having been tea drinkers for over three centuries they have evolved their own unique tea customs. One is the use of the samovar,

which many people mistakenly think is a giant teapot. It is actually a water boiler and is not used in making the tea at all. When water is brought to a boil in the samovar, it is drawn off the urn by means of a tap into an ordinary teapot with the leaves in it. The tea is made especially strong and the traditional tea glasses, held in metal cupholders with handles, are filled only partway and then topped up with more hot water from the samovar; the tea is then served with lemon and often sugar. By this method the extrastrong tea is reduced to normal strength. One should use a variation of this method if one is particularly fond of weak tea. Make tea normal strength; then add additional hot water to a partly filled cup. This will make better-tasting tea than making very weak tea in the pot.

Something like the Russian method is also an excellent idea for serving a large number of people. Here's an easy method to serve two dozen cups of hot tea:

> Pour one quart of boiling water over two-thirds cup loose tea; cover and let infuse for five minutes. Stir and strain into a teapot. Use two tablespoons of the concentrate per cup and fill with hot water.

Tea, like coffee, does not retain its goodness when reheated even if it is taken off the leaves. Making a strong tea concentrate or "essence" as above, keeping it at room temperature, and topping it in cups with piping hot water can be done for a few hours, but the flavor of normal-strength tea seems to collapse when actually reheated on the stove. In fact, even kept in a vacuum bottle, it seems to undergo a sort of disintegration of flavor that is quite noticeable.

The tea bag, like iced tea, is an American invention. The tea bag started innocently enough shortly after the turn of the century when a New York tea importer had the idea of sending around his tea samples in little hand-sewn silk bags. To his surprise, people began pouring boiling water on them, and the tea bag as we know it was born. Today almost 70 percent of the tea consumed in the United States is from tea bags. In theory, tea bags are simply a handier form of loose tea, already conveniently packaged, as it were, in individual, cup-size, throwaway "tea eggs." In practice, however, they are mostly misused. Usually they're dangled in the cup by people in a hurry until a desired shade of color is achieved, instead of being properly steeped in a pot. (The acme of such abuse is still encountered in restaurants, where

an order for hot tea will get you a cup of tepid, stale water from the coffee urn and a forlorn bag sitting on the side of the saucer. Under such conditions, no amount of massaging the immersed bag with a spoon will enable the frustrated tea drinker to extract more than a brownish-tinged cup of hot water.) In addition, many people make the mistake of trying to make a pot of tea with only one bag, not recognizing the fact that each bag contains only enough tea to make one cup.

Even properly used, there are several drawbacks to tea bags. First, they are not that much more convenient than loose tea. After all, one still has the mess of handling the sodden, dripping bag when teatime is over. Second, they are considerably more expensive. With the vast majority of tea bags, one is paying more for the expensive individual packaging than for the tea itself. Next time you're purchasing tea, price a good half-pound of tea versus the cost for one hundred tea bags of the same-quality tea. Third, under some circumstances, you can in fact taste the bag. Proper filter paper is tasteless, but tea that has been packed in bags and then boxed has a tendency with time to pick up the odors of the paper tags, the ink, and the packaging—all nuances of a highly undesirable character. Fourth, rarely do fine teas come in bags. Not only are certain grades of teas unsuitable for use in bags, but such packaging shortens their shelf life. If you look hard enough, you can find small firms and shops that will have some of their better teas put in bags for customers who insist upon it, but considering all the objections that can be leveled against the use of tea bags, their use seems foolish for fine teas and an unnecessarily expensive practice even for ordinary teas. My view is that if you're going to the trouble to use a pot, you might as well use loose tea, because a far wider selection of fine teas is available in that form.

For some tea drinkers, the best of both worlds is a "tea egg." The tea egg, sometimes called a tea ball, is really a metal tea bag with a removable top, an egg-shaped device on a chain into which tea leaves can be placed. The whole is then dropped into the pot, and boiling water is poured on top of it. Since the tea egg is perforated, the leaves can interact with the boiling water and produce a good brew. The egg or ball can then be removed at the proper time and the tea served. The egg must be big enough so that the required amount of tea fills the egg only halfway or less to allow for expansion of the saturated leaf. If the leaves are

not allowed to expand, an insipidly weak brew results. Regardless of the size of the egg, however, it does not allow the freedom of movement that the leaves have when allowed to circulate and expand throughout the entire pot. Nor can the infusion be stirred. In brief, unless carefully used, tea quality can be diminished.

On Serving Tea

Once we pass from the realm of tea preparation to tea-serving, we are passing from fact to preference, and here only a few passing remarks are in order, primarily on the suitability of teacup styles, addition of milk and other substances to tea, some suggestions on what teas to serve when, and the best way to prepare such classic variants as iced tea and spiced tea.

As mentioned in Chapter Ten, the palate is far more sensitive to moderately warm tea. If excessively hot, the tea is liable to scald the taste buds. It follows, then, that fine tea is best appreciated somewhat cooler than "piping hot." Chinese teacups are traditionally handleless, which has the advantage that one can tell by touch if the tea is ready to drink: if it's too hot to pick up, it's too hot to appreciate. Of course, tea may be drunk out of any sort of mug, but in the same way fine wine seems enhanced if served in thin crystal goblets, so too fine tea is enhanced by serving in fine china.

The Chinese and Japanese take their tea plain and would never think of adding anything, except perhaps a floating dried flower blossom on the surface. The British invariably add milk and often sugar as well; the Russians add lemon and sugar; people in the West Indies add a slice of lime; Moroccans add mint leaves; Indians may add basil leaves or a slice of orange. A great many Americans prefer their tea plain, as do Continental Europeans. If one is intent on savoring all the subtleties of a particular tea, it makes sense to take it plain. Many Darjeelings, though not all, are on the delicate side and are not improved by the addition of milk. (No one takes milk in oolong or green teas, because the flavor of the combination ranges from odd to repugnant.) On the other hand, the addition of milk to some black teas not only mellows the taste and adds body, but also enhances their fragrance, particularly Keemun. The great strength of

Assam teas seems to call for milk, as do the brisk, high-grown teas of Ceylon.

Since milk contains about 3 percent casein, it renders the tannin in tea insoluble and reduces the characteristic bite of a pungent black tea. (It also helps its digestibility.) Few people who use milk add more than enough to render the tea amber-colored—a teaspoon's worth to a cup. More milk than that and the tea loses all its refreshing astringency. The addition of cream is not recommended because true cream contains very little casein and in any case changes the flavor more than milk. Since much American cream is simply thickened milk, it is possible to use it instead of milk. Milk in moderation does not mask the flavor of good black tea, particularly for those palates that are used to the nuance milk adds. (I myself drink black teas both with and without milk, depending on the occasion and the tea.)

Users of milk in tea have long argued the rather theologically subtle point of whether the milk ought to be added to the tea last, or put in the cup first and tea poured on it. Milk-firsters insist that milk scalds perceptibly if dumped into hot tea, and therefore the milk should be warmed slowly by the addition of tea. Milk-lasters insist that one can measure the proper amount of milk to add only by watching the color of the tea change. Nonusers of milk, of course, regard the whole question as silly.

Some authorities state that a small amount of sugar enhances the flavor of some black teas, with or without milk, and even some oolong teas. I have not found this to be the case, but that may be because I do not care for sweetened tea and find, as many people do, that it disguises the flavor of the brew. For that reason, I rarely add lemon, though the lemony nuance it adds does enhance thin teas. Few people recommend adding anything but lemon to green teas. In short, the addition of milk, sugar, and lemon is much a matter of taste and custom.

The question of what teas go best with certain times of the day is again a matter of custom and taste. Keemuns were the original English breakfast teas, but now that role is taken by hearty Indian and Ceylon blends as well. I prefer Assam for breakfast, high-grown Ceylon for afternoon tea, Keemun after evening meals, Darjeeling for mid-morning or late evening, greens when in a meditative mood, and oolong anytime. Oolongs go very well with pastries and other light desserts, and though most teas are drunk after meals, a cup of fine green tea makes an unusual and bracing aperitif. In

most tea-drinking countries, the only meal with which tea is taken is breakfast, although tea is often accompanied by snacks. Discovering what teas go best with what foods and what occasions is at least as enjoyable a gastronomic exercise as trying various wine and food combinations.

Iced Tea and Other Variants

Iced tea is an American invention and is now more popular than hot tea in the United States. Essentially, iced tea is simply hot tea chilled, and the best iced teas are those that would be considered quite good if served hot. The traditional way to prepare iced tea is to make hot tea, using half again as much tea. When the tea is ready, pour over ice cubes in tall glasses. The extra strength of the tea is mitigated by the melting of the ice cubes. A handy method for making iced tea ahead of time is as follows:

> Bring one quart of cold water to a boil in a saucepan. Remove pan from heat and instantly add one-third measuring cup of loose tea. Stir, cover, and let brew five minutes. Stir again and strain into a pitcher holding a quart of cold water. Serve over ice and garnish with lemon. This makes about ten tall glasses.

Refrigeration of the tea is not recommended, however, because many teas tend to cloud when refrigerated. This has no effect whatsoever on the taste, but it makes a less attractive glass. A clouded pitcher of iced tea can be cleared by simply adding a little boiling water to it and giving it a stir. Certain teas are more likely to cloud if iced than others—Assam and high-grown Ceylon, for example, Nonetheless, any tea can be made to yield an unbitter, crystal-clear brew simply by making it by the cold-water method:

> Put six teaspoons of tea into a quart jar, add *cold* water, cover, and let stand at room temperature (or in the refrigerator) for six to nine hours. (Timing depends on the tea, so experiment.) Occasionally turn the jar upside down, then stand it up again. After a number of hours, a good deal of color and flavor has been extracted and the tea should be strained off the leaves into another jar.

The tea keeps well for days if refrigerated and always remains as clear as it is clean-tasting. This method is an excellent way to enjoy uncloudy iced Ceylon, which happens to be my favorite among iced teas, although Darjeeling can make a lovely cool drink, and jasmine makes a highly exotic summer refreshment. If iced tea is made from good tea, it retains a good deal of flavor and fragrance, and its clean astringency can be most refreshing on a summer day. Lemons, limes, mint sprigs, and other garnishes go well with it, and, of course, it keeps well. Although it is not the best way to appreciate fine tea, it is so refreshing a drink considered on its own that it is little wonder there are many Americans who never touch tea unless it's over ice!

The following recipes are for two unusual spiced teas, one hot and one iced. They are best enjoyed as "occasion teas."

Moroccan Mint Tea

1 quart water
8 teaspoons Gunpowder green tea
5 fresh mint sprigs
6 lumps sugar

Bring freshly drawn cold water to a full boil in a kettle. Put the green tea in a teapot and pour about one-half cup of the boiling water into the teapot. Swirl the water around the pot and then strain off, leaving the tea leaves in the pot. Add the mint leaves, crushing them slightly, and the 6 lumps of sugar (more if desired). Pour boiling water into the teapot and allow the mixture to brew for six to seven minutes.

Mint tea should be served in small glasses only three-quarters full so that they may be held by the top (or else use Russian tea glasses). This recipe serves about 8.

Iced Spiced Darjeeling

2 quarts water
5 cardamom pods
2 cinnamon sticks
8 cloves
½ teaspoon ground ginger
12 teaspoons Darjeeling
8 fresh mint sprigs

Bring one quart freshly drawn cold water to a boil in a saucepan, and add the cardamom, cinnamon, cloves, and ginger. Simmer for twenty minutes. Prepare one quart Darjeeling tea in a teapot, the usual way, but using 12 teaspoons of tea. Brew five to six minutes. Strain. Then pour both the water in the saucepan and the tea into one pitcher, stir, and serve over ice. Garnish with a mint sprig. Serves 8.

APPENDIX

Further Reading

There is a dearth of good books for the layman on the subjects of coffee and tea. Most popular treatments are superficial; most detailed treatments are too technical. The following brief list includes some of the better popular treatments, but most of the scholarly or technical works consulted for this book—such as *Green and Roasted Coffee Tests* (Gordian-Max Publishers, Hamburg) or Sir Percival Griffith's *History of the Indian Tea Industry*—have been omitted on the grounds of limited interest for the general reader. The list, however, includes both technical and popular works cited in the text.

Bramah, Edward. *Tea and Coffee: A Modern View of Three Hundred Years of Tradition* (London: Hutchinson, 1972).

Very readable personal account of the coffee and tea trade by onc of the few people to have been involved in both. Excellent on coffee and tea estates. Rather detailed on subjects like vending machines, and limited on others, but in sum very interesting, factual, and informative.

Haarer, A. E. *Coffee Growing* (London: Oxford University Press, 1963).

For the coffee-grower, but brief, informative, and not overly technical.

Harler, C. R. *The Culture and Marketing of Tea,* 3rd ed. (London: Oxford University Press, 1964).

Authoritative, very detailed, but quite readable reference with emphasis on cultivation and processing.

Huxley, Gervas. *Talking of Tea* (London: Thames & Hudson, 1956).

Brief, readable treatment of tea. Excellent on preparation.

Okakura, Kakuzo. *The Book of Tea* (New York: Dover Publications, Inc., 1964).

An older well-known text on the Japanese tea ceremony. Idiosyncratic, poetic, and delightful.

Schapira, Joel, David, and Karl. *The Book of Coffee and Tea* (New York: St. Martin's Press, 1975).

Written by a family of coffee merchants, this very recent book covers both beverages in depth for the consumer, but is somewhat uneven. The treatment of tasting techniques, for example, is minimal, grinding coffee at home is not discussed, and the review of the world's teas contains some inaccuracies and dated material. Well worth reading, however, for its generally sound advice and the detailed discussion of coffee types.

Shelleck, Jaime. *Tea* (New York: The Viking Press, 1972).

Beautifully designed book, but quite uneven and incomplete treatment. Not reliable as a guide to modern tea. The compilation of historical information, however, makes entertaining reading.

Sivetz, Michael, and Foote, H. Elliott. *Coffee Processing Technology*, vol. I by Sivetz and Foote; vol. II by Sivetz (Westport, Conn.: Avi Publishing Co., 1963).

Very technical and dry, but authoritative and encyclopedic. All aspects of coffee, particularly current processing, are covered, usually in great depth.

Ukers, William H. *All About Tea*, 2 vols. (New York: The Tea and Coffee Trade Journal Co., 1935).

———. *All About Coffee*, 2nd ed. (New York: The Tea and Coffee Trade Journal Co., 1935).

These marvelous, massive volumes contain a wealth of information, but are unfortunately forty years out of date; much is still useful for the scholar and entertaining for the lover of literary curiosa; other parts are now unreliable. Most popular treatments of coffee and tea since have borrowed heavily from Ukers, usually without acknowledgment. His descriptions of coffee and tea types and tastes are frequently repeated despite the fact that many are now inapplicable.

Uribé, C., Andrés. *Brown Gold: The Amazing Story of Coffee* (New York: Random House, Inc., 1954).

Entertaining popular account of the history of coffee with stress on Latin America. Much of it is now dated.

Wellman, Frederick. *Coffee: Botany, Cultivation, and Utilization* (New York: Interscience Publishers, 1961).

Authoritative, technical reference work with emphasis on coffee production.

Yu, Lu. *The Classic of Tea*, trans. Francis Ross Carpenter (Boston: Little, Brown & Company, 1974).
First complete translation of this brief work with an excellent introduction. Delightful reading.

Shopping for Fine Coffees and Teas by Mail

Coffee

The following is a brief list of some reliable outlets offering excellent-quality coffees. Most do a considerable mail-order business all over the country. Write for their price lists and ordering instructions; because of world market conditions, prices vary, but expect to pay around three to four dollars per pound for most coffees. Certain scarce coffees cost more. Capricorn and Zabar's in particular offer a number of authentic scarce coffees, including Jamaican.

Capricorn Coffees
353 Tenth Street
San Francisco, California 94003

Schapira Coffee Company
117 West 10th Street
New York, New York 10011

Simpson & Vail, Inc.
53 Park Place
New York, New York 10007

The Coffee Connection, Inc.
36 Boylston Street
Cambridge, Massachusetts 02138

Westwood Coffee Gallerie
1149 Glendon Ave.
Westwood Village, California 90024

Zabar's Gourmet Foods
2245 Broadway
New York, New York 10024

Tea

The shops listed under coffee also carry fine teas as well. In addition, the following tea importers offer a number of select, very fine teas by mail, including sample selections. Write and ask for their price lists and ordering instructions. Expect to pay from four to eight dollars per half-pound of tea. Certain rare teas cost more. Grace Tea offers a particularly wide selection.

Grace Tea Company Ltd.
799 Broadway
New York, New York 10003

O. H. Clapp, Inc.
47 Riverside Avenue
Westport, Conn. 06880

The Tea Planters and Importers Co.
55/56 Aldgate High Street
London EC3N 1AU, England

Index

Boldface numerals refer to main entries. For coffee types by country and common coffee terms, readers should consult Chapter Five, "A Guide to the World's Coffees," pp. 76–89; for coffee-tasting terms, "A Coffee Tasting Glossary," pp. 65–68. For tea types by country and common tea terms, consult Chapter Eleven, A Guide to the World's Teas," pp. 189–206; for tea-tasting terms, "A Tea Taster's Glossary," pp. 178–182.

THE SIGNET BOOK OF

COFFEE and TEA

Coffees and teas not only rank among the greatest of all pleasures of the palate—they also represent the outstanding gourmet bargain in the world today. For just pennies a cup, the knowledgeable person can sample a rich and varied assortment of tastes, scents, and satisfactions.

This unique book is designed to tell you everything you need to know to experience the full range of dining delight that coffees and teas offer. You will learn their fascinating histories, the distinct differences in their many varieties, the standards by which they are officially graded and personally judged, how and where to purchase them, their proper storage, and the secrets of how best to prepare them and serve them. Here is the one total guide to exploration of a truly exciting area of expertise and enjoyment.

NEW AMERICAN LIBRARY PUBLISHES SIGNET, MENTOR, CLASSIC, PLUME & MERIDIAN BOOKS